Public Employee Unionism

Studies of Unionism in Government

JACK STIEBER

Public Employee Unionism: Structure, Growth, Policy

THE BROOKINGS INSTITUTION
Washington, D.C.

Library of Congress Cataloging in Publication Data:
Stieber, Jack   1919–
  Public employee unionism.

  (Studies of unionism in government)
  Includes bibliographical references.
    1. Trade-unions—Government employees—United
States.   I. Brookings Institution, Washington, D.C.
II. Title   III. Series.
HD8008.S74   331.88'11'353   73-1591
ISBN 0-8157-8160-1

9 8 7 6 5 4 3 2 1

THE BROOKINGS INSTITUTION is an independent organization devoted to nonpartisan research, education, and publication in economics, government, foreign policy, and the social sciences generally. Its principal purposes are to aid in the development of sound public policies and to promote public understanding of issues of national importance.

The Institution was founded on December 8, 1927, to merge the activities of the Institute for Government Research, founded in 1916, the Institute of Economics, founded in 1922, and the Robert Brookings Graduate School of Economics and Government, founded in 1924.

The Board of Trustees is responsible for the general administration of the Institution, while the immediate direction of the policies, program, and staff is vested in the President, assisted by an advisory committee of the officers and staff. The by-laws of the Institution state, "It is the function of the Trustees to make possible the conduct of scientific research, and publication, under the most favorable conditions, and to safeguard the independence of the research staff in the pursuit of their studies and in the publication of the results of such studies. It is not a part of their function to determine, control, or influence the conduct of particular investigations or the conclusions reached."

The President bears final responsibility for the decision to publish a manuscript as a Brookings book or staff paper. In reaching his judgment on the competence, accuracy, and objectivity of each study, the President is advised by the director of the appropriate research program and weighs the views of a panel of expert outside readers who report to him in confidence on the quality of the work. Publication of a work signifies that it is deemed to be a competent treatment worthy of public consideration; such publication does not imply endorsement of conclusions or recommendations contained in the study.

The Institution maintains its position of neutrality on issues of public policy in order to safeguard the intellectual freedom of the staff. Hence interpretations or conclusions in Brookings publications should be understood to be solely those of the author or authors and should not be attributed to the Institution, to its trustees, officers, or other staff members, or to the organizations that support its research.

Foreword

The extensive literature on the development of the labor movement in the United States and its impact on the American system
of industrial relations has been largely concerned with private industry. Research on collective bargaining has likewise been concentrated on unions of workers employed in the private sector of
the economy. The growth of employee organization and collective
bargaining in the public sector during the last decade has created
a need for greater knowledge and understanding of the organizations—both union and nonunion—that represent public employees.

This book is designed to meet that need. It is the third volume
in the Brookings series of Studies of Unionism in Government,
arising from a program of research undertaken by the Institution
in 1967 with the encouragement of the National Civil Service
League and financial support from the Ford Foundation.

The first volume in the series, *The Unions and the Cities*, by
Harry H. Wellington and Ralph K. Winter, Jr., deals with the
legal problems arising from the importation of collective bargaining into the public sector. The second, *Managing Local Government under Union Pressure*, by David T. Stanley with the
assistance of Carole L. Cooper, concentrates on the influence of
unions on administrative practices of U.S. cities and urban
counties.

This study examines the various types of unions and employee associations in government and shows how their structures, growth patterns, and policies have influenced and will continue to influence collective bargaining in state and local government.

The public employees and their organizations with which this study deals are those in state and local government, exclusive of school instructional personnel and transit employees. Collective bargaining in the federal government has been excluded from the scope of all books in the Brookings series. Organizations of teachers have been omitted from this study because much has already been written about collective bargaining in schools and the organizations that represent teachers. Unions of local transit employees have a long history of collective bargaining with municipal transit authorities and have not been a part of the burgeoning organization of public employees in the late 1960s that is the focus of this book.

Because little or no research has been conducted on most of the organizations dealt with in this study, the author relied primarily on personal interviews and primary sources. He and his two assistants conducted approximately 300 interviews with union and association representatives and government officials in fifty-five cities and twenty-three states. He gratefully acknowledges their willingness to participate in this study; to preserve confidentiality, he does not identify sources of specific information.

Jack Stieber is Director of the School of Labor and Industrial Relations and Professor, Department of Economics, at Michigan State University. His assistants in this project were Philip Kienast, Assistant Professor, University of Washington, and Jerry Lelchook, U.S. Department of Labor, both formerly graduate students in the School of Labor and Industrial Relations, Michigan State University. John A. Fossum, research assistant in the School of Labor and Industrial Relations, developed the computer programs used in the preparation of statistical tables and Professor Einar Hardin of Michigan State University furnished valuable advice on the use of quantitative data.

The author wishes to acknowledge the generosity of Arnold R. Weber, John F. Burton, Jr., Paul F. Gerhart, and Charles E. Krider of the University of Chicago in granting him access to interview data and material collected for other studies in this series. The comments and suggestions of Mr. Weber, coordinator of the series, of Bob Repas of Michigan State University, and of David T. Stanley of Brookings, as well as those of anonymous readers of the manuscript selected by the Brookings Institution and of representatives of unions and employee associations described in the study, resulted in major revisions and improvements. Alice M. Carroll edited the manuscript, Evelyn P. Fisher and Genevieve Wimsatt checked it for accuracy, and Goddard W. Winterbottom prepared the index.

Mr. Stieber wishes to thank the librarian of the School of Labor and Industrial Relations of Michigan State University, Martha Jane Soltow, and her assistant, Cynthia Bullock, for cheerfully locating, usually on short notice, material he requested, and Shirley Fubara, Teresa Rompf, Cheri Sandel, and Keetsie Hinkle for typing the manuscript. Finally, he expresses his appreciation for the use of a carrel in the Michigan State University Library where he could hide from colleagues and students to work on this project.

The statements, conclusions, and recommendations in this book are those of the author, and should not be ascribed to the staff members, officers, or trustees of the Brookings Institution or to the Ford Foundation.

KERMIT GORDON
President

June 1973
Washington, D.C.

Contents

The Strike Issue *219*
Political Activity *220*
Convergence of Unions and Associations *221*

Appendixes

Index 249

Text Tables

Appendix Tables

Public Employee Unionism

Glossary

AFGE American Federation of Government Employees

AFL–CIO American Federation of Labor–Congress of Industrial Organizations

AFSCME American Federation of State, County and Municipal Employees

AGE Assembly of Governmental Employees

ANA American Nurses' Association

COPE Committee on Political Education (of the AFL–CIO)

FOP Fraternal Order of Police

IAFF International Association of Fire Fighters

IBPO International Brotherhood of Police Officers

ICPA International Conference of Police Associations

Laborers' Union Laborers' International Union of North America

NAGE National Association of Government Employees

NUPO National Union of Police Officers

PBA Police benevolent association

SEIU Service Employees International Union

SNA State nurses' association

Teamsters International Brotherhood of Teamsters, Chauffeurs, Warehousemen, and Helpers of America

CHAPTER ONE

Organizations of Public Employees

The pattern of organization among public employees in the United States is more complex than the single form of organization that is characteristic of the private sector. Public employees belong to unions and associations, which differ from each other organizationally and structurally, as well as in their purposes and policies. These organizations may be further differentiated by the level of government in which they operate, whether membership is general or specialized, and by national affiliation. Some organizations are active at only one governmental level—federal, state, or local—others at two or all three levels. Some enroll only public employees, while others include employees from the private sector. Some organizations are open to virtually all government employees, others limited to specific occupational or professional groups. Some unions and associations are affiliated with a national federation, while others are independent.

The public employee organizations analyzed in this study fall into five classifications: all-public unions; mixed unions, with both private and public employee members; state and local employee associations; professional associations; and unions and associations representing the uniformed protective services. The various types of organization that represent state and local government employees are compared in terms of structure, growth, and policies.

1

The study focuses on public sector employee organizations during the 1960s, exclusive of teacher organizations whose growth has already been well-documented[1] and unions of local transit workers which have had a long history of collective bargaining.

All-Public Unions

The largest union composed almost entirely of public employees is the American Federation of State, County and Municipal Employees (AFSCME), an affiliate of the AFL-CIO. An industrial type union, AFSCME includes employees in all state and local government functions, excepting only teachers and fire fighters, two groups excluded not by constitutional limitation but by choice.[2] Also eligible for membership are employees of quasi-public, nonprofit, or tax-exempt agencies "of a public, charitable, educational, or civic nature."[3] During the 1960s the union's membership more than doubled, increasing at a rate of over 37,000 per year in the last half of the decade. By June 1972, AFSCME claimed 550,000 members and was growing at a rate of 1,000 new members a week.[4] Although it has members in almost every state, more than half of them in 1969 were concentrated in New York, Michigan, Wisconsin, Ohio, and Massachusetts; an additional quarter were reported in California, Pennsylvania, Illinois, Minnesota, Connecticut, Washington, and Maryland.[5]

Not only is AFSCME's claimed jurisdiction wide, but, more im-

1. See Michael H. Moskow, *Teachers and Unions* (University of Pennsylvania Press, 1966); Michael H. Moskow and Robert E. Doherty, "United States," in Albert A. Blum (ed.), *Teachers Unions and Associations* (University of Illinois Press, 1969), pp. 295–332; Edward B. Shils and C. Taylor Whittier, *Teachers, Administrators, and Collective Bargaining* (Crowell, 1968); and Stanley M. Elam, Myron Lieberman, and Michael H. Moskow (eds.), *Readings on Collective Negotiations in Public Education* (Rand McNally, 1967).

2. Through its new affiliate, the Hawaii Government Employees Association, AFSCME defeated the National Education Association in a representation election for a unit of some 600 principals and officers in public schools in 1971. (Bureau of National Affairs, *Government Employee Relations Report* [GERR], No. 404 [June 7, 1971], p. B-22.)

3. Constitution of the American Federation of State, County and Municipal Employees (AFSCME) , AFL-CIO (amended, 1972), Art. 3.

4. *GERR*, No. 455 (June 5, 1972), p. B-12.

5. "AFSCME, AFL-CIO, Average Membership Report" (AFSCME, June 1969).

portant, its membership in almost every type of governmental function and in most occupational groups is substantial. Approximately half the members are employed by cities, slightly more than one-fourth by state governments, 10 percent by counties, and the remaining 15 percent by school districts, universities and colleges, nonprofit organizations, and special authorities. Occupationally, AFSCME membership is also widely distributed, with medical institution assistants (15 percent), clerical and allied employees (15 percent), tradesmen (11 percent), and domestic and custodial workers (10 percent) comprising roughly half the membership, and the remainder spread among nineteen other job categories.[6]

Mixed Unions

The most common type of union in the public sector, the mixed union, draws the majority of its members from private industry. The three mixed unions with the strongest representation in state and local government are the Service Employees International Union (SEIU) and the Laborers' International Union of North America, both affiliated with the AFL-CIO, and the independent International Brotherhood of Teamsters, Chauffeurs, Warehousemen, and Helpers of America. The construction unions, while not important in numbers of public employees, have members in many localities and, through their influence in central labor councils, sometimes play a significant role in enactment of legislation, organization, and collective bargaining for government employees.

The SEIU had an estimated 126,000 public employee members in spring 1970, all but 10,000 of whom were believed to be in state and local government. In recent years the union's growth has been concentrated in the public sector, and more than half of its locals now include government workers. By 1971, government employees accounted for about one-third of total SEIU membership of 450,000.[7]

6. *Proceedings of the 17th International Convention, American Federation of State, County and Municipal Employees, AFL-CIO* (1968), pp. 417–18.

7. U.S. Department of Labor, Labor Management Services Administration, *A Directory of Public Employee Organizations: A Guide to the Major Organizations Representing State and Local Public Employees* (November 1971), p. 44.

The SEIU construes its jurisdiction broadly: "workers, male or female, who are employed in any phases of private, non-profit, or public employment . . . or who are engaged in the maintenance, servicing, protection or operation of all types of institutions . . . whether private, public, or nonprofit and all categories of employees therein or thereabout."[8] (The prefix "Building" was removed from the union's name in 1968 as too limiting on the scope of membership.) The SEIU constitution takes two pages to specify what is meant by "all types of institutions" and to enumerate the "classifications of workers" it considers to be within its jurisdiction, and finally empowers its president to construe its jurisdiction "to embrace all classifications of workers within any establishment."[9] The SEIU has been most successful in organizing employees in hospitals, schools, and social service agencies in both state and local government. But it has also competed vigorously with AFSCME, other unions, and associations for other public employees.

The interest of the Laborers' Union in public employment is much more recent than that of either AFSCME or SEIU. Basically a union of unskilled and semiskilled construction workers, it turned to public employment in the early 1960s to halt the erosion of its membership base.[10] Although the Laborers' major interest has been at the federal level—it negotiated a merger with the Mail Handlers' Union in 1968, immediately adding 20,000 members—it claimed 24,000 state and local government members in 1970. Public employees now constitute only about 10 percent of the union's total membership of 550,000, and practically all of these members have been added since 1963.

As its name implies, the Laborers' Union defines its jurisdiction broadly and is open to all public employees. The leadership sees it moving in the direction of a "general workers' union."[11] The union has been most active among employees in sanitation, streets, and other public works departments in cities, and among state highway employees. It has tried, with only limited success, to organize white

---

8. Constitution and Bylaws, Service Employees International Union, AFL-CIO, CLC (revised and amended, 1972), Art. 3, sec. 1.

9. Ibid.

10. Derek C. Bok and John T. Dunlop, *Labor and the American Community* (Simon and Schuster, 1970), p. 143.

11. *Wall Street Journal,* July 15, 1968.

collar employees, licensed practical nurses, supervisors, and skilled craftsmen.

The Teamsters union, the largest labor organization in the United States, claims jurisdiction over "all workers" in its constitution, but designates its interest in a number of occupations in or related to transportation, warehousing, and the manufacture, processing, sale, and distribution of food, milk and dairy products, and certain other products.[12] In the public sector the Teamsters has been most active in organizing employees in street and sanitation departments of cities and in county and state highway departments. But, as in its private sector activities, it has responded to opportunities to organize employees at all governmental levels and in all occupational categories, including sheriffs, registered nurses, X-ray technicians, public school principals, and parking meter maids.

In 1970 the union had over 57,000 public employee members, 41,000 of them in municipal government, 4,400 in state, 5,200 in county, and 4,000 in school districts. One out of every five Teamster locals, 170 in all, reported some public employee membership. Approximately one-fourth of these members were employed in street and highway work and a somewhat larger proportion in sanitary services. Noninstructional education services accounted for 12 percent of public membership, public welfare 10 percent, parks and recreation 6 percent, police protection and public utilities 4 percent each, and public health and hospitals 3 percent. Practically all of the public employees were in the union's eastern and central conferences, with New York, Illinois, Michigan, and Pennsylvania having the largest number of members.[13] Public employees constitute only about 3 percent of total Teamster membership, but the leadership expects the proportion to increase and has urged locals to put more stress on organizing public employees.

A survey of municipal governments in 1970 found 19 other mixed unions reporting some 32,000 state and local government employee members, 14 others with unknown numbers of public employee members, and 5 that did not know whether or not they

12. Constitution, International Brotherhood of Teamsters, Chauffeurs, Warehousemen and Helpers of America (1971), Art. 2, sec. 1.

13. "Teamster Union Representation and Bargaining Among Public Employees, Spring 1970" (memorandum, Sept. 17, 1970).

had any government employee members.[14] The total state and local government membership of mixed unions other than the SEIU, Laborers', and Teamsters was probably about 50,000 in 1970, most of them local government employees.

Uniformed Protective Services

Police and fire fighters are usually referred to jointly as the uniformed services. Though their style of organization differs, protective service organizations have much in common: they generally include both rank and file personnel and officers; both provide protective services to the community; they are frequently accorded common treatment under state laws and municipal ordinances with respect to pay, pensions, other benefits, and collective bargaining; and it is widely assumed that strikes by their members cannot be tolerated. While the two services have these common features, an enmity has developed between police and fire fighter organizations during the last decade over the issue of parity pay.

Police officers are represented in two national associations, the Fraternal Order of Police (FOP) and the International Conference of Police Associations (ICPA); an all-public-employee union, AFSCME; several mixed unions; and many local associations not affiliated with any national organization. Despite this diversity, the organizations to which policemen belong have common objectives arising from the nature of the job, which sets policemen apart from other municipal employees.

The oldest and best known of the organizations, the Fraternal Order of Police, was founded in Pittsburgh in 1915. In 1969, though it was organized into 733 local lodges in 36 states and the District of Columbia,[15] its total membership of 80,000 was concentrated in Pennsylvania, with close to 24,000 members, and Ohio, with about 12,000 members. Any regularly appointed, full-time police officer, including those who have retired from active duty,[16] may join, and patrolmen and officers belong to the same local lodges. The FOP wishes to avoid being considered a union, and its constitution notes

14. Responses to questionnaire prepared by Jack Stieber, September 1970.

15. *FOP National Lodge, Reports, Officers and Committees, 39th National Conference* (1969), pp. 24–26.

16. Constitution and By-Laws, Fraternal Order of Police (1967), Art. 3.

that it "shall have no affiliation, directly or indirectly, with any labor union, congress, federation, or committee of like nature."[17]

The International Conference of Police Associations is a confederation of independent police associations, rather than an individual membership organization like the FOP. Founded in 1953, the ICPA was organized into over 100 state and local associations with 142,000 members in 18 states and the District of Columbia.[18] More than 80 percent of the membership is concentrated in New York, Illinois, California, New Jersey, and Massachusetts, reflecting the organization's big-city emphasis. Among its founders were independent police associations in New York, Chicago, Los Angeles, Detroit, San Francisco, Oakland, Milwaukee, New Orleans, Minneapolis, and Washington, D.C. Membership eligibility is determined by each ICPA affiliate, some taking in only patrolmen, others officers only, but most of the associations combining all ranks. Large cities, whose departments include a substantial number of officers, are most likely to have separate associations based on rank.

Among unions, AFSCME with about 10,000 police members, the International Brotherhood of Police Officers (which affiliated with SEIU in 1972) with 8,000, and the Teamsters with 2,500 are the most important. Like the FOP and most ICPA affiliates, police unions tend to include patrolmen and officers within the same locals, though bargaining units may exclude certain officer ranks. Purely local police associations are found in many cities, including some that also have unions or associations with a national affiliation. Thus, Chicago has two independent patrolmen's associations as well as an FOP lodge; Hartford and Denver have both a union and an independent police association; Cleveland, Toledo, and New Orleans have organizations limited to patrolmen that emerged in recent years to compete with FOP lodges; and Boston has two independent associations, one for patrolmen and another for officers.

Unlike their police brethren, municipal fire fighters have not divided their loyalties among several organizations. The over-

17. Ibid., Art. 2.
18. International Conference of Police Associations, "Member Associations as of July 1, 1969" (Washington: ICPA; processed). The 142,000-member estimate eliminates duplicate listing of members who belong to both state and local ICPA affiliates and excludes members in Canada and the Canal Zone.

whelming majority of fire fighters belong to the AFL-CIO International Association of Fire Fighters. The IAFF was organized in 1918 and had about 160,000 members in 1970, including some 12,000 in Canada.[19] It is the only public employee union that does not have to compete with other national organizations. No other unions have evinced any interest in organizing fire fighters, and local associations have had less success among fire fighters than among any other group of municipal employees.

State and Local Employee Associations

A major difference between the history of public employee organization and private is the existence of employee associations before the advent of unions and collective bargaining in the public sector. Most of the state and local associations were organized between 1920 and 1950. They were usually founded in order to start a retirement system; initiate or protect a civil service system; provide such benefits as life insurance, burial funds, or a credit union; or serve as a social club. Many associations had overlapping objectives, and some sought to further all four of these goals. Often a particular issue provided impetus: the Hawaii Government Employees Association was organized in 1934 to combat low salaries; the San Francisco Federation of Public Employees was started in 1932 to prevent the governor from taking over the employees' retirement fund; in the late 1950s and 1960s, a number of associations sprang up to stave off organizing efforts by unions. The state associations in Connecticut, Oregon, and Washington represented breakaway movements from AFSCME. Whatever their origin and initial purpose, almost all associations now represent their members in lobbying in state legislatures, city councils, and county boards of supervisors; many process individual grievances; and some have converted into full-fledged collective bargaining organizations. Many provide low cost group insurance, which has served as an important attraction to members.

Most state associations are affiliated with the Assembly of Governmental Employees (AGE), a very loose confederation organized

19. Report of executive officers to International Association of Fire Fighters (IAFF) conventions, 1958 to 1970.

in 1952. In 1969, 32 AGE affiliates plus 4 other state associations claimed a total of 618,000 members, about 500,000 of them state employees and the remainder local. During the 1960s, membership in the state associations increased by 47 percent, indicating that they have participated, along with the unions, in the organizational growth among public employees. The associations are a varied lot, some espousing the objectives and tactics of unions, including collective bargaining and strikes, and others continuing to promote the interests of their members through the merit system, relying on lobbying and working through civil service. All associations are united, however, in their opposition to national unions of public employees.

Local associations do not have even the tenuous ties with each other that the AGE provides for state associations. A 1968–69 Bureau of Labor Statistics survey reported 662 municipal employee associations with 264,366 members.[20] This survey, however, included many police associations affiliated with the FOP or the ICPA and some local chapters of state associations, but omitted associations in localities of less than 10,000 population. The total membership of local associations not included in national and state associations is probably around 300,000. More than half the membership is concentrated in California and the New York City area, over 80 percent is covered by civil service, and most members are employed in the uniformed services or are professional, technical, or clerical employees.

Professional Associations

One of the unusual aspects of organization among government employees has been the emergence of professional associations as collective bargaining representatives. Though unions of professional employees had existed in private industry and in nonprofit organizations, it was only with the advent of collective bargaining in government that professionals started to join together on a large scale for that purpose. Public school teachers are, of course, the prime example of professionals who have adopted collective bar-

20. U.S. Bureau of Labor Statistics, *Municipal Public Employee Associations,* Bulletin 1702 (1971).

gaining. On a much smaller scale, many other professionals in government—university professors, social workers, lawyers, doctors, dentists, accountants, engineers, architects, city planners, and so on —are now represented in collective bargaining.

An important distinction must be made between professional associations formed primarily to advance the economic and job interests of their members through collective bargaining, and those that have expanded their original purposes and objectives to include employee representation and collective bargaining. Professionals who belong to the single-purpose organization usually continue their membership in such professional organizations as the American Bar Association, American Medical Association, National Association of Social Workers, and various societies of engineers, accountants, architects, and so forth, to which they continue to look for technical information, professional guidance and stimulation, and personal recognition in their chosen careers.

The National Education Association (NEA) perhaps best epitomizes the organization that continues its concern with the professional interests of its members and, at the same time, represents them in negotiations. Another organization that has added collective bargaining responsibilities to its original purely professional interests is the American Association of University Professors (AAUP). A third—the American Nurses' Association (ANA)—is, after the National Education Association, the largest professional association involved in collective bargaining.

The ANA is an organization of registered nurses with about 200,000 members who also belong to 55 constituent state and territorial associations and about 870 district nurses' associations.[21] If the percentages of civilian registered nurses employed by governmental agencies are applied to ANA figures, approximately 50,000 would be in public employment, about 40,000 of them in state and local government.[22]

As a professional association, the ANA is interested in all aspects of nursing. Its purpose is "to foster high standards of nursing practice, to promote the professional and educational advancement of nurses, and promote the welfare of nurses to the end that all people

---

21. American Nurses' Association, *Facts About Nursing* (New York: ANA, 1969), p. 69.

22. Based on data in ibid., and correspondence and interviews with ANA staff members.

may have better nursing care."[23] Promotion of the economic interests of nurses is only one of thirteen objectives listed in its bylaws.
Others include setting standards and qualifications for nursing
practice, establishing a code of ethical conduct, providing a professional record service, assisting in the professional development
of practitioners, and promoting the general health and welfare of
the public.[24] The ANA thus differs from unions, which are dedicated primarily to improving wages, hours, and working conditions
of their members. While economic security occupies an increasingly important place in the association's activities, professional
matters still occupy the largest amount of time and resources of the
organization.

The ANA became the first professional association to espouse
collective bargaining when, in 1946, its House of Delegates adopted
a resolution urging state nurses' associations (SNAs) to seek recognition as exclusive agents of their members in negotiations with
employers. Twenty-five years later, almost every state association
represented nurses to some extent in dealing with employers. In
recent years, as a result of federal executive orders and state public
employee collective bargaining laws, an increasing amount of the
economic representation and collective bargaining activity of state
nurses' associations has been concentrated on government employees.

As a professional association, ANA is open to all registered
nurses, including educators, directors of nursing, supervisors, staff
nurses in hospitals, and nurses in private practice. In collective bargaining, state associations have sought to speak for all registered
nurses, either in all-inclusive units of supervisors and staff nurses or
in separate bargaining units. In 1970 the national policy was liberalized to permit state associations to represent other groups of
health care employees.[25]

The Extent of Representation

In less than a decade of intensive organizational activity, unions
and associations in the public sector have succeeded in organizing
a higher proportion of employees than have been organized in the

23. Bylaws, American Nurses' Association (1970), Art. 1.
24. Ibid.
25. *American Journal of Nursing,* Vol. 70 (June 1970), p. 1271.

private sector in thirty-five years of protection and encouragement under the National Labor Relations Act. Approximately one-fourth of all private wage and salary workers belong to labor unions.[26] By comparison, one-half of all federal employees were union members in 1968, and an even higher proportion of the nation's school teachers (who constitute more than one-fourth of all state and local government employees) belonged either to the National Education Association or the American Federation of Teachers.[27]

In 1970 some 2 million or 38 percent of all full-time state and local government employees, excluding teachers and transit workers, were members of employee organizations (see Table 1-1).[28]

At the local level, union membership exceeded association membership, while, in state government, associations had almost three times as many members as unions; overall, association membership was more than a third again as great as union membership. Only ten unions were active in state government as compared with about thirty engaged in organizing in cities, counties, school districts, townships, and special authorities at the local level of government.

Employee organization in state and local government, while not as large as at the federal level or among school teachers, is proportionately greater than union membership in the private sector. Unions alone have enrolled about 16 percent of all full-time non-instructional employees in state and local government (19 percent in local units only). Whether that percentage, the 38 percent represented by both unions and associations, or some in-between figure is the appropriate measure of employee organization depends on the degree to which employee associations fill the collective bargaining role. This study is an attempt to appraise realistically the contribution of unions and employee associations—both in the present and the future—in state and local government.

---

26. U.S. Bureau of the Census, *Current Population Reports,* Series P-20, No. 216, "Labor Union Membership in 1966" (1971), p. 1.

27. Harry P. Cohany and Lucretia M. Dewey, "Union Membership Among Government Employees," *Monthly Labor Review,* Vol. 93 (July 1970), pp. 16–18.

28. The percentage is based on 5.3 million full-time employees, excluding teachers and transit workers (U.S. Bureau of the Census, "Full-time Employees of State and Local Governments, by Function: October 1970," unpublished table furnished by U.S. Department of Commerce). If part-time employees are included, the proportion drops to 29 percent (U.S. Bureau of the Census, *Public Employment in 1970,* Series GE70–No. 1 [1971], p. 9).

TABLE 1-1. *State and Local Government Employee Membership in Unions and Associations, 1969–70*

Organization	Member-ship, in thousands
Union	
American Federation of State, County and Municipal Employees (AFSCME)	441
International Association of Fire Fighters (IAFF)	132
Service Employees International Union (SEIU)	124
Laborers' International Union of North America	24
International Brotherhood of Teamsters	57
Others	50
Total, unions	828
Association	
Fraternal Order of Police (FOP)	80
International Conference of Police Associations (ICPA)	142
State associations	618
Local associations	300
American Nurses' Association	40
Total, associations	1,180
Total, unions and associations	2,008

Sources: Published figures of the organizations for 1969–70, supplemented by estimates based on information from interviews, correspondence, a questionnaire survey.

Local Employee Representation

In cities of 10,000 or more population, approximately 60 percent of all public employees are represented by unions or associations, and in some cities—New York, Philadelphia, Cincinnati, Detroit, and others—representation is close to 100 percent (see Appendix A). Public employee organization is closely related to city size and geographic location. Large cities in the Middle Atlantic, New England, East North Central, and Pacific states are the most highly organized. Municipal employees in the South and the Mountain states and those working in cities with less than 50,000 population have the lowest proportion of representation. The strength and, equally important, the support of the labor movement and state collective bargaining laws for public employees have also had a positive effect on organization of state and local government employees.

Uniformed protective service employees are more highly organized than any other group of municipal employees. The most common representation arrangement is for cities to deal with three employee organizations: one for fire fighters, another for policemen, and a third for other employees. While some large cities, such as New York, Detroit, and Milwaukee, recognize many unions and associations for their nonuniformed employees, the trend is to discourage proliferation of organizations and fragmentation of bargaining by minimizing the number of different organizations dealt with on behalf of employees. AFSCME and unaffiliated all-city associations most often represent nonuniformed employees in cities dealing with only one organization. The mixed unions are likely to be found in large cities that recognize several unions, in addition to the organizations representing police and fire fighters.

CHAPTER TWO

Industrial Unions and Associations

The "industrial" type union, which regards its jurisdiction as encompassing all workers within an industry without regard to skill and occupational specialty, is epitomized in state and local government by the American Federation of State, County and Municipal Employees (AFSCME), the Service Employees Internation Union (SEIU), the Laborers' International Union, and the International Brotherhood of Teamsters. The term is perhaps something of an exaggeration for AFSCME, which excludes federal employees, and not broad enough for the mixed unions—particularly the Teamsters—whose memberships include workers in a variety of industries other than government. However, within state and local government there is no group of employees, with the possible exception of uniformed fire fighters, who are not regarded as fair game for organizing by these unions. Within their respective jurisdictions, the independent state and local employee associations are equally broad in their organizational activities.

Structure

The common organizational interests of the industrial unions and associations are pursued through vastly different structures.

AFSCME, an all-public union, has developed into an organization with power, staff, and financial resources concentrated in the national office and intermediate councils rather than in local unions. The mixed unions, long decentralized to serve the needs of their private sector operations, have integrated their public sector activities into existing structures. The associations, while paying lip service to the need for a unifying national organization, have been unwilling to surrender low dues and complete autonomy and independence for the advantages of a strong national entity.

AFSCME

The AFSCME constitution provides for three organizational levels: the international, the council, and the local union. In addition, area offices and local chapters or subunits have developed in the union. The constitution, like that of most unions, assigns considerable power to the president. He not only serves as "chief executive and administrative officer" but appoints and directs the staff, determines the jurisdiction of locals and councils, negotiates mergers or consolidations with other public employee organizations, interprets the constitution, and places subordinate bodies under suspension.[1] Although the president's actions are subject to approval of the executive board, of which he is chairman, a strong president without organized opposition—both conditions present in AFSCME since 1964—runs little risk of being challenged by his board. The international office includes as well a secretary-treasurer; he is the chief financial and recording officer of the union but has little independent power.[2]

The international convention is the highest legislative and policy-making body in AFSCME, as it is in all unions.[3] Delegate entitlement and voting strength, a controversial issue in many unions, has been particularly important in AFSCME because of the tremendous variation in local union size, the preponderance of small locals, and the relatively small number of large locals. It was a major issue in the opposition movement that led to a change in the union's leadership in 1964.

1. Constitution of the American Federation of State, County and Municipal Employees, AFL-CIO (amended, 1972), Art. 5, secs. 1, 14.
2. Ibid., Art. 6.
3. Ibid., Art. 4.

During the 1940s the maximum voting strength of the individual local was reduced considerably; in the 1950s, under pressure from large locals, the voting formula was liberalized, but the union's administration fought the attempt by "certain few centers of membership" to dominate the union.[4] The opposition, which in 1960 charged that the international staff could control policy through its right to cast votes of small locals,[5] elected a new president in 1964. The constitution has since then been amended to approximate a one man–one vote arrangement. Locals receive 1 delegate for each 100 members up to 400, and an additional delegate for each 1,000 additional members or fraction thereof.[6] Every local is entitled to at least one delegate regardless of membership. As a result, the balance of power has shifted significantly in favor of the large local unions.

Between biennial conventions, constitutional authority is vested in an executive board composed of the president, the secretary-treasurer, and one international vice-president elected from each of nineteen legislative districts, plus an additional vice-president from any district with more than 10 percent of the union's membership.[7] The board was originally intended to consist of "lay members" who would continue to work as public employees, receiving only expenses and a per diem for attending board meetings. The idea of a lay executive board to provide a link between full-time officers and rank-and-file members and to keep control of the union in the hands of the working members originated in Great Britain, where most unions have such boards. In the United States, unions tend to have full-time salaried executive boards.

While AFSCME does not allow salaried employees of the international to serve as vice-presidents, most board members hold elective or appointive office at lower levels of the union. In 1970, ten of the twenty board members were full-time directors or presidents of councils, seven were local union presidents, and one was treasurer and another business agent of a local union. Only one

---

4. *Proceedings of the 12th International Convention, American Federation of State, County and Municipal Employees, AFL-CIO (AFSCME Proceedings)* (1960), p. 242.

5. Ibid., p. 243.

6. AFSCME Constitution (1972), Art. 4, sec. 6.

7. Ibid., Art. 8, sec. 1; Art. 4, secs. 25, 26.

member held no union office and less than half of the board members were actually working as public employees.

The basic operating units of AFSCME are the councils, of which there were 72 in 1970, at least one in almost every state, Washington, D.C., and Puerto Rico.[8] The councils, which are supposed to coordinate the activities of local unions and provide services to members, vary considerably in the way they are governed. The highest policy-making body of the council is the convention, which usually meets annually or biennially. A few large councils are governed by delegate assemblies which meet monthly. Between conventions or assembly meetings, the council is governed by an executive board composed of the council officers and elected members representing local unions, geographic areas, governmental levels, or other groups with common interests. Executive board members, who serve two- or three-year terms, are usually public employees who receive only a per diem allowance and expenses; some councils pay small salaries to their president or secretary-treasurer or both.

The lowest constitutional level in the union is the local union—there were over 1,900 of them in 1970, varying in membership from 10 to 5,000.[9] Large locals are often divided into subunits or chapters according to department, occupation, area, or some other mutual interest. The international presidents have favored expanding the jurisdiction of local unions and have encouraged mergers of small locals in order to increase efficiency. Average local membership has as a result increased from about 80 in 1948 to 110 in 1958 and 230 in 1972.[10]

Because AFSCME councils and local unions have little direct contact with each other and have sometimes worked at cross purposes, the union has established area offices to coordinate their activities. The increase from five area offices in 1968 to fifteen in 1970 reflects the administration's desire to improve coordination among councils and locals in collective bargaining and political action. Each area office will eventually be staffed by a director appointed by the international president, several international representatives, and staff specialists in education, research, and public relations, who will

8. *AFSCME Proceedings* (1970), p. 508.

9. Ibid.

10. Bureau of National Affairs, *Government Employee Relations Report (GERR)*, No. 455 (June 5, 1972), p. B-13.

work closely with headquarters departments. Local unions must affiliate with appropriate AFSCME councils and also with AFL-CIO central and state bodies in their areas.[11]

Representatives of unions active in both the private and public sectors stress greater local autonomy as an important advantage of their unions over AFSCME. Many local unions have left AFSCME in search of greater autonomy. Local autonomy may, however, be used to mask other reasons for making a change—personal leadership ambition, financial inducements, internal union politics, or the desire to benefit from the economic power or political influence exercised by another union. As AFSCME has grown larger and stronger, local defections have decreased. Also, exclusive representation provisions of state laws and the AFL-CIO Internal Disputes Plan have made it increasingly difficult for local unions to change affiliation.

The constitutions of the Service Employees, the Laborers, and the Teamsters unions do not differ greatly from AFSCME's in the authority and prerogatives of the international convention, international officers, and executive boards, or in the formal relationships between local unions, intermediate bodies, and the international. Each union provides for one or more intermediate bodies with which local unions must affiliate. The SEIU has joint councils; the Laborers, district councils and regional offices; and the Teamsters, both joint councils and conferences organized on a geographical, industry, or company basis. Only the SEIU requires its local unions to affiliate with city and state councils of the AFL-CIO.

Conventions are held every four years by the SEIU, every five by the Laborers and Teamsters. Delegates are apportioned according to local membership strength, but only the Service Employees provides for per capita voting.[12] Since roll call votes almost never occur in these unions, apportionment of votes is less impor-

11. AFSCME Constitution (1972), Art. 9, secs. 11, 16.
12. Constitution and Bylaws, Service Employees International Union (1968), Art. 4, secs. 4, 10; Constitution, Laborers' International Union of North America (1966), Art. 5, sec. 4; and Constitution, International Brotherhood of Teamsters, Chauffeurs, Warehousemen and Helpers of America (1966), Art. 3, sec. 2.

tant than in AFSCME where roll calls were common occurrences prior to 1964.

Of the three mixed unions, only the Laborers has a special unit to handle public employee matters at the national level. Its Federal–Public Service Employees' Division is headed by a former leader of the Mail Handlers' Union which merged with the Laborers in 1968. State and local employee affairs are handled by a former AFSCME attorney, who was dismissed in the change of administrations in 1964. The SEIU does not have a separate division for public employee organization, but its president and one of its vice-presidents have a strong interest in public employees. The Teamsters has not considered public employment sufficiently important to organize a special national section for public employees or to assign responsibility for this area to one of its officers or staff members.

ASSOCIATIONS

The state associations, some of which have local affiliates, are very loosely linked nationally in the Assembly of Governmental Employees (AGE). Local associations have no ties to any national organization and only the most informal communication among themselves within each state.

The AGE, organized in 1952 as the National Conference of Independent Public Employee Organizations, was founded to provide a common, national voice for associations of public employees. Its very general interests, focused primarily on promoting the merit system in government, were extended in 1967 when, beset by competition from unions, the board of directors added as one of its purposes enabling affiliates to engage in "nationwide competition with international unions who raid organized independent public employee groups."[13]

The AGE has always taken pains to emphasize the distinction between state civil service associations and unions. It has stressed the complete autonomy of AGE members in determining their own policies, in contrast to union policies which "are strongly influenced and even dictated by the International councils located outside of the jurisdiction." Unions, according to AGE, advocate

13. *GERR,* No. 227 (Jan. 15, 1968), p. B-1.

pressure tactics and strikes, while associations rely on "facts and persistent yet dignified persuasion."[14] Though some associations have begun to behave very much like unions, most associations, and especially those in states that do not have laws regulating public employment labor relations, do indeed differ from unions in terms of both organizational structure and behavior.

The AGE holds annual conventions which are usually attended by one or more officers or staff members from each association. The presidency and other offices are unsalaried positions which are filled by staff members and officers of affiliated associations. The board of directors, composed of the president, past president, first vice-president, secretary, treasurer, and three vice-presidents representing geographical areas, is required to meet only once a year but has been meeting more often in recent years.[15] The AGE headquarters, maintained in the office of the California State Employees Association, is manned by a founder and past president of AGE, who also serves as consultant to the California association. In 1971 a Washington office was established in a law firm that acts as national counsel for the AGE.[16]

It takes more than a constitution, a Washington office, and occasional policy statements to make an effective national organization. Among other things, it takes a belief on the part of the members that their common objectives are more important than their differences. Equally important is the willingness to back up this belief with funds, a full-time staff, and authority for elected officials to execute policies established by the national organization. AGE affiliates have been unable to agree on such important issues as collective bargaining and the right to strike for public employees and have been unwilling to provide the funds necessary to support an effective national organization. The organization's activities are seriously hampered by a constitutional requirement of unanimous approval of all member organizations before AGE may "sponsor, support or endorse . . . any program."[17] Because their national organization is so weak, the independent associations must depend

14. Statement by board of directors, Assembly of Governmental Employees (AGE), December 1967.

15. Constitution and By Laws, AGE (1971), Art. 5.

16. Letters to the author from Executive Secretary, Oregon State Employees Association, Nov. 4, 1971, and Feb. 16, 1972.

17. AGE Constitution (1971), Art. 7.

upon leadership and resources at the state and local levels to compete successfully with AFSCME and other unions.

Most state associations limit membership to state employees; in 1969 only five claimed substantial numbers of both state and local government employee members. In a few states, state employees belong to one association, local employees to another organized on a statewide basis.[18] Most state associations have restricted their membership because of significant differences in the nature of state and local government employment, inadequate finances and staff (coupled with unwillingness to raise dues to provide additional resources), and failure to see benefits commensurate with costs from an integrated association. However, some have concluded that the addition of municipal, county, school district, and other local employees would enhance the association's influence among state legislators, all of whom are elected at the local level. A combined organization would also be in a better position to compete with unions that organize at both the state and local levels of government. A number of associations have recently opened their membership to local government employees, but enrollment has not yet significantly increased in any of these states.[19]

There is a growing tendency for state associations that do not include local employees to maintain informal ties with local associations, and for the two to assist each other as the occasion demands. Thus, in Maryland, the state Classified Employees Association helped the Baltimore Classified Municipal Employees Association in its 1969 election contest with AFSCME. In Oregon and California, state associations have also given aid and advice to local associations. The pressures for cooperation, informal relationships, and integration are bound to increase as state and local associations find themselves competing with well-organized unions that draw on manpower and financial resources much greater than those available to most independent associations.

Within states, associations are usually divided into chapters based

18. Illinois has two state associations, one for local government employees in and around Chicago, the other for state employees. New Jersey has one association for state employees, another open to both state and local government employees. Ohio has one state association that accepts both state and local government employees, and another limited to noncertified, nonteaching public school employees.

19. Letter to the author from Executive Secretary, Oregon State Employees Association, Sept. 7, 1971.

on geographical or highway districts, departments or agencies, state institutions, skills, occupations, or job classifications. The trend appears to be toward restructuring chapters along craft, occupational, and departmental lines in order to adapt to unit concepts of state collective bargaining laws. Association chapters have tended to be small and highly autonomous, but this too may change to meet the needs of collective bargaining in associations that espouse this approach to representing public employees.

Like unions, most state associations consider the convention, which usually meets annually, as the major policy-making body. Resolutions are adopted, constitutions amended, and policies set by delegate bodies, varying in size and manner of selection. Association executive boards tend to be large and almost invariably are composed of full-time government employees. Association officers, and some executive board members, are usually elected at large, and additional representatives are chosen from departments, regions, and chapters. The New York association allocates seats on the executive board to representatives of its state and county divisions. Some associations provide for representation on the basis of membership within subordinate groups. Whatever the method of selection, the unwieldy size of executive boards, ranging from 25 to 85 members, has led to the creation of small executive committees. In practice, the association president and one or two other officers, together with the full-time staff, have the strongest influence in shaping and carrying out association policies.

Minority Group Participation

State and local governments constitute the largest group of employers in the United States on whose work force comprehensive social and ethnic information is lacking. They are also the only large group whose employment practices were exempt from federal nondiscrimination requirements until 1972 when Congress extended the jurisdiction of the Equal Employment Opportunity Commission (EEOC) to employees in state, county, and municipal governments.[20] The United States Commission on Civil Rights, in 1969,

20. *Labor Relations Reporter: News and Background Information,* Vol. 79 (April 3, 1972), p. 298.

in an attempt to determine the extent and nature of minority group employment in government, studied seven major metropolitan areas of the country: San Francisco-Oakland, Philadelphia, Detroit, Atlanta, Houston, Memphis, and Baton Rouge.[21] Its findings help to explain differences in minority group membership in public employee organizations in state and local government.

Although the basic conclusion of the report was that "state and local governments have failed to fulfill their obligation to assure equal job opportunity,"[22] the commission found significant differences in employment of minority group members among different levels of government, between cities, and particularly between departments performing various municipal and state functions. In four of the eight central cities surveyed, the proportion of jobs held by Negroes was in excess of their relative numbers in the general population. A large number of local governments, however, employed no Negro workers. In state government, Negro employment was about equal to the proportion of blacks in the population generally in the North but not in the South.

In the seven areas, minority group members (of which 92 percent were black[23]) held a fourth of all state and local government jobs. In all but one area, black employment was significantly higher in government than in private industry. Negro employees, however, occupy the lower rungs of the occupational ladder. Even in the central cities where minority group members are well represented in the aggregate, they are notably absent from higher paying jobs. They are heavily concentrated in public utility and community development (primarily streets, highways, and sewerage) where they hold a majority of all laborer jobs. They are also strongly represented in public health and hospital work, and such occupations as hospital attendant, orderly, unlicensed practical nurse, nurse's aide, kitchen helper, and food handler appear to have become almost exclusively "Negro jobs." Because departments that conduct most of their business with the Negro community employ large

---

21. U.S. Commission on Civil Rights, *For All the People . . . By All the People: A Report on Equal Opportunity in State and Local Government Employment* (1969).

22. Ibid., p. 131.

23. Ibid., p. xii. Employment of Spanish-Americans was investigated in two of the areas; "more options [were] available to them than Negroes but substantially fewer options than [to] other whites" (ibid., p. 27).

numbers of Negroes, many clerical jobs in welfare and health departments are filled by Negroes.

Police and fire departments made the poorest showing in minority group employment in every city. Although 27 percent of all central city employees were policemen or firemen, only 7 percent of the Negro employees held such jobs. A Negro was two or three times as likely to obtain a civilian job in police and fire departments as to become a member of the uniformed force. Few black policemen and even fewer black fire fighters held officer rank.

Unfortunately, statistical data are not collected on minority group membership in labor organizations generally or in public employee unions and associations. However, surveys of government employee organizations in many parts of the country, including the seven metropolitan areas surveyed by the Civil Rights Commission, indicate that minority group membership generally follows the employment patterns found by the commission: it is high in unions representing unskilled and semiskilled blue collar workers; low in associations whose membership is predominantly white collar and supervisory employees; and lowest in organizations of uniformed police and fire fighters.

AFSCME

Minority group members are found at all levels of AFSCME. The union's international secretary-treasurer, elected in 1972, is a Negro. Blacks and Puerto Ricans constitute about one-third of the international executive board and have substantial representation among district council and local union officers and among the professional staff and other employees of the union. Unlike other AFSCME staff members, many of whom have come from outside the union, minority group staff are usually drawn from public employees. Approximately half of the twenty-eight staff interns in the first two classes in a program to develop union leaders from within the membership were black, Puerto Rican, or Mexican-American.[24] Convention proceedings, union publications, educational materials, in short everything visible about AFSCME, project the image of a union that is aware and sensitive to minority group members and their problems.

24. *Public Employee,* Vol. 36 (1971), pp. 6–8.

Perhaps this is not surprising in a union with a membership estimated to be as much as one-third black and with substantial numbers of Puerto Rican, Mexican-American, and Oriental-American members. Minority group participation has been facilitated by the tremendous growth in the union leadership and staff which was required to service the rapidly growing membership. It is much easier to elect or employ minority group members when an organization is expanding than it is to replace white officers and staff with such individuals, especially when the whites are entrenched in their positions and have their own following within the union.

Minority membership is, of course, directly related to the functional and occupational distribution and the geographic location of the public employees represented by the union. In the central cities where blacks hold most, and sometimes close to 100 percent, of all the low-skilled jobs in public works, sanitation, street maintenance, and hospitals, local unions are also predominantly black. In a few councils and local unions blacks are a small minority or almost nonexistent, but in most places, black membership is already large or increasing.

Not all members share the union's interest in minority group issues. An AFSCME police council in Connecticut, for instance, opposed lowering the height requirements for officers by one inch in order to aid in the recruitment of Puerto Ricans. Police locals were also unhappy about the national publicity, and particularly the photographs showing altercations between policemen and blacks, in the 1968 Memphis strike and other AFSCME strikes that have led to confrontations between black workers and white policemen. AFSCME's strong civil rights stance has undoubtedly been an obstacle to increasing membership among policemen and has contributed to the union's ambivalence toward organizing police officers. The leader of a predominantly black local said that he had never tried to organize the city police because they were "a different breed of cat" and "Wallace backers."

In New York State, one of the reasons for AFSCME's decisive representation election defeat by the Civil Service Employees Association was its identification with blacks and Puerto Ricans in New York City. In Memphis, AFSCME was so closely identified with black people that it encountered difficulty organizing white workers in hospitals in which it had 100 percent membership among blacks. On the other hand, AFSCME turned down requests to organize blacks employed by the city-owned power company because it did not wish to be charged with raiding by the International Brotherhood of Electrical Workers, which represented the white workers in the utility.

MIXED UNIONS

Minority group membership among public employees in the mixed unions is more difficult to estimate than in an all-public-employee union like AFSCME. Not only is the racial composition of the membership unknown, but also whether the members of mixed locals are private or public employees. The Equal Employment Opportunity Commission has issued some information on minority membership in the mixed unions. The data are limited to referral unions—those that "operate hiring halls or, under similar arrangements, refer persons for employment."[25] Since most local unions do not operate hiring halls and since government employers do not usually depend on unions to refer workers to them, the data are only suggestive.

In 1969, SEIU reported that 26 percent of its members in 34 local unions with 57,000 members were black, 7 percent Spanish-American, and 2 percent Oriental-American or American-Indian. The Laborers' Union reported 24 percent black, 11 percent Spanish-American, and less than 2 percent Oriental-American and American-Indian members in 428 referral locals with more than 277,000 members. The Laborers' report was based on more than half of the organization's total membership, whereas about 15 percent of the SEIU membership is in referral locals. The Teamsters union reported that 15 percent of 330,000 members in referral locals were black or Spanish-American and less than 1 percent were Oriental-American or American-Indian. The Teamsters' average was about the same as that for all referral unions.[26]

Given the concentration of public employee membership in mixed unions in the central cities and in job categories and functions with high proportions of minority group members, minorities

25. News release, Equal Employment Opportunity Commission (EEOC), Feb. 9, 1971.

26. EEOC, "Total and Minority Membership in Referral Unions in the United States, by Trade or Craft, 1969," Local Union Report EEO-3 (EEOC, 1969; processed).

must be at least as well represented throughout the unions as in the referral locals. In California, where the SEIU is the dominant public employee union, minority membership—mostly black but also Mexican-American and occasionally Indian—approached 90 percent in some locals and was very substantial in others.

While minority group officers and staff were not as visible in SEIU as in AFSCME, Negroes have attained leadership positions at both the national and local levels of the union. Two of the fourteen executive board members, four out of fifteen international organizers, two of the eight headquarters staff members, and many SEIU local union officers are black. The first black was elected to a vice-presidency in the international in 1964; he had been president for twenty-five years of New York City Local 144 with jurisdiction over hotel workers, nursing homes, and hospitals.

Minority membership is estimated at 12–15 percent of the total membership of the 2-million-member Teamsters union. A New York City local with 13,000 members, most of them in public housing and schools, was estimated to be over half blacks and Puerto Ricans. Mixed locals in Pittsburgh, St. Louis, and New Orleans reported a substantial majority of black membership among public employees. An anomaly is the Teamsters local known as the Uniformed Sanitationmen's Association, with over 10,000 members; it is largely Italian. None of the Teamsters' fifteen international executive board members are black or Spanish-American. However, minority representation among officers and staff in most public employee locals appears to be substantial.

Judging from the occupational and functional distribution of public employee membership in the Laborers' Union—largely low-skilled workers in public works, schools, housing authorities, and parks—minority group membership is probably on a par with that in other public employee unions. Two of the Laborers' eight vice-presidents are black and there is also substantial black representation among lower level union officers and staff members.[27]

ASSOCIATIONS

The relatively high concentration of white collar employees in state and local associations and the small proportion of clerical,

27. *Wall Street Journal,* July 15, 1968.

managerial, and technical jobs held by blacks and Spanish-Americans have limited the opportunities for minority group membership. The social and fraternal nature of some associations also restricts and, in some areas, rules out nonwhite membership. Thus Baltimore has two separate associations of city employees, one white, the other black.

Some associations, however, have significant numbers of minority group members and even leaders. State associations in New Jersey, Maryland, and Illinois estimate their minority membership at 20–25 percent. The New York Civil Service Employees Association must have increased its black and Spanish-American membership substantially since it was certified as the exclusive representative for state institutional and hospital employees. In Colorado, Mexican-Americans and American-Indians constitute about 15 percent of the state association and blacks an additional 5–10 percent.

Among local associations, minority membership appears to be significant only in California. The Los Angeles County Employees Association, which has now merged with the SEIU, reported about 35 percent of the membership being black or Mexican-American in 1969. The Alameda County Employees Association estimated 30–40 percent of its members were black. Several other associations in California had about 20 percent black membership. In the Midwest and the East, particularly in states with collective bargaining laws, local associations have few minority group members. Undoubtedly, this reflects the fact that they represent largely white collar and supervisory units, with unions having representation rights among blue collar employees, where blacks are found in larger numbers.

Given the low proportion of minority group membership in associations, it is not surprising that blacks and Spanish-Americans seldom hold positions of leadership. However, the president of the Oregon State Employees Association is black; the Maryland, New York, and Washington state associations have black members on their executive boards; and the Texas association has a few board members who are Mexican-American. Among local associations, minority group leadership is more limited. The Los Angeles City Employees Association, with a former three-term president who was black and a black vice-president, has had a long history of minority group leadership. Two of the fifteen members of the executive board of the San Francisco Federation of Public Employees are black.

Leadership

Not only is the locus of leadership different in unions and associations, but the relative strength of those who control the organizations' activities is vastly different. Unions concentrate power in elected, full-time officers at the international level. The older the union, the more assured the authority of its leaders. Associations, on the other hand, give little power to their officers, and whatever leadership is exerted comes from the professional staff. Association policy is determined, however, by elected officers; they are more apt to be supervisory employees than rank-and-file workers, though this situation has been changing in recent years.

AFSCME

In 1964 Arnold Zander, the first president of AFSCME, was unseated by a 21-vote margin out of 2,879 votes.[28] Jerry Wurf, the successful challenger, was relatively young for a union president, and five years later he became the youngest member of the prestigious AFL-CIO executive council. The leader in the "revolution" of young men, as Wurf called it, against the "old guard" had never worked as a public employee. He had joined the union as an international organizer in 1947, seven years after graduating from college, and subsequently became director of its largest unit, New York City Council 37.[29]

In 1972, Wurf's executive assistant was elected secretary-treasurer, succeeding a former assistant who had been elevated to the office in 1966 and was moving on to the newly created post of full-time chairman of the judicial panel.[30] The new secretary-treasurer had worked as a county engineer after attending the University of

---

28. *AFSCME Proceedings* (1964), p. 137.

29. See Irwin Ross, "Those Newly Militant Government Workers," *Fortune*, August 1968, pp. 104–7, 131–34.

30. While allegedly designed to free the judicial panel from the political processes of the union, the appointment of a full-time chairman and eight part-time members by the president for five-year terms, with the advice and consent of the executive board, would hardly seem to make the panel less political than formerly, when nine part-

California. He had been president of a predominantly white local union in California and became the highest ranking black officer in a major AFL-CIO union.[31]

The international executive board of AFSCME exercises little power in the union. The vice-presidents who serve on the board, though elected, rarely have independent power bases, having been selected by strong council directors to represent their districts. The executive board is thus one of "followers" who rarely question decisions made by the president and usually follow his recommendations. In order to assure himself of support from important council directors or presidents, the president usually checks with them before raising major issues for board action. He also involves the real leaders of the union in decision making by appointing them to study commissions charged with developing recommendations on controversial matters.

Since the change of administrations in 1964, presidential elections have been by acclamation. Executive board elections, hotly contested before 1965 when vice-presidents were elected by the entire convention rather than on a district basis, have become less competitive. There has also been a significant decrease in controversy and debate at conventions, and roll call votes have become a rarity. The changes mark the transition of AFSCME from a faction-ridden union to a more unified and disciplined organization similar to other older, more mature unions.

MIXED UNIONS

All three of the major mixed unions have experienced changes in top leadership during the last few years. In each case, the change

---

time members were elected by the executive board for two-year terms and elected their own chairman. The chairman's position, which pays the same as that of secretary-treasurer, appears to have been tailored for its occupant, freeing the secretary-treasurer's position so as to give representation to the large proportion of black members in AFSCME. The judicial panel decides charges against international officers, acts as an appeals body from decisions of subordinate tribunals, hears trusteeship cases, and, under the 1972 amendments, rules on eligibility for membership and election protests in subordinate bodies. During its first five years, the panel rendered 30 decisions, none of which resulted in a reversal of the international president or a subordinate trial body. (See Reports of the Judicial Panel to the 1966, 1968, and 1970 AFSCME conventions.)

31. *New York Times,* June 1, 1972, p. 26.

was engineered quietly, efficiently, and without involvement of the membership. David Sullivan, president of the Service Employees, who would have been ineligible for reelection because of age, resigned a year before the 1972 convention. The executive board, over which the president presides, was thus able to elevate the first vice-president and to fill his vacant office prior to the convention. In a significant departure from union tradition, the man chosen to fill the vacancy was the union's executive secretary, a specialist in public employee organization who had never held elective office in the union.[32]

During the 1960s SEIU expanded its membership by 70 percent and was particularly active in organizing public employees. The executive board grew from eight to fourteen members. Emphasis on organizing public employees can be expected to continue and increase. George Hardy, the new president, has held both local and state council offices in California, which has more SEIU public employee members than any other state. His nonideological approach to trade unionism and his willingness to give local unions a high degree of autonomy have contributed to his success in organizing public employees. In the late 1940s and early 1950s he accepted into the union United Public Workers locals that had been expelled from the CIO for being communist dominated; they are the core of the militant locals that now dominate the public employee scene in California. The SEIU in California is a strange amalgam of conventional private sector locals and local unions of public employees that run the gamut from unskilled hospital employees, park attendants, and custodians to social workers with graduate degrees.

The Laborers' Union also changed its top leadership in the 1960s. Like everything else in the operation of this union, the change was orderly. In 1968 the general executive board moved the seventy-five-year-old secretary-treasurer, Peter Fosco, to the presidency on the retirement of Joseph V. Moreschi, the union's president for fifty-two years. The board named a thirty-eight-year-old vice-president to the secretary-treasurer's job and then filled his vacated post with Fosco's son.[33]

The Laborers' Union has eight vice-presidents who, with the president and secretary-treasurer, make up the general executive board. All officers are elected by the convention which meets every

32. *Service Employee*, Vol. 32 (April 1971), pp. 12–14.
33. *AFL-CIO News*, Nov. 16, 1968, p. 3.

five years. Elections are never contested and nominations are made with all the flowery speeches, demonstrations, and hoopla generally associated with national political conventions.

The third of the mixed unions, the Teamsters, was compelled to change its top leadership in 1967 when James R. Hoffa, general president since 1957, was jailed for mail fraud and jury tampering. His hand-picked successor, Frank E. Fitzsimmons, took over when Hoffa was jailed and was elected president in his own right at the union's 1971 convention, after Hoffa's resignation.[34] None of the Teamsters' fifteen executive board members are known for their interest or activity in the public sector.

ASSOCIATIONS

Leadership in associations resides primarily in full-time staff members rather than in elected officers. The Assembly of Governmental Employees' officers, elected annually from among delegates to the convention, are usually staff members of state affiliates; they have few duties and no power. Officers in state and local associations have more constitutional authority than AGE officers but because theirs is a part-time role, day-to-day leadership usually falls to full-time executive directors. Nevertheless, the responsibility for formulating policy remains with the association officers and executive board members.

Unions have charged that associations are dominated by supervisors and other management personnel. Most state associations do indeed have substantial numbers of supervisors and middle management employees among their officers and on their executive boards. In some the preponderance of supervisors in leadership positions reflects the composition of the membership. In others it represents the advancement of employees, who have been promoted to supervisory positions while retaining membership and interest in the association. The importance of the group insurance provided by most associations to members has undoubtedly contributed to the election of supervisors to office because of their presumedly greater knowledge and expertise in selecting and administering such programs. The belief that the association should have at its helm individuals who can command the respect of top-level admin-

34. *New York Times,* July 9, 1971, p. 5.

istrators and legislators with whom they deal has probably led to the election of supervisors to policy-making positions in some associations.

Local associations appear to be less dominated by supervisors than state associations. But there are still many instances in which the president and other officers and board members hold important supervisory positions. Because local associations usually do not have full-time staff, officers play a much more active role in running the affairs of the organization than they do in state associations. In the larger local associations, with one or more full-time staff members, officers lean heavily on the staff for guidance in policy formation.

State laws prohibiting supervisors and nonsupervisory employees from belonging to the same bargaining unit or denying representation rights to supervisors have affected the leadership of associations. Some associations that engage in collective bargaining have excluded supervisors from elective office or other policy-making positions. In others, supervisors have lost interest in seeking office or even retaining membership. State collective bargaining laws have also encouraged nonsupervisory employees to become more active in their associations and to assert claims to leadership. As more associations reorient their activities toward collective bargaining, the leadership role of supervisors must of necessity be diminished, both to meet the requirements of state laws and to make the associations credible representatives in the eyes of nonsupervisory employees who constitute the bulk of the membership.

Staff

A major difference between unions and associations is the size of their staffs. Unions typically have higher ratios of staff to members than associations.

AFSCME

The AFSCME staff is a melange of former unskilled public employees and agency supervisors as well as individuals who have never worked for government; experienced organizers from other unions and those whose service in AFSCME goes back twenty or thirty years; black militants, ex-police officers, and former legislators; high school drop-outs and college graduates. Unlike most unions, which have a strong tradition or even a requirement that staff members come from the membership,[35] AFSCME's staff reads like a United Nations of unions. They formerly worked for the Automobile Workers, Machinists, Fire Fighters, Ladies Garment Workers, Meatcutters, Communication Workers, Bricklayers, Electrical Workers, Brewery Workers, Marine Engineers, Transit Workers, Teamsters, Chemical Workers, Painters, and Service Employees. Some staff members have even come from associations, which AFSCME generally refers to as company unions.

This pattern of hiring staff from outside the union has not developed by design. Quite the contrary. The union would prefer to hire people with experience in public employment and has often been criticized by competing unions and associations for employing persons who cannot understand the problems of government workers. The fact that the staff of mixed unions usually have come from private industry has not deterred them from using this charge against AFSCME in organizing campaigns.

The staff pattern of AFSCME is rooted in the nature of government employment and the history of the union. When AFSCME was organized in the 1930s, government jobs offered security. When economic conditions improved and alternative opportunities became available, those who stayed in government were more security conscious and less venturesome than others who left for greener pastures. The uncertain future and low pay of a union staff job held little attraction for government employees, even though they might be strong union supporters and eager volunteer organizers on a part-time basis. Since a leave of absence to accept a union position was unheard of in government before the 1960s, taking a union job meant a complete break in employment and the loss of civil service status and seniority. Few government employees were prepared to take this risk and the union was forced to turn to other sources.

Though the original organizers of the union and many of the early members were supervisors and white collar workers, the overwhelming majority of the membership is low-skilled and poorly educated. For many years the union relied primarily on lobbying and persuasion, rather than collective bargaining and power, and its own membership may not have seemed the best source of staff

35. Derek C. Bok and John T. Dunlop, *Labor and the American Community* (Simon and Schuster, 1970), p. 174.

to carry out these tasks. Or to put it somewhat differently, "collective begging" calls for different talents than "collective bargaining."

Finally, as a relative latecomer to the labor movement, AFSCME was in a position to hire staff who had gained experience with other unions and held responsible positions but were interested in changing jobs. One area director, for example, is a former regional director of the United Auto Workers who ran afoul of the Reuther administration. A council director had served on the staff of the Meat Cutters union and had spent several years working for the United States Agency for International Development in Turkey before joining AFSCME. A former SEIU business agent had also worked as administrative assistant to a congressman and labor adviser to a governor. Thus AFSCME has made a virtue out of the necessity of relying on outside sources for its staff. As the emphasis on collective bargaining increased, so did the union's need for people with negotiating experience who were in short supply within AFSCME.

In an effort to recruit staff from among its own members, AFSCME in 1971 revived a staff intern program that had been discontinued in 1967 (eight of the fifteen participants in the earlier program still work for the union). The new intern program is designed not only to train qualified staff with a background in public employment but to offer an avenue to upward mobility to the union's own members.[36] The first group of interns included ten men and six women, half of them minority group members, averaging thirty-five years in age. They were working at such diverse occupations as psychiatric technician, barber, engineer, bus driver, garbage collector, elevator operator, clerk, case worker, and clerk-typist. All held office or were active in their local unions.[37]

In the spring of 1970, AFSCME employed 589 full-time professionals at all levels of the union to service some 450,000 members.[38] The staff has grown from 61 in 1948 when the union had 90,000 members and 165 in 1958 when it had 185,000. Thus there was 1 staff member for every 764 union members in 1970 as compared to

---

36. *AFSCME Proceedings* (1970), pp. 431–32.

37. *Public Employee,* Vol. 36 (January–February 1971), pp. 6, 7.

38. Professionals include all staff members other than those engaged in secretarial, clerical, maintenance, or custodial work.

1 for 1,500 twenty years ago and 1 for 1,100 a decade ago.[39] The international employed 38 professionals in the headquarters office in Washington, D.C., and 101 in the field. Most of the remaining 450 worked for councils and some for local unions as full-time staff representatives or business agents.

The council director is the key staff member in AFSCME and, collectively, the directors constitute the backbone of the union. Though he is generally appointed by and constitutionally responsible to the executive board, the director is usually the most powerful individual in the council in making as well as carrying out policy. The director personifies the council to the membership and government officials and, more than any other single individual, is responsible for the success or failure of the union in the area within his jurisdiction. The job calls for a combination of talents: politician, administrator, negotiator, public speaker, social worker, and curb-stone lawyer.

The council director appoints and supervises other staff members and determines their salaries, usually subject to approval of the executive board. The number of professional staff members varies from one or two in the smallest councils to about a hundred in the largest. Few councils have more than ten full-time staff members. The full-time staff is supplemented by members who work for the union on a part-time basis and, during important organizing drives, representation election campaigns, and strikes, by international representatives.

International field staff, some council staffs, and all office employees of the union are represented by unions. The issue of organization for international staff was first raised at the 1964 convention by staff members who feared for their jobs after a change in presidents. The new president assured the delegates that rumors that he was about to "axe" the entire staff were "so much nonsense."[40] The motion to recognize a staff union was referred to the newly elected executive board, which deferred action until 1970.

Despite his assurances, Wurf "cleaned house" when he took over in 1964. AFSCME continued to have considerable staff turnover

39. By 1972, AFSCME staff had increased to 920 and membership to 550,000, a ratio of 1 staff member for every 600 members (*GERR*, No. 455 [June 5, 1972], pp. B-12, 13).

40. *AFSCME Proceedings* (1964), pp. 158–62.

even after the original change in administration. Wurf's volatile temper and hard driving leadership style have sometimes been blamed for the high turnover. But some former staff members resigned to advance their careers elsewhere, others were fired for incompetence, and still others left because of internal differences that develop in any growing, dynamic, and highly political organization.

MIXED UNIONS

Unlike AFSCME, whose staff is concentrated in the international and the councils, the overwhelming bulk of the staff of the mixed unions is employed by local unions. In 1970 the SEIU, AFSCME's major union competitor, maintained a professional staff of only 26 in Washington, 18 of whom were international organizers. The union's 350 locals and regional offices employed about 600 staff representatives. The ratio of professional staff to total membership, including both private and public sector employees, was about 1 to 655, somewhat higher than AFSCME's ratio.

The lesser role of the international in the operations of the SEIU is reflected in expenditures for organizing and providing services to members. In 1967 the SEIU international spent only $232,114 on salaries of representatives and organizers, and $143,438 for organizing expenses.[41] AFSCME, with about the same number of members as SEIU, spent $363,818 on organizers' salaries and $507,342 on other expenses related to international organizational activities during the last six months of 1967 alone.[42] Thus, AFSCME appears to have had about five times as many representatives working out of international headquarters and expended almost five times as much money supporting organizing activities as did the SEIU. Another service stressed much more by AFSCME than SEIU is research and education, for which the all-public-employee union spent over $200,000 in 1967 as compared with only $15,000 by SEIU in 1965, the highest year on record during the 1960s.[43] In 1972 SEIU's new president reported that 70 new organizers and 8 research and negotiating specialists had been added to the union's

41. Service Employees International Union, *Proceedings of the Fourteenth General Convention (SEIU Proceedings)* (1968), Financial Summary, Exhibit B.
42. *AFSCME Proceedings* (1968), p. 368.
43. *SEIU Proceedings* (1968), Financial Summary, Exhibit B; *AFSCME Proceedings* (1968), p. 369.

staff.[44] Despite the lesser role played by the international in the affairs of the SEIU, its financial situation is much better than AFSCME's. As of December 31, 1967, SEIU's net worth was $5,679,862 compared with $505,338 for AFSCME.[45]

The local union in SEIU provides many of the services that the council and the international provide in AFSCME. The officers and executive board members of public employee locals are generally full-time government employees. The professional staff are a varied group. In one Los Angeles local the business manager—a woman—is a former federal government economist who was instrumental in organizing the local and has held positions as shop steward and president. This local of 5,500 unskilled hospital and institutional employees has an assistant general manager and 6 staff representatives.

The executive director of a statewide local of 3,500 government social workers has a bachelor's degree in sociology and a master's degree in political science. He and the 3 full-time staff representatives who work with him have been described by a university professor as "dedicated men who believe they are cadres in a social revolution."[46] The general manager of a local with 3,200 members is a black former sanitation worker who joined the union while he was still a probationary employee, organized employees in the Department of Public Works, and has held various elective offices in the union. His local also employs 3 staff representatives.

The Laborers' Union, whose public employee membership represents about 13 percent of its 550,000 members, considers the public sector less important than the construction laborers and employees in allied industries that it serves.[47] The officers and almost all of the international and local staff come from the construction industry and have only a limited understanding of government employment. Exceptions are the union's general counsel, who is a key man in the Laborers' hierarchy, and the few staff members of the Federal–Public Service Employees' Division who recognize the potential in public employees as a source of union membership. But

44. *Service Employee,* June 1972.

45. *SEIU Proceedings* (1968), Financial Summary, Exhibit A; *AFSCME Proceedings* (1968), p. 363.

46. Letter to the author from Archie Kleingartner, University of California at Los Angeles, Dec. 2, 1971.

47. Bok and Dunlop, *Labor and the American Community,* p. 157.

their efforts to increase the Laborers' emphasis on public employee organization have met with only limited success.

The Laborers' Union is run in a paternalistic manner. Salary increases and other adjustments are promulgated by the president at regular intervals. The 120 international representatives, who are assigned to regional offices, do not have a union but are better paid than staff members of AFSCME and SEIU who do. Some additional 1,500 full-time representatives are employed by the union's 600 locals, which have full responsibility for determining their salaries and perquisites. Turnover is high among the representatives who service public sector locals because of their unfamiliarity with the field and the "somewhat ambiguous position [of this area] at international headquarters."[48]

Only a small proportion of the local union representatives devotes any time to organizing or servicing state and local government employees. A few locals or councils have enough public employee members to warrant the employment of full-time staff members. Construction councils and private sector locals assist public employee locals during election campaigns or when an unusual effort is called for. For example, in 1968 when the Laborers' Union was competing with AFSCME and a city association to represent sanitation and public works employees in Baltimore, surrounding area locals sent more than a dozen organizers to help the three full-time staff members assigned to the area; in Providence, local representatives were reinforced by staff from construction locals to help defeat AFSCME in an election for all of the city's blue collar employees; and in San Francisco the single full-time representative working in public employment was aided by some forty additional representatives when the union was organizing at the Tracy Ordnance Depot.

The usual arrangement is for the business agent of a construction or other private sector local union to decide whether to organize or accept government workers into his local, and to spend some of his time servicing them until the local can afford a second full-time person or the public employees are able to establish their own local. Some Laborers business agents are not interested in organizing public employees, feel unqualified to operate in the public sector, or do not want to bother organizing a relatively small number of low-

48. Ibid.

paid potential members who may turn out to be more trouble than they are worth. Almost invariably the decision whether and whom to organize is made at the local level. The international might be called in for help after the organization effort has gotten under way, but only in situations where large installations or government departments with a substantial number of employees are involved would the decision originate with the international.

In the Teamsters union almost all staff members—90 percent according to one officer—work for and are paid by local unions or other subordinate bodies.[49] Only about 50 general organizers are assigned to the international, while several thousand business agents and other staff members are employed by the 4 area conferences, 49 joint councils, and 764 Teamster locals. In keeping with officers' salaries, which are the highest of any union, Teamster staff members at all levels, though unorganized, are generally better paid than professionals in other unions.[50]

Teamster public employee locals differ greatly in the number of staff members employed. The largest staff, of 15 to 20 professionals, includes 2 lawyers, an economist, a welfare fund director, a director of organization, and several business agents. Locals that include both public and private employees generally assign one or more staff members to service government workers. A few locals with public employee members have no staff assigned to the public sector.

The burgeoning movement to organize public employees has resulted in a very active and competitive labor market for union representatives with public sector experience. The 1964 change of command in AFSCME benefited the Laborers, SEIU, Teamsters, and other mixed unions and some associations as well. As a result of the interchange of staff among public employee organizations, it is not unusual to find men who once worked together competing against each other in organizing public employees.

49. H. J. Gibbons, "Centralization in the Teamsters Union," in Joel Seidman (ed.), *Trade Union Government and Collective Bargaining* (Praeger, 1970), p. 151.

50. The Teamsters' constitution (adopted in 1971) also contains a unique safeguard against salary reductions. The salary of an officer or business agent of a local or subordinate body "may not be reduced an unreasonable amount as a subterfuge to force his resignation." Salary reductions during a person's term of elected office may be made only for financial reasons "as attested to by the General Secretary-Treasurer of the International Union." (Constitution [1971], Art. 22, sec. 3, p. 136.)

ASSOCIATIONS

Almost all state associations have full-time professional and clerical staff. The largest, with 170,000 members in 1969, employed 45 professional and about 80 clerical employees and the second largest 60 professionals and 50 clerical employees to service 120,000 members. Excluding the few associations without professional staff, the number of members served per staff member in state associations ranged from 9,000–10,000 to about 600.

The associations most active in competing for members have as many or more full-time professionals as their AFSCME counterparts. In most states, however, AFSCME councils have more professional staff members than the associations and almost always boast a better ratio of staff to membership. This advantage in professional expertise at the state level is increased by the services provided by AFSCME's national headquarters and area offices which have no counterpart in state associations.

Association staff members are drawn from a variety of sources and backgrounds. A high proportion are college graduates and, as a group, they have had more formal education than union representatives in the public employment field. Associations often recruit former state employees because of their familiarity with civil service regulations and procedures. Several association directors are attorneys and a number of staff members have worked for unions. Thus, the director of one state association is a former president of an AFL-CIO city council; in another two staff members came out of the Longshoremen's Union; and the executive secretary of a third association is a former business agent of the International Brotherhood of Electrical Workers.

Most associations set staff salaries and provide benefits equivalent to comparable positions in state service. Salaries thus vary considerably among state associations, but, on the whole, salaries and fringe benefits of association staff compare favorably with those of union representatives. At least three associations are known to have staff organizations. Two of them, Oregon and New York, were also the first to espouse collective bargaining and have been highly successful in competing with unions to represent state employees. Having brought the benefits of collective bargaining to the membership, it appears that association employees want to do likewise for themselves.

Association staff members engage in a wide variety of activities including organizing, collective bargaining, processing grievances, testifying before legislative bodies, drafting legislation, lobbying, research, public relations, and administering insurance programs. In effect, they perform many of the same functions as the staffs of international unions. However, priorities differ, depending on the orientation and emphasis of the association. In particular, insurance services often account for considerable staff time. For example, one-fourth of the professional staff of one association is occupied in selling and administering life, income, disability, and health insurance. Insurance operations also require large numbers of clerical employees, and this accounts for the relatively high ratio of clerical to professional staff in state associations as compared with unions.

The organization and direction of staff is usually a responsibility of the association executive director, who is appointed by and responsible to the board of directors. This arrangement is similar to that in AFSCME councils. In some associations the director and staff exercise considerable authority in making as well as carrying out policy. In most states, however, the elected executive board has jealously guarded its authority to make policy and, in some states, to hire and supervise staff members. The precise division of responsibility and influence on policy between the executive board and association director depends on the personality and ability of the director, the history and traditions of the association, and the individuals elected to board positions. On the whole, association executive boards appear to have retained more authority and influence on policy than boards of AFSCME councils in which the council director has often emerged as the dominant figure and sometimes occupies the joint position of director and president.

Among independent local associations, only the very largest employ full-time professional staff. Most associations are run by one or two clerical employees, while elected officers spend as much time on association business as they can spare from their jobs, evenings and weekends. California, the stronghold of local association activity, is an exception, with several of the larger local associations employing sizable professional and clerical staff. For example, the 35,000-member Los Angeles County Employees Association, before its 1971 merger with the SEIU, employed 25 to 30 professionals and about an equal number of full-time clerical workers. Its activities were conducted through four divisions: representation, consumer services, public relations, and internal administration. The largest division had about 15 professionals, who represented members in processing grievances, handling wage and salary claims, and in negotiations. Most staff members had college or law degrees and some had previously worked for unions or private industry. The enactment of the 1968 Meyers–Milias–Brown Act and local ordinances governing labor relations in public employment has changed the emphasis on insurance and other consumer services in some associations and led to recruitment of additional staff members with experience or training in collective bargaining.

Many directors, general managers, and chief administrative officers of California state and local associations belong to the Public Employee Staff Organization (PESO), which in 1969 had 42 members. PESO, organized in 1952, is primarily designed to provide an opportunity for top staff members of employee associations to exchange ideas and compare notes. The very existence of this organization indicates the advanced state of employee associations in California.

Finances

Local union dues and per capita taxes to support higher echelons of the organization are the life blood of a union. The degree of control exercised by the leadership and support for the international officers can be gauged reasonably well by their success in obtaining increased revenues by raising per capita taxes. Opposition to per capita increases, which come out of local dues, has been a perennial rallying point for dissident movements in unions. Denial of necessary funds to run an effective organization can give rise to charges of inefficiency, failure to increase membership, and inadequate service, and eventually lead to defeat of incumbent officers. Few issues call for greater political skill on the part of a union's leadership than guiding a per capita tax increase proposal through a convention without stirring up a major debate and leaving a substantial minority dissatisfied no matter what the outcome.[51]

51. John T. Dunlop, "Discussion," in Seidman, *Trade Union Government and Collective Bargaining*, p. 204.

Local union dues in AFSCME were generally $4 or more per month in 1969; a few locals assessed dues at the minimum permissible level of $3, some charged as much as $7, and others had variable dues related to earnings. Dues of SEIU and Laborers public employee locals were usually set at around the constitutional minimum of $4, which was lower than the average dues of private sector locals in these unions. In the Teamsters union, public employee locals were often classified as "extreme hardship cases" by the executive board, permitting them to set dues below the $7 minimum established by the constitution.

A major difference between AFSCME and the mixed unions is in the distribution of membership dues. In AFSCME only a small portion of the dues dollar remains in the local union treasury after it has made mandatory per capita payments to the international, the council, and the AFL-CIO bodies with which it is affiliated. This situation is reversed in mixed unions, with the local union retaining most of its membership dues to use as it sees fit.

In 1969, AFSCME locals paid $1 per month per capita to the international, about $2 to their councils, and $0.20 to state and local AFL-CIO bodies. For most locals, per capita charges claimed well over half of all monthly dues receipts. The 1970 convention increased the international per capita payment to $1.50 in two steps, forcing many locals to raise dues.

Contrast the AFSCME dues distribution with arrangements in the mixed unions. In 1969, SEIU locals were obligated to pay per capita taxes totaling about $1.30 per month, less than one-third of membership dues. Per capita payments in the Laborers' Union ranged from $1.75 to $2 per month, depending on whether the local chose to affiliate with AFL-CIO state and local councils. For most public employee locals, this was less than half their dues income. Teamster locals paid somewhat more than $2 per capita to the international, joint councils, and area conferences, but a Teamster vice-president estimates that local unions retain 75 percent of all dues payments.[52] Some mixed union representatives are reluctant to organize public employees because the new locals would not be self-sustaining financially for some time, if ever, and would have to be subsidized by councils. The major difference between

52. Gibbons, "Centralization in the Teamsters Union," p. 151.

AFSCME and the mixed unions is in the per capita fee paid to councils, which furnish AFSCME local unions most of the services that locals in the mixed unions provide for themselves.

A major advantage claimed by employee associations in competing with unions is their low dues structure. In 1969, state association membership dues ranged from $5 to $36 per year, exclusive of premiums paid by members who purchased insurance through their associations. Highest dues were charged by associations in the West. Dues in independent local associations tend to be even lower than in state associations, typically ranging from $1 to $6 a year in 1969. But in California and Washington, local associations charged $12 to $48 a year.

The major distinction between associations with high and low dues is in the nature of the organization and the services provided. Associations charging dues of $12 a year or less are generally fraternal, social, or insurance-selling organizations with no professional staff and few services other than an occasional newsletter mailed to members. Those with higher dues often engage in collective bargaining or other forms of employee representation, usually employ one or more full-time staff members, represent their members before legislative bodies, and have a regular publication and public relations program.

The only per capita tax paid by state associations is $0.10 per year, with a minimum charge of $100 per organization, to the Assembly of Governmental Employees.[53] This very low assessment enables state associations to keep dues much lower than unions, a point that they repeatedly call to the attention of public employees. State associations generally return only a small portion of membership dues to local chapters—usually 10–25 percent. A few also remit small sums to regional or other subordinate bodies.

Increases in the international per capita tax have encountered much greater opposition in AFSCME than in mixed unions, where raises have been voted at conventions with little or no discussion. Local union dues in AFSCME are relatively low because of low earnings of members, and an increase in per capita is almost certain to require a dues increase. Moreover, per capita payments to councils are much higher than in most other unions. During the late

---

53. Letter to the author from Executive Secretary, Oregon State Employees Association, Feb. 16, 1972.

1950s and early 1960s the per capita issue became the means of expressing confidence in or opposition to the administration.

The per capita fee, which had been $0.35 in 1935, had increased only to $0.65 by 1966. Within six years of the accession of the new administration the per capita tax had risen by 130 percent—to $1.50 per month. One favorable factor was probably the huge increase in membership from 234,000 in 1964 to 460,000 in 1970. The Wurf administration was the beneficiary of the increased confidence that AFSCME members and convention delegates felt toward their union which, in less than a decade, had risen from nineteenth to seventh in size within the AFL-CIO. Convention delegates also apparently approved the administration's moves to reduce the union's financial commitments. At the same time, the constitutional amendment that gave a proportionately greater voice to large locals favored the new administration. Finally, there was no organized opposition to exploit the per capita increase issue.

Insofar as there is a relationship between financial independence and local autonomy—and most union officials consider the two to be very closely related—locals in the SEIU, Laborers, and Teamsters can lay claim to considerably more autonomy than AFSCME locals. Differences between the mixed unions and AFSCME in the distribution of local union dues can, in large part, be explained by differences in local union size. AFSCME with 1,900 local unions for over 500,000 members has more than twice as many locals as the Teamsters, which has 2 million members, three times as many as the Laborers, with about the same membership as AFSCME, and five times as many as the SEIU, with somewhat fewer members. Because of its small size, the average AFSCME local cannot afford to employ even one full-time staff representative and therefore must depend on the council and the international for services that most locals in mixed unions provide. While public employee locals in mixed unions tend to be smaller than private sector locals, they are still larger, on the average, than AFSCME locals. The net effect is that, despite apparent similarities in their constitutional prerogatives, locals in mixed unions are in fact more autonomous than AFSCME locals because they are larger and more independent financially.[54]

When unions are compared with independent associations, dif-

54. For a discussion of union structure and local union size, see Bok and Dunlop, *Labor and the American Community,* pp. 150–55.

ferences show up in both total membership dues and the distribution of the dues dollar. While most association dues are substantially lower than those paid by union members, the difference is much narrower in associations that engage in collective bargaining, grievance processing, and other responsibilities of employee representation. Associations claim that they can charge less because all their income is used to provide services to members, rather than for administrative expenses of higher echelons and for political and other peripheral activities that do not directly benefit the membership. But unions hold that they furnish a much broader range of services than associations and that legislative and political action are necessary if collective bargaining is to be effective.

Summary

Unions and associations of state and local government employees are decentralized in order to adapt to the governmental structure in which they operate. Decisions are made by units that correspond to the level of government in which their members are employed. For unions, this is generally the local union or a council representing several locals; for associations, it is the chapter, lodge, district, or some appropriate grouping of these units. The national organization exercises little authority over subordinate units in their relationships with government employers.

Despite this basic similarity in structure, there are significant differences in coordination, services, and general policy influence exerted by national and intermediate echelons of public employee organizations. Among the unions, AFSCME is most heavily involved in these activities through its national and area offices and state and district councils. The council is the focal unit in AFSCME, employing full-time staff, providing assistance and other services to local unions, and representing the union in the area in which it has jurisdiction. AFSCME's objective appears to be decentralized but coordinated decision making, with centrally provided staff services.

The mixed unions are decentralized both in servicing and decision making. Local unions employ full-time staff and, except in special situations, receive little assistance from intermediate or national offices of their unions. The unions have made few adjustments to meet the needs of public sector locals that are relatively small in size, poorly financed, and have specialized needs. While the national offices of these unions encourage subordinate bodies to organize government employees, the final decision is usually made at the local level on a cost-benefit calculus that does not extend beyond the jurisdiction of the local leadership. The success of the mixed unions in the public sector has depended on the interest and ability of a few individuals in each organization rather than a deliberate plan to organize public employees, developed at the national level and implemented throughout the union.

State employee associations are essentially single-level organizations in which power, financial resources, and staff are all concentrated at the state level. The national Assembly of Governmental Employees serves more as a communications link between state associations than a higher echelon or even a coordinating organization. The relationship between state associations and their local chapters more closely resembles that between AFSCME councils and local unions than the relationship between intermediate bodies and locals in mixed unions.

A recent development, not discernible in the formal organizational structures of either AFSCME or the mixed unions, is the extension of almost complete autonomy and independence to associations that have affiliated with these unions. Both AFSCME and SEIU have consummated merger agreements with associations in the past few years, and new mergers are being reported almost every month.[55] While the agreements vary from case to case and are not always made public, they represent a significant trend in the structure of public employee unions.

Minority group membership is relatively large in public employee unions and blacks wield considerable influence, most often in local unions but occasionally at the intermediate and international levels. In contrast, blacks and other minority groups constitute only a small proportion of association membership and occupy few leadership positions. This has put associations at a disadvantage in competing with unions among blue collar workers in public employment.

In the realm of union government, AFSCME has, for most of its history, been readily distinguishable from the mixed unions by its

55. See Chapter 5 for a discussion of union–association mergers.

open conventions and active internal political life. National union offices have often been contested and important issues debated and decided on the floor of the convention rather than in hotel rooms and committee meetings. The SEIU, Laborers, and Teamsters are more disciplined unions than AFSCME. The international president's authority is rarely questioned, at least not publicly; officers and executive board members invariably are elected by acclamation, and conventions are used to ratify previously made decisions rather than to provide a forum to debate and discuss issues. Disagreements and power struggles undoubtedly occur, but they are settled in private and not permitted to disturb the membership, let alone come to the attention of the general public. Since the ascendancy of Wurf to the presidency in 1964 and the disintegration of an organized opposition to the administration, AFSCME with each passing year appears more and more to resemble other unions in the government of its internal affairs. However, it is still something of a maverick within the AFL-CIO.

CHAPTER THREE

Uniformed Services

Fire fighters and policemen are often linked in the public mind because of the essential protective services they perform in the community. However, the organizations these two groups of uniformed employees have formed to represent them differ greatly. Most fire fighters belong to an international union affiliated with the AFL-CIO while police officers are distributed among two national non-union organizations, several unions, and many local independent associations.

Structure

The international level in the fire fighters' union is more powerful than that of either of the associations to which policemen belong, but less powerful than the international offices of the general public employee unions. State associations are more important bodies than the international, though large-city locals often refuse to belong to them. The locus of power for both uniformed services is in the local chapter.

INTERNATIONAL ASSOCIATION OF FIRE FIGHTERS

As in all unions, the biennial international convention is the "supreme authority" and the "highest legislative, executive and judicial body" of the International Association of Fire Fighters

51

(IAFF). Between conventions, authority is vested in the union's executive board: the president, secretary-treasurer, and sixteen vice-presidents who are elected by convention delegates from each district. The international president has less power than in most unions, the executive board and the local unions being the prime beneficiaries of the relative weakness of the presidential office. Thus, the constitution makes no provision for the establishment of trusteeships over subordinate bodies, a power usually vested in the president subject to approval of the executive board. A proposed amendment to give the president such authority was rejected by delegates to the 1970 convention.[1]

The issue of delegate representation and voting strength at conventions has plagued the IAFF since its inception. The original constitution, adopted in 1918, provided for 1 delegate for each local with less than 100 members, 2 for 101–250 members, 3 for 251–500, and a maximum of 4 for locals with 501–1,000 members. Each delegate carried one vote. When New York City Local 94, with over 3,000 members, joined the IAFF in 1919, the constitution was amended to allow 1 additional delegate for every additional 1,000 members or major fraction thereof, but the voting provision remained unchanged. Despite repeated efforts by the larger locals to gain greater representation and voting strength at conventions, this provision of the constitution remained unchanged until 1970.

Like the American Federation of State, County and Municipal Employees (AFSCME), where convention voting strength has also been an important issue, the IAFF is a union of predominantly small locals. Three-fourths of them have less than 100 members, and some fewer than 10. On the other hand, a number have more than 1,000 members and New York City Local 94 more than 10,000. With 1,700 local unions and 160,000 members, the IAFF probably has more locals for its size than any other union. Historically, the union has been dominated by small locals which have been greatly favored by the representation and voting rules. For example, at the 1968 convention, 424 locals with a total membership of about 29,000 had 517 votes, while 29 locals of more than 1,000 members each, representing 39,000 fire fighters, cast only 109 votes.[2]

---

1. *Report on Convention Proceedings, International Association of Fire Fighters, AFL-CIO, CLC, 30th Convention* (1970), p. 2.

2. Notes taken at Metro Caucus Meeting, Dec. 14–15, 1968, New Orleans, La.

The 1968 convention defeated, by a substantial majority, a move to elect international officers of the union on a one man–one vote principle. This action, together with adoption of an amendment making affiliation with state IAFF associations mandatory for all locals, precipitated a convention walkout and a threat to quit the union by delegates from the large locals, which in 1966 had organized themselves into the Metropolitan (Metro) Caucus. The delegates returned when the date for mandatory affiliation was postponed until after the 1970 convention and the president was charged with appointing a special commission to study the matter and "report a proper resolution" to that convention.[3]

During the interim the Metro Caucus withheld per capita payments to the international. The amount was substantial since the caucus represented 30 percent of the total IAFF membership. Eventually a compromise was worked out with the help of a three-member committee appointed by AFL-CIO President George Meany. It liberalized the number of convention delegates authorized for large local unions, provided for per capita voting in the election of international officers and on roll call votes, and permitted proxy voting by locals with 100 or less members.[4] The changes were adopted at the 1970 convention over the objection of delegates from the smaller locals. The large locals also had their way when affiliation with state associations was made voluntary rather than mandatory.[5] Like AFSCME, the IAFF has shifted power from the small locals to the larger, stronger, and more militant local unions.

STATE FIRE FIGHTER ASSOCIATIONS

Reflecting the high degree of local union autonomy in the IAFF, state associations and joint councils are chartered by request of a majority of the local unions in an area rather than on the initiative

3. *Resolutions, 29th Biennial Convention, International Association of Fire Fighters, AFL-CIO and CLC* (1968), p. 13.

4. "Decision and Recommendation of the AFL-CIO Advisory Panel Appointed by President George Meany in IAFF Internal Dispute Over Representation and Delegate Voting at Conventions" (Jan. 8, 1970; processed). Under the new provision, all locals with 751 to 10,000 members were entitled to more convention delegates than under the replaced provision. However, New York City Local 94, with more than 10,000, lost delegates.

5. *Report on Convention Proceedings, IAFF* (1970), p. 16.

of the international president or the executive board.[6] The proper role of state associations is another subject of controversy between large and small locals. In 1919 a delegate from Cambridge, Massachusetts, saw the state association as an intermediate body designed to improve communications, channel requests for assistance, and generally act as a vital link between the local unions and the international. By contrast, a delegate from Chicago felt that "everything we have got, we have gotten by our own efforts. No man in the International can come into Chicago and render me any assistance. We are able to take care of our own condition, and do not have to call on anyone."[7]

Those differences continued to be fairly representative for the next forty years, the small locals seeking help, the large locals preferring to look after their own interests. Though they have rejected assistance from IAFF state associations, the large locals value their ties with AFL-CIO city and state councils because of the political pressures these bodies can exert on elected officials. They have stayed in the IAFF, even though they believed they were being inequitably treated, to preserve their AFL-CIO relationships.

Despite the controversy over them, state associations grew in number from 8 in the 1930s to 42 in 1970. Their role is primarily to represent local affiliates in state legislatures on such issues as achieving civil service status for fire fighters, improving pension systems, and lobbying for the two-platoon system. Local unions in large cities that have home rule charters[8] or are singled out by special state legislation prefer to do their own lobbying on issues that concern them. In many instances, large city locals and state associations have taken opposing positions on legislation, leading to attempts to authorize the international to revoke the charter of such locals.

Not all large locals denigrate the value of state associations. Some rely on their lobbying activities to reach small-town legislators, whose votes count just as much as those from big cities. On the

6. Constitution and By-Laws, International Association of Fire Fighters (1970), Art. 14, sec. 1.

7. *Proceedings, International Association of Fire Fighters, 2nd Convention (IAFF Proceedings)* (1919), pp. 60–61.

8. The IAFF is opposed to home rule charters for cities, characterizing them as "the most modern challenging, perplexing, and insidious issue ever perpetrated." (*IAFF Proceedings* [1960], p. 308.)

whole, local union officials have less use for the international than for state associations. Many hold the IAFF affiliation important largely as a means of maintaining ties with the AFL-CIO.

During the 1960s, state associations became increasingly active in states with collective bargaining laws governing public employees generally and fire fighters specifically. They have issued reports comparing fire fighter wages and benefits in various localities, conducted training sessions and collective bargaining seminars, and provided staff support in negotiations. While the state associations' value has been enhanced, their financial resources have been correspondingly strained—hence the unsuccessful effort to require all locals to affiliate with state bodies.

NATIONAL POLICE ASSOCIATIONS

The two major independent national associations of police officers—the Fraternal Order of Police (FOP) and the International Conference of Police Associations (ICPA)—are much more loosely structured than the IAFF and other unions of public employees. Both emphasize local autonomy and vest little power in their national officers. Even local police associations affiliated with unions have a high degree of autonomy and are regarded, both by themselves and their international unions, as different from other local unions.[9] Originally organized primarily for fraternal, benevolent, public service, and professional reasons, both organizations have in recent years placed greater emphasis on economic objectives. The FOP has done this without changing its original statement of objectives, which makes no mention of wages and working conditions,[10] while the ICPA added "the establishment and maintenance of equitable wages, hours, retirement and working conditions" to its objectives in 1967.[11]

9. Jerry Wurf, "Current Issues of State, Local and Municipal Collective Bargaining," in "Proceedings of the Second Labor Relations Symposium on Labor-Management Relations in the Public Sector" (Labor Education Center, University of Kentucky, 1969; processed), p. 50. The National Union of Police Officers, which in 1972 became a division of the SEIU, is also completely autonomous and has "complete freedom of action." (*New York Times*, Feb. 25, 1972, p. 29.)

10. Constitution and By-Laws, Fraternal Order of Police (1967), Preamble. This is the latest edition obtainable; the FOP considers its constitution an internal document available only to members (letter to the author from FOP National Secretary, July 13, 1972).

11. By Laws, International Conference of Police Associations (1967), Art. 2.

In 1969 the FOP and the ICPA issued a joint resolution opposing the formation of a national police union which, under the
leadership of a former president of both the New York City Patrolmen's Benevolent Association and the ICPA, was seeking an AFL-
CIO charter. The resolution said that "the public can best be
served by police organizations being distinctly separate and not
affiliated directly or indirectly with labor unions"; it established a
joint council "to bring about a closer relationship for the purpose
of uniting, organizing and professionalizing all law enforcement
officers."[12] Nothing has since been heard from the council. However, in 1971 the ICPA in a policy statement said that it was not
"anti-labor or anti-union" and wished to continue to have good relationships with labor and professional associations.[13]

Policemen were not always opposed to being a part of the labor
movement. Prior to the First World War, local associations of
policemen and fire fighters developed along parallel paths, as fraternal and benevolent associations that also functioned as political
pressure groups. Both groups made significant moves toward
unionism during the first two decades of the twentieth century.
Despite considerable antagonism toward policemen because of their
often repressive role in strikes and picketing in labor disputes, the
AFL had by September 1919 issued charters to thirty-three police
local unions, most of them in cities that also had IAFF local
unions.[14]

The Boston police strike of September 1919, which was marked
by rioting, looting, and violence, put an end to the burgeoning
unionism. Congress banned unions in the protective services, police
and fire, in the District of Columbia and many cities and states followed suit. With the strike the parallel development of police and
fire fighter organizations ended.[15] Though growth of the IAFF was
seriously impeded during the 1920s, the organization survived and

---

12. Bureau of National Affairs, *Government Employee Relations Report (GERR)*,
No. 329 (Dec. 29, 1969), p. B-7.

13. "Policy Statement of the International Conference of Police Associations,"
ICPA By Laws (revised, July 1971).

14. Philip Kienast, "Policemen and Fire Fighter Employee Organizations: A Comparative Study of Historical and Sociological Factors Affecting Employee Organization
Structure" (Ph.D. dissertation, Michigan State University, 1972).

15. Sterling D. Spero, *Government As Employer* (New York: Remsen, 1948), p. 281;
see also, pp. 236, 272.

recovered. Not so with police unionism. It was twenty years before an AFL union, AFSCME, ventured to issue a charter to a local of police officers. Now, more than fifty years after the Boston police strike, stirrings of unionism are again evident among policemen, but the major national police organizations are nonunion and against affiliation with the labor movement.

The national FOP holds biennial conferences composed of one delegate for every fifty members of each subordinate lodge and three delegates from each state lodge. Between conferences the board of directors (president, immediate past president, vice-president, secretary, treasurer, conductor, guard, and one trustee from each state lodge) is empowered to "exercise all administrative powers." However, since the board is required to meet only once between conferences, the president generally speaks and acts for the organization.[16] The FOP national office is located in the home city of the secretary; it thus may move as often as every two years, whenever the secretary changes, a rather cumbersome administrative arrangement. The FOP publishes an official *Police Journal* and an annual survey of police salaries.

The ICPA was organized in 1953 by a number of independent police associations that rejected an invitation to join the FOP because they wanted to retain their independence and yet have the benefits of a national confederation. They also wished to avoid any conflict with city administrators and police commissioners, many of whom considered the FOP a union and had prohibited their police officers from joining that organization. By adopting "professionalization" of police as a major objective and by stressing the collection, study, standardization, and dissemination of data as its major function, the ICPA succeeded in allaying the fears of city officials.

ICPA member associations are assured of complete autonomy, including the right of each association to determine its own membership eligibility requirements. Until 1971, each association was allocated only 1 accredited voting delegate to the annual conference; since then, each association has been allowed 1 voting delegate for every 500 members of the first 2,000 and 1 for each additional 2,000 members or portion thereof.[17] The leadership viewed

16. Constitution and By-Laws, FOP (1967), Art. 7.
17. ICPA By Laws (revised, July 1971), Art. 5, sec. 2.

this as a necessary first step to persuade the larger ICPA affiliates to vest greater authority in the annual conference and the national officers. A full-time paid executive director, appointed by the board of directors, is in charge of the national office in Washington, D.C., and serves as treasurer, general manager, and public relations officer of the conference. The ICPA publishes a monthly *Newsletter,* a quarterly magazine, and an annual survey of police salaries and fringe benefits. Unlike FOP affiliates, which are clearly designated as local lodges of the Fraternal Order of Police, ICPA member associations are usually called police benevolent associations or some other name that carries no indication of ICPA affiliation.

STATE POLICE ASSOCIATIONS

Police and fire fighters, more than any other group of municipal employees, work under conditions that are mandated by state legislatures.[18] State associations are thus much more important to them than are national organizations. Every state has at least one state police association and a number have two or more, reflecting different national affiliations, big city–small city interest conflicts, desire to limit membership to patrolmen or officers, and organizational rivalry among local police groups.

The major activity of state associations is to lobby state legislatures for measures favorable to police officers. In several states, compulsory arbitration laws for police and fire fighters were enacted largely as a result of pressure from state associations representing those groups, with each claiming major credit for the law. State associations also claim credit for the enactment of pension plans which are usually much more liberal than those of other city employees. With the advent of collective bargaining for public employees, state police associations have started to collect and disseminate information on comparative wages and conditions of employment, and some have organized training programs to improve negotiating skills of police representatives.

At the local level there is little difference between one kind of police organization and another. While FOP lodges are required to belong to state lodges, where they exist, they are virtually as

18. Advisory Commission on Intergovernmental Relations, *Labor-Management Policies for State and Local Government* (Washington: ACIR, 1969), pp. 260–63.

autonomous with respect to collective bargaining, establishment of membership dues, and determining policy as ICPA affiliates, for whom state affiliation is optional, and local independent police associations.

Minority Group Participation

While information on the membership of minority groups in national organizations of police and fire fighters is scant, considerably more is known about their representation in the uniformed services than in other government functions. This is more true of police departments than of fire departments, because of the 1967 riots and the much greater concern over relations between police and the black community in urban areas.

POLICE

Since 1968, when the Report of the National Advisory Commission on Civil Disorders drew national attention to the small number of blacks and other minorities on the police forces of major cities, only a few cities have succeeded in significantly increasing their proportion of nonwhite policemen. In Washington, D.C., 36 percent of the 5,000-member force was black in 1970 as compared with 20 percent in 1968; in Atlanta the proportion rose to 28 percent from 10 percent; in Baltimore from 7 percent to 13 percent; and in Detroit from 5 percent to 11 percent (see Table 3-1).[19] In no city with a significant black population is the percentage of black policemen close to the proportion of blacks in the general population. The facts are even more discouraging than the figures in Table 3-1 suggest, because the 1968–70 period was one in which cities were supposedly engaged in a major effort to recruit minority group members and particularly blacks into their police forces.[20]

The record was worse for superior officers. In the 28 cities surveyed by the National Advisory Commission on Civil Disorders,

19. The increases in the proportion of blacks were probably somewhat larger than the figures indicate because the 1968 percentage includes all nonwhite policemen while the 1970 figures are for black policemen only.

20. Carolyn Stieber, "Recruiting Minority Police: Some Lessons to Learn," *Michigan Municipal Review*, March 1969, pp. 55–58, 64.

TABLE 3-1. *Black Policemen as a Percent of the Total Police Force in Selected U.S. Cities, 1968 and 1970*

City	Blacks as percent of total population	Nonwhite policemen, 1968[a]		Black policemen, 1970	
		Number	Percent of total force	Number	Percent of total force
Washington, D.C.	71.1	559	20.5	1,797	35.9
Gary, Ind.	52.8	n.a.	n.a.	130	31.3
Atlanta, Ga.	51.3	98	10.1	260	27.6
Philadelphia, Pa.	33.6	1,377	20.0	1,347	18.6
Chicago, Ill.	32.7	1,842	16.6	2,100	16.5
Newark, N.J.	54.2	184	9.8	225	15.0
St. Louis, Mo.	40.9	224	11.0	326	14.7
Mobile, Ala.	35.5	n.a.	n.a.	36	13.0
Baltimore, Md.	46.4	208	6.8	420	12.7
Hartford, Conn.	27.9	38	11.1	60	12.0
Wilmington, Del.	43.6	n.a.	n.a.	32	11.5
Detroit, Mich.	43.7	227	5.2	567	11.1
Miami, Fla.	22.7	n.a.	n.a.	74	10.3
Cleveland, Ohio	38.3	165	7.4	191	7.8
New York, N.Y.	21.1	1,485	5.4	2,400	7.5
Portsmouth, Va.	39.9	n.a.	n.a.	14	7.2
Shreveport, La.	34.1	n.a.	n.a.	25	7.2
Louisville, Ky.	23.8	35	6.2	42	6.7
Charleston, W.Va.	10.3	n.a.	n.a.	10	6.6
Winston Salem, N.C.	34.3	n.a.	n.a.	20	6.6
Pittsburgh, Pa.	20.2	109	7.0	105	6.4
Jackson, Miss.	39.7	n.a.	n.a.	17	6.3
New Orleans, La.	45.0	54	4.1	83	6.1
Los Angeles, Calif.	17.9	n.a.	n.a.	350	5.2
Dayton, Ohio	30.5	16	3.8	22	5.2
Memphis, Tenn.	38.9	46	5.3	55	5.0
San Francisco, Calif.	13.4	102	5.8	90	5.0

only 92 of 7,040 sworn officers holding the rank of lieutenant or higher were nonwhites, a ratio of 1 to 77 as compared with a ratio of 1 to 17 for white policemen. The relative ratios were somewhat better for sergeants, 1 to 26 for nonwhites and 1 to 12 for whites. Practically never did a city show a lower ratio in any rank for nonwhite as compared with white policemen.[21]

Black policemen, more than any other public employee occupational group, have tended to form their own organizations. Virtu-

21. *Report of the National Advisory Commission on Civil Disorders* (1968), p. 169.

TABLE 3-1 *(continued)*

City	Blacks as percent of total population	Nonwhite policemen, 1968[a] Number	Nonwhite policemen, 1968[a] Percent of total force	Black policemen, 1970 Number	Black policemen, 1970 Percent of total force
Oakland, Calif.	*34.5*	27	*4.1*	34	*4.7*
Charlotte, N.C.	*30.3*	n.a.	n.a.	22	*4.5*
Providence, R.I.	*8.9*	n.a.	n.a.	18	*4.5*
Milwaukee, Wis.	*14.7*	n.a.	n.a.	50	*2.3*
Boston, Mass.	*16.3*	49	*2.0*	60	*2.1*
Birmingham, Ala.	*42.0*	n.a.	n.a.	13	*1.9*
Dallas, Tex.	*24.9*	n.a.	n.a.	32	*1.9*
New Haven, Conn.	*26.3*	31	*6.9*	n.a.	n.a.
Cincinnati, Ohio	*27.6*	54	*6.1*	n.a.	n.a.
Kansas City, Mo.	*22.1*	51	*5.5*	n.a.	n.a.
Baton Rouge, La.	*27.8*	12	*3.8*[b]	n.a.	n.a.
Oklahoma City, Okla.	*13.7*	16	*3.7*	n.a.	n.a.
Houston, Tex.	*25.7*	56	*3.5*[b]	n.a.	n.a.
Tampa, Fla.	*19.7*	17	*3.3*	n.a.	n.a.
Buffalo, N.Y.	*20.4*	37	*2.7*	n.a.	n.a.
Phoenix, Ariz.	*4.8*	7	*1.0*	n.a.	n.a.

Sources: U.S. Bureau of the Census, *Census of Population, 1970, General Population Characteristics,* Final Report PC(1)-B1 (1972), Table 67; *Report of the National Advisory Commission on Civil Disorders* (1968), p. 169; U.S. Commission on Civil Rights, *For All the People . . . By All the People: A Report on Equal Opportunity in State and Local Government Employment* (1969), p. 17; *New York Times,* Jan. 25, 1971, p. 14, and May 19, 1971, p. 39; International City Management, *The Municipal Year Book, 1969,* pp. 338–39; and *Ebony,* May 1971, p. 124.
a. Nonwhite includes blacks and other nonwhites.
b. Figures are for 1967.
n.a. Not available.

ally every major city has a black policemen's organization.[22] Some are affiliated with such national groups as the National Society of Afro-American Police Officers, the Afro-American Patrolmen's Association, and the Guardians. Many local organizations belong to the National Council of Police Societies, which claims to represent 10,000 black policemen in 20 cities.[23] The council was organized because of a widespread belief among black policemen that the predominantly white police associations do not represent their interests, outside of the areas of pay and economic benefits.[24]

22. *New York Times,* Sept. 28, 1969.
23. Ibid., June 6, 1970, and June 13, 1971.
24. Ibid., June 11, 1971.

Detroit, in addition to chapters of two national groups, has a militant Black Police Officers' Caucus, which was formed in 1965 to protest the absence of blacks on the executive board of the Detroit Police Officers Association (DPOA). When this and other demands were presented by 175 black officers at a DPOA meeting, "they laughed at us," said a cochairman of the caucus, and "we walked out of the meeting." Since this confrontation the caucus has opposed the DPOA on many issues. The caucus differs from other black police groups not so much in objectives—both want to upgrade the image of the black policeman in the black community and to obtain equal treatment for black officers in the department—as in methods. Caucus members are younger, more direct, and more militant in their opposition to the established order, whether it be the city, the department, or the DPOA. They have remained members of the DPOA because of supposed benefits, the most important being legal defense against charges related to performance of police duties. But some caucus members favor leaving the DPOA to form their own organization.

Incidents that have served to widen the gulf between black and white policemen have occurred in cities throughout the country. The issues involved have varied: endorsement of George Wallace for United States president by the national president of the Fraternal Order of Police (FOP); support by police associations of white mayoralty candidates in contests with blacks; charges of police brutality; use of dogs and excessive use of firepower against blacks; Mayor Daley's shoot-to-kill order to Chicago policemen in dealing with looters; use of epithets by white policemen in referring to black members of the force; alleged discrimination against blacks in upgrading and promotions; and a brawl between white and black policemen at an annual FOP picnic, reportedly started when a black youth danced with a white girl.[25] These and similar incidents have helped to convince black policemen that they need their own organizations to represent them.

While most of the altercations and charges of discrimination have occurred in cities with affiliates of the FOP or the ICPA, blacks have also had their differences with local unions affiliated with AFSCME.

25. See ibid., Sept. 28, 1969, April 29, 1970, Aug. 2, 1970; and *Newsweek,* Aug. 4, 1969, p. 54.

In January 1970 the Hartford, Connecticut, Guardians charged that the AFSCME police local had discriminated against black members by refusing to represent them with legal counsel in grievances against the city, while providing legal aid to three white policemen named in a federal suit charging Hartford police with discrimination against blacks and Puerto Ricans.[26] The Portland, Oregon, local was challenged for its opposition to a plan by the city to add six blacks to the eight-hundred-man force—only five of them black—by taking them on as temporary employees until they were sufficiently trained to pass the civil service examination.[27] The Portland local has since left AFSCME to join the International Brotherhood of Police Officers. The Hartford local has also left the union, to affiliate with the National Association of Government Employees.

FIRE FIGHTERS

Black firemen are still a rare breed in most cities. New York, Philadelphia, Washington, Chicago, and Gary, Indiana, were the only cities with more than 100 blacks in their fire departments in 1969–70. Gary, whose population is about 55 percent black, had 103 black fire fighters out of a force of 282, the largest percentage by far of any American city. Even cities that have had some success in recruiting black police officers have only token representation of blacks in their fire departments. Many cities with sizable black populations have less than 5 percent blacks in their departments (see Table 3-2). Fire chiefs express surprise and disappointment over their inability to recruit blacks, but black fire fighters offer reasons: discrimination, civil service tests designed for whites, recruiting of nonresidents in competition with ghetto dwellers, and automatic elimination of applicants with token police records.[28]

Fire departments have been subjected to less pressure than police departments to recruit blacks by civil rights organizations. On the other hand, opposition to recruitment of blacks has been greater among fire fighters than policemen because of the greater social interaction in the firehouse, including eating and sleeping in the

26. *GERR*, No. 332 (Jan. 19, 1970), pp. B-12–B-13.
27. *GERR*, No. 258 (Aug. 19, 1968), p. B-14.
28. *New York Times*, June 27, 1970.

TABLE 3-2. *Black Fire Fighters in Selected U.S. Cities, 1969–70*

City	Black fire fighters	
	Number	Percent of total
Gary, Ind.	103	*36.5*
Washington, D.C.	260	*18.6*
Philadelphia, Pa.	500	*14.7*
Hartford, Conn.	45	*10.6*
St. Louis, Mo.	70	*5.7*
Pittsburgh, Pa.	60	*5.5*
New York, N.Y.	700	*5.0*
Oakland, Calif.	28	*4.4*
Chicago, Ill.	202	*4.0*
Cleveland, Ohio	50	*3.9*
Detroit, Mich.	45	*3.5*
Houston, Tex.	40	*2.7*
Los Angeles, Calif.	53	*1.5*
Buffalo, N.Y.	15	*1.2*
Wilmington, Del.	3	*1.2*
Youngstown, Ohio	3	*1.1*
New Orleans, La.	10	*1.1*
Denver, Colo.	8	*1.0*[a]
Boston, Mass.	17	*0.9*
Milwaukee, Wis.	8	*0.8*
Des Moines, Iowa	2	*0.6*
Seattle, Wash.	4	*0.4*
Los Angeles County, Calif.	7	*0.4*
Miami, Fla.	2	*0.3*
San Francisco, Calif.	4	*0.2*
Portland, Oreg.	0	*0.0*
Madison, Wis.	0	*0.0*

Sources: *New York Times*, June 27, 1970; *Newsweek*, July 21, 1969; and interviews.
a. Includes 20 Mexican-Americans.

same quarters in many cities. The president of the International Association of Black Professional Fire Fighters estimates that only 4,500 or less than 3 percent of the nation's paid fire fighters are black.[29] Because of its concern over maintaining civil service standards for its members, the IAFF successfully resisted a proposal by the Department of Housing and Urban Development that cities "eliminate artificial barriers to employment and occupational advancement, including Civil Service requirements, which restrict em-

29. *GERR*, No. 474 (Oct. 16, 1972), p. B-16.

ployment opportunities for the disadvantaged."[30] Instead, the union in 1971 devised a pilot recruitment program, financed by the Department of Labor, to recruit and train 1,200 Vietnam veterans from minority groups in twelve urban areas.[31] A year after inauguration of the program, the AFL-CIO Civil Rights Department praised it. The president of the association of black fire fighters charged that it was ineffective; he claimed that local black firemen's organizations had not been involved in the program and as a result few blacks were recruited in several cities.[32]

Black fire fighters, like their police counterparts, tend to belong to the local organization in their city, which is usually an IAFF affiliate. Black organizations are not common, probably because few cities have enough black fire fighters to provide the nucleus for a separate organization. In Washington, D.C., a black Professional Firemen's Association (PFA) was formed after 170 blacks resigned from the IAFF because the local union opposed the promotion of five black firemen on the ground that they were not qualified under civil service rules. In St. Louis, a black captain started an organization of black fire fighters with the avowed objective of obtaining greater assignment of black firemen to black neighborhoods. The blacks charged that being spread out over the entire city left them isolated and subject to harassment and discrimination.[33]

In November 1969 five black fire organizations—one each from Hartford, Philadelphia, and New York City, and two from New Jersey—launched a national organization of black fire fighters. The mood of the conference, summed up by one delegate, was moderate: "We want to work with, not against."[34]

The International Association of Fire Fighters did not take official notice of the racial issue, either within the union or the nation as a whole, until the early 1970s. However, delegates to the 1972 convention departed from past practice by passing a resolution deploring "any discrimination on the basis of race, creed, color or national origin" and by changing the constitution to include an ex-

30. Leon E. Lunden, "International Association of Fire Fighters Convention," *Monthly Labor Review,* October 1972, p. 54.

31. *AFL-CIO News,* Oct. 30, 1971, p. 7.

32. GERR, No. 474 (Oct. 16, 1972).

33. GERR, No. 390 (March 1, 1971), pp. B-8–B-10.

34. GERR, No. 322 (Nov. 10, 1969), p. B-17.

plicit prohibition against discrimination in membership eligibility or treatment.[35]

Leadership

Both the police and fire fighters depend for their leadership on elected officials. Very little financial incentive is offered either at the international level or in the majority of local organizations to aspiring leaders. Fire fighters not only have a wide advantage over the police in the IAFF's membership in the AFL-CIO, but the nature of the fire fighter's working schedule concentrates his off-duty hours into full days that can be put into his union duties. Police have neither of these benefits and they suffer the disadvantage of public antipathy to police unionization.

INTERNATIONAL ASSOCIATION OF FIRE FIGHTERS

The IAFF resembles AFSCME in the factionalism that existed within the union during the early 1960s and the tradition of open conventions that admitted considerable debate. The important turning point in the IAFF came in 1968, when the Metro Caucus came to the convention intending to elect their candidate to the presidency, achieve proportionate representation and voting at conventions, and eliminate the constitutional prohibition on strikes. Two years later they were successful in changing the representation and voting arrangements and the no-strike rule. While the caucus failed to elect its presidential candidate, it helped to elect a compromise replacement for the outgoing president who, recognizing he could not be reelected, chose to retire. The new president, William H. McClennan, is the first nonofficer to be elected to that position.

The IAFF maintains a small professional staff at its headquarters in Washington, D.C., depending on part-time vice-presidents and per diem representatives to provide organizing and other services to local unions. In 1969 the staff included an assistant to the president, three legislative representatives, two research specialists, and eight

35. Lunden, "IAFF Convention," p. 54.

general field representatives, all hired since 1959. In addition, the union employs legal counsel and an outside public relations consultant. The growth in international staff and services has been particularly helpful to locals in small and medium-sized cities.

Under the IAFF constitution, vice-presidents are responsible for advising local unions and other subordinate bodies, providing professional and technical assistance, organizing, and performing other services as directed by the international officers.[36] Since they are also employed as fire fighters, their IAFF responsibilities are normally carried out during off-duty hours. Their work schedules and the fact that they are permitted to trade work days with other members of the department make the arrangement practicable.

Local officers also are working fire fighters whose off-duty time comes in one- or two-day blocks. Even on duty, fire fighters have considerable "free" time, and most chiefs, who also belong to the union, are liberal in the way they permit such time to be used. Fire departments often allow union officers to take time off with pay to attend union meetings and legislative and city council hearings and to handle grievances. In some cities, union officers are given special assignments to facilitate their availability for union business. When special jobs such as lobbying in the state legislature require extra time, local unions commonly pay an off-duty member to work for an officer. Most local unions pay their part-time officers small salaries, ranging from a few hundred to a few thousand dollars a year, in addition to expenses.

Cities with full-time officers follow varying practices with respect to salaries. In New York the president of IAFF Local 94 is on leave with full pay from the fire department and in addition receives a salary from the union. The president of the Chicago local is on leave without pay from the department and receives $25,000 a year from the union, an incentive that, coupled with the city's practice of promoting the president, has made the presidency a much-sought-after position. In Kansas City the full-time local union president since 1953 is a retired battalion chief, who is paid only a nominal salary to supplement his pension.

Both fire officers and men participate actively in local union affairs. The president of an IAFF local union is as likely to hold the

36. IAFF Constitution (1970), Art. 6, sec. 3.

rank of lieutenant, captain, or assistant chief as he is to be a rank-and-file fire fighter. In Buffalo and Denver, local unions prohibit superior fire officers from serving as union officials, while in Oakland, California, officers above the rank of captain may not hold office.

IAFF local unions do not generally employ full-time professional staff who are not themselves fire fighters. Liberal leave and substitute policies permit union officers to perform the functions for which other unions ordinarily employ full-time representatives or business agents. Lawyers are generally employed on a retainer or hourly basis to handle disputed pension claims and workmen's compensation cases and to represent members in civil service disciplinary proceedings.

POLICE ASSOCIATIONS

The current president of the FOP, a retired police sergeant, in 1965 defeated a retired lieutenant who had been president for nineteen years. The election represented a shift from a "soft sell" leadership to a highly vocal, flamboyant one. "He speaks the cop's language" is a phrase often used by police officers to describe FOP president John J. Harrington. His reelection to three successive terms indicates that he represents the views of the average policeman. In 1968, local FOP lodges reacted favorably to his proposal for a police "holiday" to dramatize the slaying of three Cleveland police officers, even though it conflicted with the FOP constitutional prohibition on strikes or "concerted action to cause a cessation of the performance of police duties."[37] His endorsement of George C. Wallace in the 1968 presidential campaign, also in conflict with the "strictly nonpolitical" character of the FOP, was approved at the 1969 FOP convention in a unanimous vote of tribute to "that honorable statesman."[38]

The president, who also heads the Philadelphia FOP Lodge and is paid only $200 a year by the national FOP, believes his office should be a full-time job.[39] He is indefatigable in his activities on

37. *National Police Journal,* Autumn 1968, pp. 8, 23.

38. National Lodge, Fraternal Order of Police, "Proposed Resolutions," 39th Biennial Conference (1969). Wallace also delivered the keynote address to the 1967 FOP conference.

39. *FOP National Lodge, Reports, Officers and Committees, 39th National Conference* (1969), p. 12.

behalf of the FOP. Between 1967 and 1969 he reported spending 335 days on FOP business.[40] But of $15,945 spent on travel, only $503 was for "organizing travel," the rest being for "regular travel" to appear on television, speak at state FOP meetings, and meet with government officials. Similarly, twenty-five Grand Lodge officers and trustees spent only $4,698 of a total of $38,684 in travel expenses for "organizing purposes."[41]

Until 1972 the ICPA presidency was a part-time post and more an honorary than a leadership position. The 1972 convention elected Edward J. Kiernan, formerly president of the New York City PBA, and established a two-year term for the president at a salary of $20,000 per year; it also raised dues to finance a more active national office. With a full-time, paid position, the president will be able to devote more time to organizing and recruiting new members.

Except in a few large cities, elected officers of local police associations serve their organizations while continuing to work as full-time policemen. In some departments the association president is assigned to duties that enable him to devote practically full time to organizational affairs. In others, local officers believe they are given punitive assignments because of their association activities. Many associations pay their part-time officers a small monthly stipend, rarely exceeding $300 plus expenses. In New York City the PBA president is on leave with full pay and receives a $10,000 expense allowance from the association; in Detroit the three top officers are on leave and their salaries are shared equally by the city and the association; in Chicago the president, a patrolman, is on leave without pay and receives a sergeant's salary from the association; and in Philadelphia three full-time officers are paid at a rate two grades above their departmental rank.

Associations that include policemen of all ranks tend to vest leadership in patrolmen rather than in superior officers, who dominated the associations in earlier years. The various offices and membership on the board of directors commonly are divided among several ranks, with a clear majority for patrolmen and sergeants. The trend toward leadership by patrolmen reflects increased militancy, especially among younger policemen. It is also indicative of greater job security as civil service has been extended to police de-

40. *FOP National Lodge, Reports* (1969), pp. 1–13.
41. Ibid., p. 31.

partments. Younger policemen now seek union office, often in contests with superior officers in their own departments. A more significant factor is state public employee collective bargaining laws that do not permit policemen and supervisory officers to be members of the same bargaining unit; associations naturally turn to patrolmen for leadership, and superior officers lose interest in running for office.

The only full-time staff in most local police associations are office employees who work under the direction of the elected officers. However, every association employs an attorney, usually on a retainer basis, to represent members in internal department hearings and civil service proceedings, and to defend policemen against charges brought by individual citizens. The importance of state legislation and local ordinances in determining salaries, pensions, and other economic benefits for policemen has also led to increased reliance on lawyers to draft legislation, testify at hearings, lobby legislators, and otherwise serve as advisers to association officers. Associations have also turned to attorneys for assistance in collective bargaining and representation under grievance procedures. The fact that policemen have daily contact with lawyers in their work may lead them to think more in terms of legal representation than other public employees. Expenditures for legal services is invariably the largest item in a police association's budget.

Some police associations have retained public relations representatives and consultants for special technical assignments, such as preparation of pension demands. The New York City association not only retains a public relations firm but in 1968 employed ten full-time staff members. Police locals affiliated with AFSCME and other unions have available the services of staff representatives who, though lacking in knowledge of police work, are experienced in negotiations and processing of grievances.

Finances

The comparative weakness of national and state levels of police organizations as compared to the IAFF and other unions shows up in their dues structure. Typically, dues are low, and most of what is collected remains in local coffers.

FIRE FIGHTERS

Unlike other public employee unions, the IAFF has no minimum dues requirement.[42] Local union dues are required only to be sufficient to cover the per capita tax to the international and "the necessary expenses of conducting business of the local."[43] In 1969 most IAFF locals charged dues of $4 or $5. The monthly per capita tax to the international—$1.25 effective in 1971—includes $0.10 earmarked for an emergency disputes fund.[44] State associations establish their own per capita taxes, usually about $0.50 a month; membership, of course, is not mandatory, and many large unions do not belong to state associations. However, almost all IAFF locals belong to state and local AFL-CIO councils, at a cost of about $0.20 to $0.25 per member each month.

Total monthly charges therefore run about $2 a month, or less than half of the membership dues in the average local union, and considerably less in those not affiliated with state associations. Some locals derive income from benefits, dances, shows, and other events, and a few offer comprehensive insurance programs supported by extra payments in addition to monthly dues. Special assessments are levied occasionally to support lobbying activities and referendum campaigns and for other purposes.

Historically, per capita increases have been voted over the opposition of the large local unions; the larger the local, the more likely are its delegates to oppose any increase in the resources and authority of the international and state associations. Small and medium-sized locals, recognizing their need for help from higher echelons of the union, have generally supported increases. Since the 1970 voting amendment, the large locals have had power to defeat proposals for per capita increases. The $0.50 increase voted at the 1970 convention suggests that the large local unions will exercise this power responsibly now that they have achieved their objective of having a voice in union affairs proportionate to their membership.

42. However, the secretary-treasurer of the IAFF has urged local unions to adopt "the IAFF policy on union dues, which is 1 per cent of a month's salary of the base pay of the first-grade Fire Fighters, with the absolute minimum of $4 per month." (*Reports, 30th Convention, IAFF* [1970], p. 11.)

43. IAFF Constitution (1970), Art. 13, sec. 4.

44. Ibid., Art. 8, secs. 5, 10.

POLICE

There is great variation in dues charged by local police associations. These groups depend much more heavily than fire fighters on fund-raising benefits and on the sale of publications, advertising, and miscellaneous items. Another source of revenue, confined almost entirely to the FOP, is associate memberships.

In general, dues are lowest in FOP lodges and highest in union-affiliated and big-city ICPA or independent associations. Local FOP dues in 1968–70 ranged from less than $1 to $4 a month. Independent associations and ICPA affiliates in large cities generally assessed monthly dues of $2 to $5, while AFSCME police locals usually charged $4 to $5 a month. A Tacoma, Washington, police local affiliated with the Operating Engineers' Union charged 1 percent of salary, averaging $7.90 per month.

Many FOP lodges and some ICPA and independent associations derive substantial revenue from shows, dances, and other fund-raising events. Union police locals do not generally engage in such activities and some nonunion associations strongly oppose fund-raising schemes because they consider them demeaning and unprofessional. The Oakland Police Officers Association withdrew from the ICPA, in part, as a reaction against commercialism injected into the annual meeting by the Chicago Patrolmen's Association which netted $15,000 by selling advertisements for a convention booklet. In general, the higher the dues structure of an association, the less likely it is to engage in external fund raising.

An even more questionable source of revenue is the sale of associate memberships in FOP lodges. The FOP constitution gives official sanction to "associate lodges" made up of businessmen, professional people, and other citizens.[45] Local FOP lodges tend to have about half as many associate members, who pay $10 to $20 a year dues, as regular active police members. An extreme example is Chicago, where 4,000 associates paid annual dues of $12 at a time when the FOP lodge had only 6,000 police members who paid less than $1 per month in dues. As with benefits and other fund-raising events, many police associations deplore the practice of selling associate memberships as unworthy of professionals and contributing to the impression that police favors can be bought.

45. FOP Constitution and By-Laws, Art. 16.

Still another source of revenue are special assessments to finance referendum campaigns, to reimburse policemen for lost time due to "job actions," and to pay extraordinary legal expenses. In 1967 the Detroit association levied a $10 special assessment on each member to pay lost wages to policemen participating in a "blue flu" job action, and $20 the following year to finance a referendum campaign against a change in the police pension plan. Associations in New York, Chicago, and Cleveland have also used special assessments to meet extraordinary expenses.

Affiliates of the FOP and the ICPA pay much lower per capita taxes than do union locals. Local FOP lodges pay only $1 per member a year to the Grand Lodge (and at the last three conventions have refused to increase the amount) and from $1 to $5 a year to state lodges. In 1969 the ICPA, reacting to the formation of a national police union, raised dues to $0.60 per member per year to finance expanded organizing activities and, in 1972 to $1.20 per capita with a minimum of $75 for any association in order to pay a full-time president and increase national office activities. ICPA affiliates and independent associations usually pay $1.50 to $3 a year per member to state police associations to which they belong.

The small scale on which the national office of the FOP operates is apparent from its financial statement for the two-year period July 1, 1967–June 30, 1969: $263,000 received from sale of decals, emblems, and other merchandise, and $153,000 from per capita taxes; $82,000 spent for "purchase of merchandise for resale" and $91,000 for "membership activities" including conference expenses, travel, salary surveys, and meetings.[46] The ICPA budget was even more modest; for the fiscal year 1969–70, anticipated income was only $21,322, of which $13,000 was from dues, and proposed expenditures were $19,615, including $9,600 for salaries and $3,500 for general office expense.[47] By comparison, AFSCME's per capita tax income in 1968 of about $130,000 for 10,000 police members was not much less than the 80,000 FOP members contributed in per capita dues over a two-year period.[48] The International Asso-

46. *FOP National Lodge, Reports* (1969), pp. 28–30.

47. International Conference of Police Associations, "Budget and Anticipated Income for Fiscal Year 1969–70" (n.d.; processed).

48. *Proceedings of the 17th International Convention, American Federation of State, County and Municipal Employees, AFL-CIO* (1968), pp. 366, 416.

ciation of Fire Fighters collected over \$1.5 million in per capita taxes in fiscal year 1970 and spent \$134,000 in organizing new members.[49] The difference in the scale of operations between these two public employee unions and the two national police associations suggests the vast difference in the roles played by the respective national organizations in relation to their local affiliates.

Summary

In structure, government, and administration, the IAFF resembles other unions more than other organizations of uniformed protective service employees. It has a trilevel structure comprising national, intermediate, and local echelons, full-time paid officers, a small but growing international staff, and a dues structure similar to that of other public employee unions. The IAFF has a strong tradition of local union autonomy which results in less power being centered in the international office, especially the presidency, than either AFSCME or the mixed unions. Like AFSCME, the IAFF has a lay executive board composed of working fire fighters. However, AFSCME has full-time council directors or presidents on its board, whereas none of the IAFF board members are full-time employees of the union. The IAFF also resembles AFSCME in its open conventions and active internal political life. In both unions the balance of power has shifted from small and medium-sized locals to larger local unions during the last decade. In AFSCME the shift was initiated by the international, but in the IAFF the large local unions forced the international to accede to their demands for influence more commensurate with membership size.

The major police organizations, the FOP and the ICPA, grant complete autonomy to local units and vest minimal authority in national and state echelons. Professional staff is virtually nonexistent and membership dues and per capita payments are usually set at low levels. Unlike unions, many local police associations, particularly FOP lodges, derive substantial income from benefits, special assessments, and associate memberships. With the advent of collective bargaining, some local associations have increased dues but there appears to be little inclination to provide adequate financial resources to enable national offices to play a larger service

49. *IAFF Proceedings* (1970), pp. 50–52.

role. Administratively, police organizations follow the association model rather than the union model of the fire fighters and other public employee unions.

Police and fire fighter jobs were until recently considered "white" occupations by the cities, the men who held the jobs, and the black community. Obviously, the organizations formed by policemen and fire fighters had the same complexion and the same philosophy as their members. While the number of black policemen and fire fighters has increased in recent years, blacks are still too small a group in all but a very few cities to affect the election of leaders in the local organizations to which they belong or to influence policy. There is little question that the FOP, ICPA, IAFF, and local police and fire fighter organizations could significantly increase the number of black policemen and firemen if they really wanted to. Instead, they have often insisted on rigid adherence to standards regarding physical attributes, education, police records, and civil service procedures that make it difficult to recruit minority group members.

The 1919 Boston police strike was a turning point in the early development of police organizations toward unionism. But there were other reasons why policemen might not have followed the fire fighters' example of forming an international union within the labor movement. As early as 1897 the American Federation of Labor denied a request for a police union charter on the ground that "policemen are often controlled by forces inimical to the labor movement."[50] That feeling, which continued to exist for many years, was undoubtedly engendered by the frequent use of local police forces to break strikes and disperse pickets in labor disputes. Also contributing to the discouragement of affiliation of police associations with the labor movement were the opposition of politicians, for whom control of police departments was an essential element in the operation of big-city political machines, and the antagonism of police chiefs, who argued that police unions were incompatible with professionalization of the police function.[51] These obstacles to unionization, which were not present for fire fighters, help to explain the different organizational development among the two uniformed protective services.

50. Emma Schweppe, *The Firemen's and Patrolmen's Unions in the City of New York* (New York: King's Crown Press, 1948), p. 25.
51. Kienast, "Policemen and Fire Fighter Organizations."

CHAPTER FOUR

American Nurses' Association

The American Nurses' Association (ANA) and its constituent units are similar to mixed unions in that they draw membership from both the public and the private sector. Neither the national nor the state associations now make any distinction between their public and private members, despite the different laws, rules, and procedures that apply to the two groups. The essential similarity in the nursing function, regardless of place of employment, and the ANA's emphasis on clinical aspects of the profession make the lack of division natural, and the mobility between public and private employment only makes a sorting of the two more difficult. As collective bargaining assumes greater importance in the profession, special arrangements will probably have to be made for nurses in public employment, for it is there that the major changes are occurring.

The National Association

The major policy-making body of the American Nurses' Association is the biennial convention, called the House of Delegates. Every constituent association is entitled to three delegates-at-large and one additional delegate for every two hundred members, each carrying one vote.[1] Conventions are usually attended by about a thousand voting delegates from the fifty-five state and territorial associations and several thousand additional ANA members and guests.[2]

The House of Delegates reflects the new structure of the association which was adopted in 1966 after eight years of study. Representation was made "a little more equitable for members in small and large states."[3] At the national level, four commissions were established to develop and implement the ANA's interest and activity in nursing education, nursing services, nursing research, and economic and general welfare. These commissions, each composed of six elected members and three appointed by the ANA board of directors, have considerable autonomy and much more authority than the committees they replaced.[4] Commission members, who are supposed to be "experts" in their field, serve four-year terms and are limited to two consecutive terms.[5]

A second major change resulted in the establishment of five divisions focusing on the clinical interests of nurses: community health, geriatrics, maternal and child health, medical-surgical, and psychiatric and mental health.[6] Under the previous ANA structure, nurses were identified by the nature of their employment; now occupational interests are centered at the state level and occupational forums are held at the biennial convention.[7] The major thrust of the reorganization was to direct attention at the national level to clinical and professional interests, and to allocate major responsibility for employment and occupational concerns to state associations which would receive guidance and support from the ANA Commission on Economic and General Welfare.[8]

1. Bylaws, American Nurses' Association (ANA) (1970), Art. 24, secs. 1, 2, 3.

2. *Proceedings, House of Delegates, Divisions on Practice, 46th Convention, American Nurses' Association (ANA Proceedings)* (1968), pp. 1, 96; *Summary Proceedings, 1970 House of Delegates, American Nurses' Association* (1970), p. 78.

3. ANA, *Proposed Plan for Functions and Structure of ANA, 1965 Supplement* (1965), p. 7.

4. ANA, "ANA Regional Conferences on Structure and Bylaws, 1967" (ANA; processed), p. 3; "Proposed Amendments to ANA Bylaws," *American Journal of Nursing,* April 1966, pp. 918–38.

5. ANA Bylaws, Art. 12.

6. Ibid., Art. 13.

7. Ibid., Art. 20.

8. "ANA Regional Conferences, 1967," p. 4.

Minority Group Participation

The ANA has long had a commitment to equal employment opportunity and civil rights generally, and specifically with respect to the nursing profession. In 1946 the association launched a campaign to eliminate segregation and discrimination in nursing;[9] the convention called on all state and district associations to drop racial barriers to membership (they existed in some southern states in violation of ANA policy). In 1948 the ANA adopted a policy that meetings be held only in integrated facilities and created a special category of direct membership for Negro nurses in the four states still practicing discrimination. This assurance of ANA membership led to the disbandment of the National Association of Colored Graduate Nurses. By 1964 all state and district associations had removed racial barriers to membership.[10]

The ANA headquarters staff has for many years included blacks. In 1969, 25 percent of the general staff and 4 percent of the professional staff were minority group members.[11] In 1970 a black professor of nursing was elected to the ANA board of directors.[12] ANA policy calls for inclusion of nondiscrimination provisions in collective bargaining agreements. In 1969, two-thirds of all contracts negotiated by state nurses' associations contained such clauses.[13]

The association's efforts to aid minority groups appear to have helped little. The 1960 census reported that 6.5 percent, or about 37,000, of the professional nurses in the United States were nonwhite.[14] In 1966, about 4,000—2.9 percent of all students of nursing —were Negro, and about one-third were enrolled in "predominantly Negro programs." About 3 percent of the graduates that year were Negroes.[15] There were more licenses issued to registered

9. ANA, "The ANA Record on Civil Rights" (ANA, 1969; processed).
10. Ibid.
11. "Number and Percent of ANA Professional and General Staff from Minority Groups, 1946–1969," table furnished by ANA.
12. *ANA in Action*, Vol. 2 (Summer 1970).
13. "The ANA Record on Civil Rights."
14. U.S. Bureau of the Census, *Statistical Abstract of the United States, 1970*, p. 228.
15. ANA, *Facts About Nursing: A Statistical Summary* (ANA, 1968 edition), pp. 98–99.

nurses from foreign countries in 1966 and 1967 than there were Negro nursing students.[16]

Despite recruitment programs and demonstration projects sponsored by the ANA and the National Student Nurses' Association (NSNA), the number of black Americans graduating from nursing education programs has declined since passage of the Civil Rights Act of 1964.[17] "This fact indicts the nursing profession," said the Minnesota State Nursing Association. "It means that the closing of the predominantly Negro schools has affected Negro student graduations more than . . . the federal law which makes it obligatory for any nursing education program utilizing federal funds to make special efforts to recruit and educate minority students."[18]

ANA Leadership

The ANA by-laws call for each constituent association to allocate its convention delegates "among the organized state sections and unorganized occupational interests to assure equitable representation of its members."[19] State associations apparently have not interpreted "equitable" to mean "proportionate" representation. In both 1968 and 1970, general duty nurses, who comprise over half of the nursing profession, were represented by only about 25 percent of all delegates, while nursing administrators and educators, about 7 percent of all nurses, made up 35 percent of the delegate body.[20] Even assuming that a higher percentage of administrators and educators than of general duty nurses are ANA members, the distribution of convention delegates obviously does not give anything approaching proportionate representation to occupational interests. A motion to amend the by-laws to explicitly require "proportionate representation" was defeated at the 1970 convention.[21]

16. Ibid., p. 60. These figures may include both nurses registered for the first time in the United States and those previously licensed in another state or territory of the United States.

17. ANA, *House of Delegates Reports, 1968–70, 47th Convention* (1970), p. 120.

18. Ibid.

19. ANA Bylaws, Art. 24, sec. 3.

20. *ANA Proceedings* (1968), p. 1, and (1970), p. 1; ANA, *Facts About Nursing*, pp. 18–22.

21. *ANA Proceedings* (1970), pp. 62–63.

Between conventions, responsibility for conducting the affairs of the ANA resides in a board of directors—six officers and ten directors—that meets three times a year. The president, three vice-presidents, secretary, and treasurer are limited to two terms of two years each in the same office. Five directors are elected at each biennial convention; they may not serve more than two consecutive four-year terms.[22] Officers and board members receive no salaries and continue to work at their regular jobs while fulfilling their ANA responsibilities. They are elected from a "ticket" prepared by a nominating committee and structured "so as to result in the election of directors representative of the occupational groups in nursing."[23] Nominations may also be made from the floor of the convention.

Again, educators and administrators are overrepresented. General duty and other nonsupervisory nurses are rarely elected to top ANA offices. The six officers elected at the 1970 convention were either deans or professors in schools and departments of nursing or nursing administrators (as were most of those elected to office in 1968). The three persons elected to the Commission on Economic and General Welfare were a university professor, an executive director of a state association, and a "medico-legal" consultant. The ANA executive director is a former university professor and dean.[24]

The dominant role of educators and administrators reflects the strong emphasis on professional objectives and clinical interests in the ANA. Candidates standing for office at the 1970 convention, for instance, stressed quality and adequacy of nursing, nursing education, clinical practice, utilization of nurses, patient care, and recruitment at least as much as the economic status of nurses.[25]

Persons with advanced academic degrees or supervisory positions are probably chosen for office because they are considered capable of providing effective leadership. They not only tend to be more experienced than general duty and other nurses, but they are better able to allocate time to the unpaid positions in the ANA. Despite the growing interest and activity of the ANA in promoting the economic status of its members through collective bargaining, the

22. ANA Bylaws, Arts. 6 and 7.
23. Ibid., Art. 21, Sec. 3.
24. *ANA in Action*, Vol. 2 (Summer 1970).
25. *American Journal of Nursing*, Vol. 70 (March 1970), pp. 571–81.

association's leadership continues to be drawn from the relatively small group of those interested primarily in the professional aspects of nursing.[26]

The problems that a part-time, nonsalaried board of directors presents were spelled out in a 1970 "Report of ANA's Financial Situation" prepared by the association's controller and the executive director (who was elected president at the 1970 convention). They compared the ANA to an industrial enterprise or a university, whose board members are selected for the kinds of expertise or help needed. Because they continue in office for long periods, often indefinitely, board members develop a "first-hand knowledge and grasp of problems as they evolve and become related to new and emerging problems in the work of the corporation."[27] The ANA board, on the other hand, is an "elected representative, political board." Members are chosen for their expertise in some aspect of nursing, rather than for knowledge necessary to the operation of a large organization. Frequently, they serve for only two or four years. "Thus the *ANA Board is a continuing mechanism* with continual changes occurring in its membership and in the kinds of expertise thus brought to the task. Under these conditions it is rarely possible for Board members to be fully aware, on the basis of direct first-hand experience, of a slowly developing problem."[28]

Its three meetings a year add to the need of new members to be "re-oriented" to continuing problems. But more frequent meetings would make it impossible for some nominees to accept election to the board and would add expenses that the ANA is not in a position to incur. The board is required to make "many 'tough-minded' decisions but its members, by the requirements of nursing, are likely to be 'tender-hearted,' finding hard decisions difficult except under the most compelling circumstances."[29]

Authority and responsibility for the design and conduct of internal operations have of necessity been centered in a full-time, paid executive director appointed by the board. "The power to choose and to screen information—to embellish or distort it, to

26. Joel Seidman, "Nurses and Collective Bargaining," *Industrial and Labor Relations Review*, Vol. 23 (April 1970), p. 339.

27. Hildegard E. Peplau and Gerald A. Dorfman, "Report of ANA's Financial Situation" (ANA, April 28, 1970; processed), p. 5.

28. Ibid.

29. Ibid., pp. 6–7.

expand or to limit it, to present or to withhold it—lies in the hands of the Executive Director."[30] (In 1969 the board had commissioned an outside study of the ANA's operations which led to a complete reorganization of the national office and to tight budget controls.)

It is interesting that the ANA officials chose to compare the organization to a private corporation or university rather than to a union, whose economic objectives and tactics more closely resemble those of the ANA. The typical union differs from the ANA in that its major officers—the president and secretary-treasurer—are elected full-time paid officials, who are responsible for conducting the affairs of the union in accordance with policy decisions of the convention and the international executive board. The vice-presidents who, together with the officers, make up the executive board, also usually hold full-time union positions or devote considerable time to union business. The ANA would more closely resemble a union if its board consisted largely of executive directors and officers of state nurses' associations, who have a continuing association with the membership and the affairs of the organization, rather than of educators and administrators whose primary interest and concerns are likely to be different from those of most ANA members. As the ANA increases its emphasis on improving the economic status of its members, the structure that has served it well as a purely professional organization may prove to be unsuited to dealing with the complex and controversial issues that are an integral part of the collective bargaining and legislative processes.

State Associations

A major accomplishment of the 1966 reorganization was to differentiate the role and structure of the state and district nurses' associations from those of the national association. The ANA now has responsibility for setting standards through its national commissions. The task of translating standards into reality in the practice of nursing lies with the state and district associations. State associations are divided into occupational sections that serve as a mechanism for promoting the occupational and economic interests of the members.

30. Ibid., p. 6.

Officers and members of the board of directors of state associations are elected at annual or biennial conventions and serve without pay while continuing to work at their regular jobs. Most state nurses' associations (SNAs) have a president, two vice-presidents, a secretary, and a treasurer and a board of directors, including the officers, that varies from fifteen to thirty members. Officers are usually limited to two years, other directors to four years in office. Some directors are elected at large and others by occupational sections, such as general duty nurses, administrators, head nurses, private duty nurses, educators, public health nurses, and office nurses. A full-time staff headed by an executive director, and varying in size among states from one to thirty-four, is responsible for conducting the day-to-day business of the association and provides continuity to the organization.

As in the national organization, nurse administrators, educators, and supervisors tend to occupy leadership positions in state associations. However, this situation is changing in SNAs that are most active in collective bargaining. Thus in the California SNA, a militant state association and one of the first to engage in collective bargaining, general duty and other nonsupervisory nurses have exercised considerable leadership. In Michigan, where one-third of the members are in bargaining units, each occupational section has a member on the board of directors, and delegates to state and national conventions are elected to give proportionate representation to occupational groupings. There is evidence that this does not entirely satisfy nonsupervisory nurses. In 1971, general duty nurses at one hospital voted to decertify the Michigan Nurses' Association (MNA) as their bargaining representative and formed a new organization open only to nonsupervisory nurses and graduate student nurses. Similar actions were reported under way in several other hospitals. The schism was precipitated by a 1970 decision to dissolve the separate MNA division established in 1968 to carry out the collective bargaining functions of the association. Its functions were integrated into the association's general operations and the consulting firm that had been conducting collective bargaining activities was replaced by MNA's economic security professional staff.[31]

31. *Michigan Nurse Newsletter,* Vol. 43 (September 1970), p. 3.

A majority of the bargaining units represented by the MNA are in public employment. The troubles within that association may be indicative of what will happen generally as collective bargaining assumes greater importance in the nursing profession. State associations may find it necessary to create structures or at least staff specializations to deal with the special status and problems of nurses in public employment.

Economic Security Program

The Economic Security Program, initiated in 1946, is the organizational vehicle through which the ANA and its state affiliates represent the economic interests of nurses and engage in collective bargaining and other forms of negotiation. The ANA Commission on Economic and General Welfare is charged with developing and implementing general economic standards and programs, recommending policy on legislative matters, and evaluating the economics of health care and nursing. Because the objectives of the program were not being effectively carried out, the commission introduced a "new approach" in 1967. National staff was made available to assist state associations in economic security matters. The commission required that the state make some monetary commitment to each project; usually, ANA provided salary for the staff while the SNA financed travel, consultation, public relations, office space, and secretarial service.

Between late 1967 and the end of 1969 the commission approved fourteen projects involving some 11,000 nurses. The services it provided—"offering representation to new groups, assisting groups in organizing, gaining recognition in negotiating agreements, preparing briefs, developing educational programs, conducting workshops, giving advice on collective bargaining legislation, analyzing surveys, and recruiting membership"[32]—are very similar to those provided by a national union to local affiliates that need help in organization and collective bargaining.

When the new approach was suspended in March 1970 (for financial reasons), seven projects had been completed, seven were incomplete, and several projects and requests for assistance were

32. ANA, *House of Delegates Reports, 1968–70,* p. 74.

awaiting action. The basic goal of preparing SNA staff to implement new programs without extensive reliance on ANA staff had not been achieved.[33]

Staff

The headquarters staff of the ANA has fluctuated considerably in recent years. Between August 1967 and September 1969 the professional staff rose from 56 to 68, then fell to 32 in May 1971 after the financial crisis of 1969. The Economic Security Division, which had grown from 5 to 15, was particularly hard hit, only 2 persons retaining their positions. Clerical personnel were also reduced substantially. The dues increase voted in 1970 has permitted the ANA to start rebuilding its staff.[34]

The ANA staff has tended to be about evenly divided between registered nurses and nonnurses. The nonnurses have generally been employed in public relations, business and film service, and similar divisions. At its high point, the Economic Security Division consisted of four nurses, including the director, and eleven other professional staff members, nine of them men. The nonnurses had come from such places as the International Ladies' Garment Workers, Oil and Chemical Workers, American Federation of Government Employees, and the Industrial Union Department of the AFL-CIO. The ANA negotiates and has written agreements with a professional staff organization and an AFL-CIO union representing general staff employees.[35]

At the state level, SNAs employed 359 staff members, about equally divided between professional and clerical employees, in March 1968. About 75 percent of the professional staff and an even higher proportion of the executive directors were nurses. The largest staff, California's, included 34 professional members, New York's 11, and Pennsylvania's 9. Twenty states had only 1 professional staff member and four associations had none. Some two-thirds of all professional staff below the rank of executive director had been hired since 1965; three-fourths of the executive directors had been in their positions since 1962. Less than 10 percent of the district nurses'

33. Ibid., p. 21.
34. Headquarters staff lists for various dates, 1967–71, supplied by ANA.
35. *ANA Proceedings* (1966), pp. 9–10.

associations had any professional staff, and that was usually only an executive director.[36]

Twenty-two state associations in 1968 identified 51 professional positions—about 25 percent of the total—as having been established for their economic security programs, about half of them for that purpose solely or as major program responsibility. Since then, economic security staff has been increasing in SNAs—in fact, several of the professionals laid off in the ANA financial crisis have been employed by state associations. In addition to or in place of their own staff, twenty states in 1968 retained industrial relations consultants and forty-eight legal consultants, some of whom advised on industrial relations.[37]

In 1969 the median salary of SNA professional staff members, including executive directors, was somewhat more than $11,000 per year. Individual salaries ranged from $6,000 to over $27,000, with the larger associations generally paying the higher salaries. Half the states employed no professionals other than an executive director. Salaries were highest in the West, followed by SNAs in the North Central, Northeast, and South, in that order. Salaries of SNA executive directors and professional staff members appear to be comparable to those paid to public employee union and association staff representatives, but fringe benefits are much less generous. Sixteen state associations have written contracts with professional staff members. Only eight of these covered professional staff members other than the executive director.[38]

While SNAs, like the parent ANA, prefer to employ registered nurses, many economic security staff members are nonnurses, both male and female. The specialized knowledge required in collective bargaining and related activities is rarely found among nurses, and SNAs have not hesitated to employ persons outside the nursing profession. Economic security staff members generally perform the same duties as union representatives, relying on committees made up of nurses to advise them on technical matters. In 1967, SNAs conducted 41 collective bargaining conferences, workshops, and institutes (more than in any other program area); since many states

36. ANA, Research and Statistics Department, "Summary of Annual Reports from State Nurses' Associations, March, 1968" (ANA, 1968; processed), pp. 6, 7, 59.

37. Ibid., pp. 8–17.

38. ANA, Research and Statistics Department, "Survey of Salaries and Other Employment Conditions for Professional Staff Employees of State Nurses' Associations, October, 1969" (memorandum, April 3, 1970).

have enacted collective bargaining laws for public employees and nurses since then, educational programs in economic security have undoubtedly increased. Some SNAs already employ more staff members on economic security than in any other program, and this will no doubt soon be the case everywhere.[39]

Finances

Membership dues vary from state to state and also among districts. In response to the financial crisis, national dues were increased from $12.50 to $25 per year by the 1970 convention. Full membership privileges were extended, at one-half the regular dues rate, to unemployed nurses, nursing students, new graduates for the first year of membership, and nurses eligible for old age benefits under social security.[40] In addition to national dues, ANA members pay varying dues to state and district associations. Twenty-eight SNAs increased their dues between 1966 and 1968, partly because of expanded economic security activities. Total national, state, and district charges in 1968 ranged from a high of $72.50 in Michigan to a low of $25 in Mississippi.[41] The 1970 national dues increase raised these levels by $12.50. These figures indicate that nurses' dues are more comparable to those charged by public employee unions than by employee associations.

At the end of 1969 the ANA had a deficit of $619,013 in its operating fund.[42] As the 1970 "Report of ANA's Financial Situation" noted: "At a most critical time in the history of nursing, at a time when the power of organized nursing should be strong and clearly influential in health affairs at the national level, ANA finds itself in a serious financial crisis."[43] It proposed an appeal to members for contributions to a $1.6 million emergency fund. If successful, "it will be possible for ANA to rebuild at the end of 1970; if it is not successful, some plan to pay off debts will have to be made and this process will slow up for years to come the forward thrust of ANA."[44]

39. "Summary of Annual Reports from State Nurses' Associations, March, 1968," pp. 8–16.

40. *ANA in Action*, Vol. 2 (Summer 1970).

41. "Summary of Annual Reports from State Nurses' Associations, March, 1968," p. 4.

42. ANA, *House of Delegates Reports, 1968–70*, p. xiii.

43. "Report of ANA's Financial Situation," p. 1.

44. Ibid., p. 13.

Summary

Though unique in its professional orientation, the American Nurses' Association has some of the same problems as the other kinds of organizations included in this study. Like the mixed unions, the ANA includes both private and public employees within its ranks and must adapt to the special problems of nurses covered by state public employee collective bargaining laws. It shares with the employee associations the problem of a leadership made up of the elite of the profession who may have different priorities than the bulk of the membership, especially with respect to economic security. Like organizations of fire fighters and to a lesser degree policemen, the ANA is an all-inclusive organization whose members feel a strong community of interest regardless of position in the hierarchical structure of the profession. Their problems pertaining to composition of bargaining units have thus been similar. Because collective bargaining is not the major function of the ANA, nurses have the additional problem of fitting this relatively new activity into the overall structure of their national, state, and district associations. Though much more sympathetic to minority group membership than the uniformed services, the ANA has not succeeded in substantially increasing the number of blacks in the profession.

The ANA and its state affiliates have learned that collective bargaining is a costly and time-consuming activity. With a dues structure that is already high, especially for general duty and other nonsupervisory nurses, it will be increasingly difficult to furnish effective representation in collective bargaining without decreasing services in professional areas. Some nurses oppose shifting resources, while others favor increasing emphasis on collective bargaining whatever the expense. The split is likely to be along occupational lines, with nurse educators, administrators, and head nurses on one side and general duty and other lower level nurses on the other. Given the decentralization of the collective bargaining function in the ANA, this issue will have to be resolved by the state associations rather than the national organization.

CHAPTER FIVE

Conflict and Cooperation

Public employment represents the major new area for union organization since the 1930s when the Congress of Industrial Organizations (CIO) was formed by unions dedicated to organizing workers in the mass production industries. Just as the issue of industrial unionism led to bitter strife within the labor movement, so also has the organization of government employees given rise to interunion conflict. The issue has been further complicated in public employment by the presence of employee associations, many of them predating unions of government employees.

Disputes among AFL-CIO unions, between those unions and independent unions, and between unions and associations have characterized organization efforts in the public sector at all levels—federal, state, and local.[1] The overlapping jurisdictional claims and interests of the major unions active in state and local government—the American Federation of State, County and Municipal Employees (AFSCME), the Service Employees International Union (SEIU), the Laborers' International Union, and the International Brotherhood of Teamsters—have resulted in interunion conflicts in organizing, in representation elections, and in charges brought under the AFL-CIO Internal Disputes Plan. Other unions have also entered the fray. While the conflict generally has been between

1. See Leo Kramer, *Labor's Paradox—The American Federation of State, County, and Municipal Employees, AFL-CIO* (Wiley, 1962).

89

two unions competing for a group of workers, coalitions have at times involved several unions in a contest.

The SEIU, Laborers, and Teamsters have one common advantage over AFSCME in organizing and representing public employees. Each can draw on its private sector local unions and memberships for money and manpower to support organizing campaigns and to exert pressure on government employers. Sometimes the mixed unions can provide jobs in private industry to striking public employee members. The SEIU and the Laborers have considerable influence in state and local AFL-CIO councils; the Laborers' Union is also affiliated with the AFL-CIO Building and Construction Trades Department, whose members often control central labor bodies. The Teamsters, though independent, maintains excellent relations with many AFL-CIO unions, especially those in the building trades. The mixed unions have sometimes collaborated against AFSCME, which all other unions consider their major adversary in state and local government.

Police and fire fighter organizations, while not in competition with each other for members, are extremely jealous of any advantage that one may gain over the other in wages or other benefits. The International Association of Fire Fighters has often benefited from the support of AFL-CIO state and local labor councils in negotiations with city officials and in influencing legislative bodies. Police organizations tend to be "loners" in representing their members, but have in some instances associated themselves with the fire fighters and other employee groups in dealing with city officials.

Employee associations compete with all unions and, in the process, sometimes behave in ways that make it difficult to differentiate them from unions.[2] Some, at both the state and local level, have entered into mergers or other joint arrangements with unions. In a few instances the two types of organizations have cooperated, especially on legislative matters.[3] But, for the most part, the relationship between associations and unions is characterized by conflict and competition. Given their independent status, associations

---

2. The Executive Secretary of the Oregon State Employees Association writes: "We are a union—and our membership promotion material and other publications say so—but an independent union rather than an AFL-CIO affiliate." (Letter to the author, Aug. 16, 1971.)

3. Ibid.

are not in a position to help each other, except by exchanging information, and thus are at a disadvantage in competing with national unions. However, antipathy between unions has in some instances resulted in the alliance of a union with an association against another union.

The American Nurses' Association (ANA) is the major professional association, outside of education, that has espoused collective bargaining. Limiting itself to one specialized group of employees, registered nurses, it has had little competition in its organizing efforts, although it has been challenged for the right to represent nurses in some institutions. The ANA, and particularly the state nurses' associations which are the locus of collective bargaining activity, cooperates with other employee organizations but considers itself different from them because of its professional orientation.

Interunion Competition

AFSCME's jurisdiction was cloudy from its birth. It was given a direct charter as a local union by the American Federation of Labor in May 1932.[4] Its efforts to win a national charter were at first blocked by the American Federation of Government Employees (AFGE), a union of federal employees that amended its constitution in 1935 to include state, county, and municipal employees. At that point AFSCME intended to enter AFGE as an autonomous union for state and local government employees, with its own officers and constitution. However, internal problems in AFGE and the split within the labor movement resulting from formation of the CIO helped AFSCME to obtain its own charter as an international union in October 1936.[5]

The AFL executive council was persuaded to grant the charter because the AFSCME constitution excluded from membership persons over whom "jurisdiction has been granted to other national or international unions by the American Federation of Labor," and provided for dual membership so that government employee crafts-

---

4. AFSCME was chartered as a "federal" union not affiliated with any international union.

5. Kramer, *Labor's Paradox*, pp. 12–23.

men could belong to both AFSCME and a craft union. In 1952 all reference to jurisdiction was removed from AFSCME's constitution because other unions were using its language to prove that AFSCME did not have complete jurisdiction over all state, county, and municipal employees.[6]

The union's major competitor during the 1950s was the Service Employees.[7] In 1951, AFL President William Green demanded that AFSCME turn over to the SEIU all janitors, janitresses, and custodians. AFSCME refused, charging that the craft union intent of the order was in direct conflict with its own doctrine of industrial unionism.[8] When George Meany, the new AFL president, ruled a year later that SEIU had jurisdiction over custodians and janitors in schools, AFSCME accepted the ruling. In return, SEIU conceded jurisdiction over clerical and professional employees in public service and agreed to stop organizing employees in government hospitals and institutions. But the agreement was never signed because AFSCME refused to force its existing locals to join SEIU. The failure to consummate this agreement resulted in a continuation of warfare between the two unions.[9]

6. Ibid., pp. 51–52. The international executive board described the jurisdictional muddle:

> We were introduced into this picture in 1936 with a jurisdictional definition difficult if not impossible to understand and certainly beyond the comprehension of ordinary mortals. It says at the outset that our jurisdiction is over state and local government employees over whom jurisdiction was not granted to unions chartered prior to October 12, 1936. It follows that our jurisdiction is defined by the jurisdictions of unions in existence as of that date. . . . Each time another national or international union raises a jurisdictional question we must ask the American Federation of Labor for the definition of that organization's territory as officially granted to it prior to 1936. . . . Then, we were advised that in the case of some unions there is no stated definition of their jurisdiction but that they can take into membership whatever is generally implied in the title of their organization. This means, and in our experience specifically has meant, that our jurisdiction will be defined differently at different times by people in authority in the organizations without specific grants. An agreement reached by us with such an organization will be kept in the form of a verbal understanding and it will then be subject to change with changing attitudes on the part of those in authority in other unions.

(*Proceedings of the 8th International Convention, American Federation of State, County and Municipal Employees, A.F. of L. [AFSCME Proceedings]* [1952], p. 256.)

7. The union was at that time named the Building Service Employees' International Union. Of this union, AFSCME's executive board wrote in 1952: "It is evidently their official position that we are to be wiped out." (Ibid., p. 257.)

8. Ibid., p. 259.

9. *AFSCME Proceedings* (1954), pp. 236–39.

Relations between the two unions improved after 1960, and they finally reached a no-raiding agreement. In 1962 the AFL Internal Disputes Plan was created to resolve jurisdictional disputes among AFL affiliates. Competition for government employees and charges of raiding continued, however. In 1966, AFSCME's president accused SEIU of uniting with the Teamsters in Michigan against AFSCME. He also charged that the Laborers' Union, fortified by several former key staff members from AFSCME, was raiding AFSCME in Rhode Island and a few other states. Even the Communications Workers of America "suddenly decided that they wanted to organize clerical workers. . . . They are even changing the emblem of their union. They are taking off the telephone. I don't know what they are going to substitute, a typewriter or something."[10] AFSCME regards these unions as interlopers, who have no understanding or interest in public employees and their problems, but are "simply looking for a sideline."[11]

Other unions see the situation differently. The Service Employees International Union scoffs at the suggestion that AFSCME has a legitimate claim on the entire state and local government field, noting that its interests and success in organizing public employees date back to the early years of the union, which was formed in 1921. Hospital employees, both public and private, have always represented one of the most important sectors of SEIU membership, and nonacademic school, college, and university employees were added to the union's jurisdiction by constitutional amendment in 1950.[12] The SEIU considers itself a "unique organization," equally at home in three major sectors—public service, the service industries, and nonprofit institutions.[13] It regards AFSCME and other unions as latecomers to the organization of public employees.

State and local governments are a less important source of new members in the Laborers' Union than in SEIU. For the Laborers, jurisdictional disputes, when they arise, are usually with AFSCME. In 1941 the union complained about infringements by AFSCME on the Laborers' jurisdiction in several states, citing AFSCME's

10. *AFSCME Proceedings* (1966), p. 19.
11. Ibid.
12. *Proceedings of the Fourteenth General Convention, Building Service Employees' International Union, AFL (BSEIU Proceedings)* (1950), p. 203.
13. *BSEIU Proceedings* (1960), p. 11.

pledge not to interfere with the jurisdiction of other unions.[14] In 1942 the Laborers charged AFSCME with infringement of its charter in another area. It was finally reported at the 1956 convention that an agreement had been reached between the unions' presidents in which AFSCME conceded that all new construction as well as alteration, repair, and maintenance was within the jurisdiction of building trades unions.[15]

But these early disputes were mild compared with the frequent and bitter conflicts that occurred after 1964, when the Laborers established a Federal–Public Service Division staffed by several former AFSCME representatives. In Providence, Rhode Island, the Laborers' Union won a major victory in March 1968 when it defeated AFSCME in a citywide election to gain exclusive representation for about 1,000 city employees.[16] The tables were reversed in Baltimore a year later when AFSCME defeated the Laborers and a city employees' association in an election called after the AFSCME local had called a sanitation department strike. In both cities, former AFSCME representatives led the Laborers' campaign and both sides called in reinforcements from other areas.

Like the SEIU, the Laborers have been able to settle most differences with other unions in the public employment field amicably and have sometimes made alliances against AFSCME.[17] Only AFSCME has proved an implacable opponent, resulting in numerous cases brought before the AFL-CIO Internal Disputes panel. Even as recently as 1966, the Laborers still contended that AFSCME's 1936 charter from the AFL covered only white collar workers and that the union had "overstepped its jurisdiction" by organizing blue collar workers.[18]

As an independent union which recognizes no jurisdictional boundaries, the Teamsters presents a formidable challenge in any

14. "Report of the General President," in *Report of Proceedings of the Eighth Convention, International Hod Carriers', Building and Common Laborers' Union of America (Laborers' Proceedings)* (1941), pp. 276–77.

15. *Laborers' Proceedings* (1956), p. 198.

16. *Spotlite,* Vol. 2 (April 1968).

17. Bureau of National Affairs, *Government Employee Relations Report (GERR),* No. 392 (March 15, 1971), p. B-6. In January 1971 the Service Employees, Laborers, and Operating Engineers cooperated against AFSCME in representation elections involving some 20,000 Pennsylvania state employees. *(GERR,* No. 419 [Sept. 20, 1971], pp. B-2–B-4.)

18. *Laborers' Proceedings* (1966), p. 172.

field it seeks to organize. Until the 1960s the union did not exhibit much interest in public employment, preferring to concentrate on private sector employees who were easier to organize and could better afford to pay the relatively high dues charged by most Teamster locals. As more states passed collective bargaining laws covering government workers, the Teamsters started to pay more attention to the public sector and by 1970 claimed some 57,000 members among state and local government employees.[19] True to its philosophy as a union for all workers, the Teamsters has enrolled public employees in a wide range of occupations: garbage collectors, truck drivers, school principals, policemen, housing superintendents, and hospital workers.

The Teamsters, though not subject to the AFL-CIO Internal Disputes Plan, has not raided other unions any more than have AFL-CIO affiliates. Its locals have negotiated bilateral no-raiding agreements with the Service Employees, the Laborers, and AFSCME in a number of cities. In some areas the Teamsters has joined with one or more other unions in organizing public employees and, like the SEIU and the Laborers, its most frequent opponent has been AFSCME.

Two of the largest Teamster public employee local unions located in New York City are former AFSCME affiliates. One of those locals had a major confrontation with AFSCME Council 37 in 1965 over the representation of 34,000 hospital workers. A personal letter of support for AFSCME from AFL-CIO President George Meany to every hospital employee was credited with playing an important role in AFSCME's victory, which made it the dominant organization among hospital workers in New York City.[20] The Teamster local subsequently attacked AFSCME for endorsing the establishment of the tripartite Office of Collective Bargaining to regulate labor-management relations between the city of New York and its employees. A few years later, however, the Teamster local joined the group of unions that support the Office of Collective Bargaining and it now has amicable relations with AFSCME, sealed by a no-raiding agreement.

In another conflict, a Teamster local in Milwaukee succeeded in

---

19. "Teamster Union Representation and Bargaining Among Public Employees, Spring 1970" (memorandum, Sept. 17, 1970).

20. *AFSCME Proceedings* (1966), p. 313.

separating a few hundred truck drivers and equipment operators from a much larger unit of city employees represented by AFSCME. The Teamster campaign emphasized the benefits of a small craft union over the industrial union that must accommodate a multitude of interests.[21] The AFSCME council was subsequently replaced by the Teamster local as the drivers and operators' collective bargaining representative.

Union autonomy has proved in some cases to be disadvantageous. For example, several thousand New York City welfare workers who decided to leave AFSCME returned after a few years of independence, convinced of the need for affiliation with a large public employee union and the labor movement. The breakaway group, the Social Service Employees Union (SSEU), was organized in 1961 as an independent union. In 1964 it defeated the AFSCME local in a representation election for a unit of case workers, children's counselors, and home economists. The two unions fought one another until 1969, when the SSEU voted to rejoin AFSCME. The decision recognized the close relationship between employees represented by the two unions. Also, the only way for SSEU members to influence negotiations on citywide issues for all social service employees was to become a part of the AFSCME council that was the recognized bargaining agent on such issues. The independent union had learned from bitter experience that it could not conduct a successful strike without the support of the labor movement. Moreover, its membership added to the AFSCME local would make that the largest local union in the council, with the ability to exercise considerable influence on policy decisions.

AFL-CIO Internal Disputes Plan

Many disputes between AFL-CIO unions active in public employment have resulted in charges brought under the Internal Disputes Plan. The original plan, a no-raiding program, was designed to protect the established bargaining relationships of affiliates of the Congress of Industrial Organizations against raids by American Federation of Labor unions, and vice versa, shortly before

21. Leaflets issued by Teamsters Local 242 (April 26 and June 18, 1968; processed).

TABLE 5-1. *AFL-CIO Internal Disputes Determinations Involving State and Local Government Unions, 1962–70*[a]

Contending unions	Number of cases	Number of cases sustained for				
		AFSCME	SEIU	Laborers	Other union[b]	Neither contestant[c]
AFSCME–SEIU	16	6	9	...	...	1
AFSCME–Laborers	14	12	...	2	...	...
AFSCME–Other union[b]	13	6	...	...	4	3
SEIU–Other union[b]	7	...	5	...	2	...
Laborers–Other union[b]	2	...	...	2	0	...
Other unions	4	...	...	...	4	...
Total	56	24	14	4	10	4

Sources: AFL-CIO, *Index Digest of Determinations of the Impartial Umpire Under the AFL-CIO Internal Disputes Plan, 1962–69* (AFL-CIO, n.d.); and individual case decisions for 1970.
a. First seven months only of 1970.
b. Union other than AFSCME, Laborers, or SEIU.
c. Both unions found to be in violation of Article 20 of the AFL-CIO constitution (1969).

the two organizations were reunified in 1955.[22] It was binding only on those unions that elected to become signatories to the agreement. In 1958 the no-raiding principles were extended to all unions, while the umpire's rulings, formerly binding, were given the status of recommendations which could be appealed to the AFL-CIO executive council. In 1962, circulation of defamatory literature in organizing campaigns was prohibited. Unions that do not comply with decisions of the umpire or the executive council are denied the protection of the plan, the noncompliance findings are publicized, and all affiliates are enjoined from rendering assistance to the offending unions.[23]

Between 1962 and July 1970, about 15 percent of all umpire decisions under the plan involved unions in state and local government (see Table 5-1). (Many more cases were settled through mediation.) More than half of the 56 decisions occurred during the last two and one-half years, and 16 during the first seven months of 1970 alone. Forty of the cases involved a violation of Article 20 of the AFL-CIO constitution, which sets forth the principles governing interunion competition in organizing workers. In nine out of ten

22. AFL-CIO Constitution, as amended by the Eighth Constitutional Convention of the AFL-CIO (1969), Art. 20.
23. Ibid.; and David T. Cole, "The Internal Disputes Plan: A Working Reality," *AFL-CIO American Federationist,* Vol. 76 (June 1969), pp. 16–21.

cases the charge was attempting to organize employees for whom another AFL-CIO affiliate has secured "an established collective bargaining relationship."[24] In the other 10 percent the alleged violation was use of defamatory matter by one affiliate against another in an organizational campaign.[25] Although sustained in a majority of cases, AFSCME has declared its dissatisfaction with "the merely negative restraints" on jurisdictional warfare provided by the Internal Disputes Plan. A 1972 convention resolution called for a program to deal with the "allocation and, if necessary, reallocation of jurisdiction" but made no specific proposal on how to draw jurisdictional lines among competing unions.[26]

In one particularly significant determination, in November 1964, the umpire held that an affiliate could have an "established collective bargaining relationship," as defined in the AFL-CIO constitution, even though exclusive representation was not possible.[27] In a case involving AFSCME and the Laborers' Union over the representation of employees at Massillon State Hospital and four other Ohio state institutions, the umpire held that the Laborers had violated the AFL-CIO constitution by soliciting membership and encouraging employees to disaffiliate from the State, County and Municipal Employees. AFSCME had been recognized as the representative for its members in these hospitals with check-off privileges and the right to handle grievances, and discuss merit increases, sick leaves, seniority, choice of shifts, and vacation periods. AFSCME had not, however, been recognized as the exclusive bargaining representative for all employees, nor did it represent a majority of the employees in any of the institutions, there being no legal provision or policy of granting exclusive representation for state employees in Ohio.

The Laborers claimed that AFSCME did not have the kind of employer recognition contemplated by the AFL-CIO constitution as the basis for the creation of an "established collective bargaining relationship."[28] In rejecting its argument, the umpire held that in state employment, where written agreements are not used

24. AFL-CIO Constitution (1969), Art. 20, sec. 2.
25. Ibid., sec. 5.
26. *GERR*, No. 455 (June 5, 1972), pp. 2–3, 4.
27. Cole, "Internal Disputes Plan," p. 20.
28. AFL-CIO, *The AFL-CIO Internal Disputes Plan Determinations, 1964–65* (AFL-CIO, 1966), pp. 83–87.

and exclusive bargaining rights are not normally granted, recognition creates an established bargaining relationship which other unions must respect. "If such a relationship could be protected only if the recognized union has exclusive bargaining rights or represents a majority of the employees, this would amount in practical terms to a denial of such protection and an open invitation to raiding and chaos."[29]

The AFL-CIO executive council, in sustaining the umpire's decision, limited the ruling to situations "where laws, regulations or practice restrict affiliates to the representation of their members only and no broader collective bargaining relationship can be established." In such cases, the council said, affiliates are entitled to protection only as to the employees whom they represent, but not for nonmember employees.[30]

In a second important decision, the AFL-CIO executive council refused to permit a union in state and local government to seek exclusive recognition in a bargaining unit for which another affiliate already held a lower form of recognition.[31] This ruling is in conflict with a decision of the New York City Office of Collective Bargaining (OCB), which in 1969 modified its rules to permit a union to petition for exclusive representation on a citywide basis of employees in a job classification for which another union had previously been recognized on a departmental basis.[32] (Citywide recognition enables a union to bargain over a much wider range of issues than departmental recognition.) The AFL-CIO determination has deterred unions in New York from petitioning for citywide certification for fear that they will be charged with raiding by unions holding departmental recognition. The OCB charged that the AFL-CIO position denies employees their maximum bargaining rights and defeats the purposes and policies of the New York City collective bargaining law.[33]

Twelve Internal Disputes cases have arisen in New York City, and five of them have involved departmental versus citywide rep-

29. Ibid., p. 85.
30. Ibid., p. 87.
31. "Special Committee on the Application of Article XXI to Collective Bargaining Relationships with Government Agencies" (statement by AFL-CIO Executive Council, Sept. 11, 1967; processed).
32. Press Release, Office of Collective Bargaining, New York City, July 22, 1969.
33. Ibid.

resentation. Until the conflict between the New York City representation procedures and the executive council application of the AFL-CIO constitution is resolved, this issue will continue to pose difficult problems for public employee unions.

Union-Association Relations

By 1970, interunion conflict had become more structured and formalized as a result of representation procedures established in states with public employment collective bargaining laws, the AFL-CIO Internal Disputes Plan, and improved relations among the competing unions. The same cannot be said of the relations between unions and associations. The two types of organizations would appear to be natural enemies because of their differing philosophies of public employee representation. Unions denigrate employee associations as "company unions," "scabs," and "insurance brokers." But, at the same time, union leaders admit that the associations can be formidable competitors and often constitute their major opposition in the public sector. Association strength in some states and localities has led unions to twist an old strategy to their own use: if you can't beat them, get them to join you.

The difference between unions and associations was spelled out at the 1968 convention of the Hawaii Government Employees Association (HGEA).[34] The advocate of associations as representatives of state and local government employees pointed to their long history and the fact that some were groups that had broken away from unions because of dissatisfaction with the representation they were getting. Association leaders, he argued, are better qualified to represent employees in collective bargaining than union representatives because of their better understanding of the structure and operations of government agencies. Moreover, their broader goals enable associations to do a better job in lobbying, testifying before committees, influencing government officials, and processing grievances.

Their membership often includes supervisors, who are effective representatives before some government bodies and in some types of activity; in states where supervisors may not belong to organiza-

34. Transcript of debate between Jerry Wurf and Thomas Enright.

tions representing nonsupervisory employees, they can be accorded associate membership. The association spokesman termed unions' per capita payments to their national bodies needlessly high, their support from private sector unions and AFL-CIO central bodies unreliable, and their political influence exaggerated.

The president of AFSCME, trying to persuade HGEA to merge with his union, emphasized the union's single-minded concern for the worker. He argued that collective bargaining is the only way to improve wages and working conditions. Though local unions in AFSCME are independent in their operations (and in their membership policies), they may call on the international union for staff services in research, organizing, education, public relations, and other areas. They can also count on the support of the 15-million-member AFL-CIO. AFSCME leaders, their international president argued, are more effective than association officers because they are elected by and accountable to the membership. Staff members who have not come out of government employment bring experience from other unions, and with proper training and supervision they can deal effectively with problems of public employees.

One month after the convention debate the HGEA board of directors voted unanimously against affiliating with AFSCME, despite overwhelming staff support for the merger.[35] The main reasons were a strong desire for local autonomy and unwillingness to shoulder per capita payments to a national union. Three years later, however, the board voted unanimously to affiliate with AFSCME. At the same time, the independent United Public Workers (UPW) voted to merge with AFSCME. The three-way merger was surprising because of the bad relationship between the conservative, predominantly white collar, supervisor-dominated HGEA and the radical, blue collar UPW, which had been expelled from the CIO in 1949 as a communist-dominated union.[36]

A major factor influencing the merger was the enactment, in 1970, of a collective bargaining law for public employees by the Hawaii legislature. The HGEA and the UPW apparently decided that they stood to gain more from cooperating than from fighting each other and other unions for the right to represent Hawaii's 40,000 government employees. Under the affiliation agreement, the

35. Bob Repas, "From Associationism to Unionism" (n.d.; processed), p. 11.
36. Ibid., p. 9.

HGEA and the UPW retained their autonomy, including the right to hire their own staff, and were given a two-year waiver on the payment of per capita dues to the international. All new employees in blue collar classifications were required to join UPW, and white collar employees to become members of HGEA. With the merger, AFSCME, which had previously had no members in Hawaii, gained 28,000 members and became the major union in Hawaii.[37]

Another such merger, of the Rhode Island State Employees Association and AFSCME in July 1972, ended a bitter rivalry and gave AFSCME more than 12,000 of Rhode Island's 14,000 public employees.[38] The union has made overtures elsewhere to state associations, with varying degrees of success.

At the local level, AFSCME's greatest success has been the merger approved in 1971 by the 12,000-member Los Angeles All City Employees Association, the nation's largest independent association of municipal employees.[39] Mergers have also been consummated with local associations in other parts of the country; these successes will undoubtedly help to attract other local groups to AFSCME's banner.

Ranking in importance with the AFSCME success in Hawaii is the capture of the 32,000-member Los Angeles County Employees Association (LACEA) by the Service Employees International Union. For years the two had been competing for some 60,000 county employees (with AFSCME running a poor third in enrolling members). SEIU leaflets denounced the association for trying to block the county collective bargaining ordinance, enacted in 1968, and for continuing to "peddle pills, theatre tickets, and blue chip stamps."[40] The LACEA responded by calling the union leaders "rabble rousers." In a dramatic about-face, in June 1969, they formed an alliance to cooperate in representation elections. Under the "mutual cooperation plan" the association continued as an independent organization for those county employees who did not want a union to represent them, and the two organizations agreed not to challenge each other in representation elections. They hailed the agreement as an "historic document ending the 20-year war"

37. *Public Employee*, Vol. 36 (January–February 1971), pp. 1, 11.
38. *GERR*, No. 460 (July 10, 1972), p. B-20.
39. *Public Employee*, Vol. 36 (August 1971), p. 3.
40. Leaflet issued by SEIU Local 434 (n.d.).

between them and ushering in a "new era of joint action on behalf of County workers for decent wages and fringe benefits."[41] After two years of cooperation, LACEA affiliated with SEIU, retaining its title as an autonomous unit with its own elected officers and staff. The merged organization, representing 50,000 county employees, insures SEIU dominance among public employees in Los Angeles County.[42]

The notable success of a small, craft union—the 11,000-member Marine Engineers Beneficial Association (MEBA), AFL-CIO—in attracting local employee associations to its banner is indicative of the wide-open nature of public employee unionism. Within two years of forming a public employees' division, MEBA succeeded in persuading a variety of associations with twice its own membership to affiliate with it. The MEBA guaranteed that the associations would be permitted to retain their autonomy and, at the same time, benefit from the financial support, professional assistance in collective bargaining, and political influence of the parent organization.[43]

Why has a century-old small union of skilled craftsmen embarked on a campaign to organize government and other nonseagoing employees? The choice, according to MEBA's president, "is either to go forward, to greater strength and influence, or to decline in relative importance and ultimately in our ability to provide adequate representation for the engineers themselves. . . . An increasing number of trade unions have been casting aside their old traditional lines of jurisdiction in order to reach out to groups and individuals hitherto outside the labor organizations."[44]

While mergers can be expected to continue between unions and associations, competition and rivalry will for some time to come dominate their relationship. Thus far, the contest appears to be a standoff, with unions dominant in some states, associations in others. At the local level, unions and associations have fared about equally well in representation elections in four states for which

---

41. "Memorandum of Understanding Between SEIU, AFL-CIO and LACEA," *GERR*, No. 322 (Nov. 10, 1969), pp. E-1, E-2.

42. *GERR*, No. 386 (Feb. 1, 1971), p. B-11.

43. *GERR*, No. 366 (Sept. 14, 1970), p. B-16; No. 388 (Feb. 15, 1971), p. B-19; and No. 398 (April 26, 1971), p. B-18. In 1972 the largest MEBA association voted to disaffiliate because MEBA had not lived up to its promises. (*GERR*, No. 476 [Oct. 30, 1972], p. B-19.)

44. *American Marine Engineer*, Vol. 20 (March 1970), p. 9.

statistics are available—New York, Connecticut, Michigan, and Wisconsin.[45] However, in most instances in which government employers have granted recognition without elections, associations have been the recipients of that voluntary recognition.

Nurse-Union Relations

The state nurses' associations have little competition from either unions or civil service associations to represent registered nurses in collective bargaining. While there are exceptions—in Philadelphia, for example, AFSCME represents all nonuniformed city employees —nurses are usually represented by state affiliates of the American Nurses' Association (ANA) or not at all. Under most state laws, registered nurses qualify as professionals entitled to be represented in a separate unit if they wish.[46] AFSCME has tried to organize registered nurses in a number of government hospitals without much success. In 1968, nurses represented only 0.2 percent of AFSCME's total membership.[47] The Service Employees, Teamsters, and the New York Civil Service Employees Association represent nurses in some areas, but these are aberrations rather than trends.

Despite the ANA's increasing acceptance of collective bargaining over the last twenty years, most nurses still regard unions with apprehension and bridle at the suggestion that their association can be equated with a union, even in the area of economic security. In New York City the nurses' association does not belong to the committee of labor organizations that support the city's Office of Collective Bargaining, but it does utilize the OCB's services. Most state nurses' associations see themselves as having little in common with unions and believe that the strongest argument a hospital administrator can make against the association is to label it a "union." Nurses, who can be militant at the bargaining table, threaten mass resignations, and even strike, still cringe at being called a union.

The ANA and its state associations cooperate with the AFL-CIO

45. See Chapter 7.
46. Advisory Commission on Intergovernmental Relations, *Labor-Management Policies for State and Local Government* (Washington: ACIR, 1969), pp. 160–219; *GERR*, No. 237 (March 25, 1968), p. B-1.
47. *AFSCME Proceedings* (1968), p. 417.

and unions in lobbying for legislation, serving on advisory committees, and sometimes in bargaining collectively. Nurses do not usually seek the support of AFL-CIO central labor councils in disputes with employers in the belief that such support could prove damaging to their cause. On the whole, the relationship between nurses' associations and unions can be characterized as friendly and cooperative but aloof.

Uniformed Services

There is more interorganization rivalry to represent policemen than fire fighters. While there are many independent associations of fire fighters, especially in California and New Jersey, there have been few conflicts between the dominant International Association of Fire Fighters (IAFF) and other organizations. The picture is rather different for police. There is a proliferation of police organizations of all types: national associations, local unaffiliated associations, local unions affiliated with all-public unions, locals that belong to mixed unions, and a national independent police union. No single organization dominates the field.

For a while, during 1969–70, it appeared that the AFL-CIO might support the formation of a national union of policemen, following the request of the International Brotherhood of Police Officers (IBPO) for an AFL-CIO charter. AFSCME, which had long been ambivalent about its 10,000 police members and had made little effort to expand membership among law enforcement officers, indicated it would not oppose the granting of a charter. However, its attitude changed when the IBPO succeeded in winning over several of AFSCME's police locals but showed no signs of attracting support elsewhere. AFL-CIO President Meany concluded that there was no "demand or real desire for a policemen's international union throughout the country," and in February 1971 the AFL-CIO turned down the IBPO's request for a charter.[48] In 1972 the IBPO was merged into the Service Employees Union as a separate and autonomous division under the name of the National Union of Police Officers.

48. *John Herling's Labor Letter,* Feb. 21, 1971.

At about the same time that the IBPO was being organized, the National Association of Government Employees (NAGE), whose membership consists almost entirely of federal government employees, also announced its intention of organizing policemen. It has succeeded in winning over several former AFSCME locals in New England,[49] including one that voted to disaffiliate because AFSCME's "services were minimal while the expense was great."[50]

The advent of competition appears to have helped AFSCME resolve its ambivalence toward organizing police. The 1970 convention eliminated AFSCME's long-standing prohibition against strikes by locals of law enforcement officers, an action that police locals had sought for a long time.[51] At a conference of AFSCME police locals, the international president told the assemblage: "We want policemen in AFSCME . . . and we're going to get them."[52] He urged police locals that were in the IBPO to join AFSCME and promised a drive to organize policemen. At about the same time, in what might be interpreted as an oblique invitation to New York City policemen, he commented that a wildcat strike "was apparently as much against the police organization leadership as it was against the city" and was evidence of "widespread distrust among patrolmen of the leadership of the Patrolmen's Benevolent Association."[53]

POLICE–FIRE FIGHTER RELATIONS

There is little interest among the uniformed services in joint organizations of police and fire fighters at either the national or local level, and only one such group exists in a major city—the Los Angeles Fire and Police Protection League. A more interesting and live issue is the relationship between local organizations of police and fire fighters, which ranges from close cooperation in some cities to extreme hostility in others.

Policemen and fire fighters have much in common and until the 1950s the two groups worked closely together in efforts to promote

49. *GERR*, No. 353 (June 15, 1970), p. B-14, and No. 404 (June 7, 1971), p. B-21.

50. In the Matter of City of Hartford (Police Department) and Local 234 of Council 15, AFSCME, Case No. MPP-2021, Decision 977, March 17, 1971, Connecticut State Board of Labor Relations.

51. *AFSCME Proceedings* (1970), p. 288.

52. *Public Employee,* Vol. 36 (March 1971), p. 3.

53. Ibid. (January–February 1971), p. 2.

the economic interests of their members. The alliance was generally more advantageous to the police than to the fire fighters, who are skillful operators in the political arena and have the benefit of a national organization and the support of the labor movement. Police association leaders in many cities admit that for years they "rode the broad coattails" of the fire fighters to improved wages, pensions, and fringe benefits. Parity pay between the two services was an established and accepted fact in almost all cities.

The change that began in the 1950s continued through the 1960s as a result of the related phenomena of racial conflict, the preoccupation with law and order, and the drive toward professionalization of police departments. Police organizations found themselves no longer dependent on the political clout of the fire fighters, as it became apparent that the public and elected political officials would support, and in some cases even initiate, efforts to improve police salaries and other economic benefits over and above what they were prepared to do for fire fighters and other public employees. Many cities, often at the instigation of police organizations, began to question the concept of parity pay for police and fire fighters. Tradition and the political influence of the IAFF were the major obstacles to separate pay scales.[54]

The fire fighters were understandably miffed by what they regarded as a lack of appreciation of the function they performed and the hazards involved in their occupation.[55] They were particularly outraged by the eagerness with which their police brethren were pressing to break parity arrangements that had existed for years. Nevertheless, parity still prevails in most cities; in 1967, among 386 communities with IAFF locals, disparity existed in only 80. The trend to pay police more than fire fighters is evident, however; during 1966 and the first five months of 1967 twenty cities voted against parity,[56] whereas referendums to institute disparity had been defeated in forty-nine cities during the preceding twenty years.

Fire fighters are prepared to incur considerable costs to fight dis-

54. See, for example, the opinion of the arbitration panel in the case involving the City of Detroit and IAFF Local 344, dated Jan. 4, 1971 (*GERR*, No. 387 [Feb. 8, 1971], pp. B-14, B-15).

55. See the advertisement, "We Die Nine Years Sooner..." *New York Times*, April 15, 1971, p. 59, placed by IAFF Local 854.

56. IAFF, Research and Statistics Department, "Report of the 1967 Survey on Disparity" (IAFF, n.d.; processed).

parity. When San Francisco in 1963 attacked its difficulties in recruiting and retaining policemen by granting a wage increase to policemen but not to firemen, the IAFF local union embarked on a campaign to amend the city charter to require parity between the two services. The local spent $100,000, raised by membership contributions of 5 percent of gross monthly salary. Radio, television, newspaper advertisements, posters, bumper stickers, visits by firemen to schools and homes were employed in the campaign. The charter amendment was approved by a margin of less than 0.5 percent of the votes cast and parity was reestablished.[57]

Organizations of police and fire fighters continue to have good relations in many cities. They cooperate in lobbying activities, job actions, demonstrations, referendum campaigns for salary increases, joint negotiations, and occasionally in strikes. In other cities, however, the two organizations have little contact with each other, each going its own way in representing the interests of its members.

Organized Labor and Public Employee Unions

The labor movement, until recently, showed little interest in public employees and could not be counted on to support, let alone actively assist, unions trying to organize government workers. Many union leaders, including AFL-CIO President Meany, had reservations about the extent to which collective bargaining was applicable to public employees and opposed strikes against government employers. These attitudes changed during the 1960s. Collective bargaining, including the right to strike, is now generally supported for all public employees with the possible exception of police and fire fighters, and the labor movement can usually be counted on to throw its weight and influence behind efforts to organize public employees. However, conflicts of interests between private and public sector unions sometimes result in nonsupport and even opposition of state and city central labor bodies and individual unions to public employee objectives. At times the two opponents compete for AFL-CIO support, posing a difficult problem for a central labor body.

57. Eugene J. Devine, *Analysis of Manpower Shortages in Local Government: Case Studies of Nurses, Policemen, and Teachers* (Praeger, 1970), pp. 79–80.

AFL-CIO councils can be most helpful to public employee unions by exercising political influence and by lending support in crisis situations such as strikes. Their support may be essential to the enactment of state laws extending collective bargaining to public employees and providing for compulsory arbitration in police and fire fighter disputes. In Michigan, for instance, the state AFL-CIO worked closely with AFSCME and the IAFF in lobbying for the 1965 Public Employment Relations Act and, in 1969, joined the fire fighters in support of compulsory arbitration for unresolved police and fire disputes. In return, the IAFF gave up its effort to enact a compulsory arbitration law that was tied to a workmen's compensation bill opposed by the labor movement. AFL-CIO support has been similarly instrumental in the enactment of comprehensive laws governing collective bargaining for public employees in other states.

On the other hand, the withholding of labor support has been a major obstacle to the enactment of legislation favorable to public employees in a number of states. In Illinois, AFL-CIO opposition to a bill was attacked by AFSCME's president as a move to protect a patronage arrangement in Chicago.[58] In Indiana, private sector unions and the state federation opposed or refused to support legislation favorable to public employees. And in Colorado the AFL-CIO, which is dominated by the building trades, supported a bill to prohibit moonlighting by policemen and fire fighters who worked as skilled tradesmen during their off-hours.

At the local level, public employee unions are particularly dependent on the support of central labor councils in states that do not have public employment bargaining laws. Union recognition in such jurisdictions can be attained generally through political connections with the administration or by a successful strike, and labor support is essential to success through either route. Craft unions, influential in AFL-CIO councils, often have prevailing rate arrangements for their members in city employment, giving them a stake in opposing collective bargaining for public employees. In Cleveland, where the AFL-CIO central labor council refused to support striking AFSCME workers involved in a jurisdictional dispute with the Teamsters union, AFSCME President Wurf charged

58. *AFSCME Proceedings* (1968), p. 262.

that "thirteen old line unions . . . turned themselves into scabs in the classic sense of the word."[59] In several other cities, representatives of public employee unions described central labor councils as hostile or disinterested in helping public employee unions.

On the other hand, the AFL-CIO central labor council in New York often used political influence with Mayor Wagner on behalf of public employee unions before the passage of the state's Taylor Act and the city's collective bargaining ordinance. In Cincinnati and Baltimore, AFL-CIO councils supported strikes of public employees and used their political influence with the city to obtain favorable settlements. And in Los Angeles County the AFL-CIO played an important coordinating role among public employee unions competing under a 1969 ordinance granting collective bargaining rights to public employees.

The IAFF particularly recognizes the assistance of state and local central labor councils. During the 1968–69 voting-rights dispute within the IAFF, many local leaders stated their allegiance to the International rested only on their fear of jeopardizing their relationship with the AFL-CIO. Fire fighters are active and often serve as officers and executive board members in AFL-CIO councils. State federations are important to IAFF locals because economic benefits and conditions of employment of their members are often mandated by state legislatures. In several states, AFL-CIO councils have been influential in advancing fire fighter interests.

Fire fighters have also benefited from labor support at the local level. Because its members are reluctant to resort to strikes, the IAFF can be greatly helped by unions that will not cross its picket lines, will exert influence on elected city officials to accede to its demands, and will lend support in voter referendums on wage increases. In Boston, Teamsters have respected informational picket lines around city hall manned by fire fighters. In Cranston, Rhode Island, unions refused to cross IAFF and police picket lines set up around city projects and buildings. In Youngstown, Ohio, the AFL-CIO and especially the Steelworkers (the major union in the city) interceded on behalf of fire fighters and police during their strike in 1967. In Seattle the AFL-CIO has appeared before the city coun-

59. *Ohio Public Employee,* September 1969.

cil in support of fire fighter demands. It is obvious why this group of city employees attaches importance to affiliation with the labor movement.

COALITION OF PUBLIC EMPLOYEE ORGANIZATIONS

The 1970 AFSCME convention passed a resolution endorsing a proposal, advanced by President Jerry Wurf, that the officers explore "the possibilities and potentials of a coalition of all public employee unions, including AFL-CIO affiliates, unaffiliated unions and the postal labor organizations."[60] The primary purpose of the coalition would be to increase the political influence of public employee unions on Congress, state legislatures, and the executive branches of government. Wurf defined the scope of the coalition as "organizations which represent exclusively public employees," thus excluding mixed unions and associations of private and public employees.[61]

Consequently, it came as a surprise when Wurf and the president of the 1.1-million-member National Education Association (NEA), a professional association of teachers, principals, and school administrators, announced the formation of the Coalition of Public Employee Organizations and invited other unions and associations to join. It was particularly surprising that Wurf should choose a professional association and the chief rival of another AFL-CIO union, the American Federation of Teachers (AFT), as the organization with which to launch the coalition. The AFT president, who had been hailed at the 1970 AFSCME convention for "his outstanding leadership of a sister union,"[62] immediately attacked the coalition as a "publicity stunt." He questioned the alliance with a nonunion association and urged AFL-CIO central bodies and other unions to ignore the coalition.[63] The International Association of Fire Fighters responded by joining the coalition shortly thereafter, but no other union has joined.

60. *AFSCME Proceedings* (1970), Resolution 108, pp. 652–53.
61. *Public Employee*, Vol. 36 (April 1971), p. 2.
62. *AFSCME Proceedings* (1970), Resolution 107, pp. 651–52.
63. *GERR*, No. 395 (April 5, 1971), p. B-7.

Summary

State and local government is not the place to look for a rational structure of employee organization. Only the IAFF commands anything approaching undisputed jurisdiction, and even it is challenged by local all-city associations and independent organizations limited to fire fighters. All other employees are considered fair game for unions vying with one another and with associations for members and representation rights. The only limitations on the competing organizations are self-restraint, of which there is very little, financial resources, and the AFL-CIO Internal Disputes Plan, which has played a constructive role in mitigating disputes among unions. Despite AFSCME's demand for "a more rational mechanism for determining jurisdiction,"[64] it is difficult to see how the conflicting claims and interests of AFL-CIO unions in the public employee field can be resolved. While competition between unions and employee associations continues, mergers are being consummated at a rate that suggests this may become the dominant method of resolving or averting conflicts between the two during the 1970s.

A potential major conflict area is representation of policemen. Many policemen are unhappy with the representation they have been getting from their organizations, whether the Fraternal Order of Police, the International Conference of Police Associations, AFSCME, mixed unions, or independents. Policemen are fed up with what they regard as the "raw deal" they have been getting from Congress, the Supreme Court, civil rights organizations, black militants, and student activists. One way of giving vent to their frustration is to demand more money, better pensions, and more control over working conditions. While they have made progress in all three of these areas, stringent budgets and citizen revolts against tax increases have made officeholders more resistant to economic demands, not only of policemen but of all city employees. The police consider their demands more justifiable than those of other employees and are inclined to blame their organizations and leaders for any short-fall between demands and settlements. If, during the next few years, AFSCME and the SEIU-affiliated National Union of Police Officers (NUPO) fail to increase their police

64. *GERR,* No. 455 (June 5, 1972), p. G-2.

membership substantially, there may yet be a new national police union chartered by the AFL-CIO, despite its recent refusal to charter an independent union. The next decade may see the emergence of two major organizations, one an AFL-CIO union combining locals from AFSCME, the SEIU–NUPO, and independent union-oriented police organizations and the other a national association of policemen who want to remain outside the labor movement.

The formation of the Coalition of Public Employee Organizations, at the initiative of AFSCME, represents a bold bid for leadership in the public employee field. As long as the coalition excludes the Service Employees, Laborers, Teamsters, and other mixed unions, it cannot hope to obtain support from either the national AFL-CIO or state and city central labor councils. Wurf obviously knew this and must have reasoned that an alliance with the largest association of professional employees and the all-public IAFF was worth the price of further alienating unions with which AFSCME was competing in organizing government employees.

CHAPTER SIX

Collective Bargaining

Until the last decade, collective bargaining for public employees was practiced in only a few government jurisdictions and was considered illegal in most states. In 1972, twenty-three states had collective bargaining laws that applied generally to public employees in either state or local government or both. Of these, only seven were mandatory laws extending full bargaining rights to all public employees on wages, hours, and conditions of employment. The others omitted some employees from coverage, excluded some subjects from bargaining, or merely authorized but did not require employers to bargain.[1] Despite its brief life span and the limited arena in which collective bargaining in public employment has been promoted by statute, it is now certain that this process will be used increasingly to determine the wages and working conditions of government employees. Not only unions but civil service and professional associations and even public employers have begun a process of self-examination and restructuring in order to prepare themselves to perform their assigned roles in collective bargaining.

Attitudes toward Collective Bargaining

Collective bargaining was not generally considered applicable to public employment until the late 1950s. The doctrine of state sovereignty, the domination of state legislatures by rural and anti-

1. *Report of the President and Headquarters Departments, International Convention, American Federation of State, County and Municipal Employees, AFL-CIO* (1972), pp. 30–32.

114

labor interests, unqualified acceptance of the prohibition against strikes by public employees, and the weakness of unions in public employment all contributed to the view that it was not a viable approach to improving the economic status of civil servants. The labor movement generally shared this view and, in any event, was too busy organizing and representing union members in private industry to pay much attention to public employees. The few unions that were active in government concentrated their efforts on civil service and politics.

AFSCME

The American Federation of State, County and Municipal Employees (AFSCME) was organized to protect and promote civil service for state and local government employees. In the union's early years, "the AFSCME leadership saw itself as part of a great movement to reform government," and one of the union's primary objectives as "the extension of the merit system to all nonpolicy determining positions of all governmental jurisdictions."[2] The union placed great stress on civil service and enhancing the image of public employees. States and cities that adopted or improved civil service statutes were regularly praised at the union's meetings, and those where the patronage system still held sway were criticized.[3] In 1948 the union instituted an annual "Public Servants Week" (later called "Public Employees Week"). Locals made special efforts to inform citizens about the work of public employees through literature, speeches to civic groups, radio and television programs, and tours of police departments, institutions, and government offices.

Collective bargaining, a long-range goal, was regarded as highly desirable but not essential, since a good civil service system was considered the best protection for public employees. Not until 1960 was "collective bargaining resulting in working agreements and contracts" incorporated in the constitution as a method of achiev-

2. Leo Kramer, *Labor's Paradox—The American Federation of State, County, and Municipal Employees, AFL-CIO* (Wiley, 1962), p. 27.

3. *Proceedings of the Ninth International Convention of the American Federation of State, County and Municipal Employees, A.F. of L. (AFSCME Proceedings)* (1954), pp. 10–11; (1956), p. 271; (1958), p. 285; (1960), pp. 341–44; (1962), p. 340; (1964), p. 271.

ing the union's objectives.[4] This lukewarm approach was challenged and in 1968 the constitution was amended to read: "We are committed to the process of collective bargaining as the most desirable, democratic, and effective method . . . to promote the welfare of the membership and to provide a voice in the determination of the terms and conditions of employment."[5] Henceforth, collective bargaining was to be the cornerstone of AFSCME's policies and philosophy.

Public Employees Week was dropped as a union observance shortly after the election of a new president in 1964. The constitution proposed by a union commission to a special constitutional convention in 1965 omitted all mention of civil service. Only an amendment from the floor preserved "civil service legislation and career service in government" as a union objective.[6] President Jerry Wurf's view that civil service is "a thing of the past" and "the managerial system of the boss—he owns it"[7] is widely held by AFSCME staff members throughout the country who believe that, except for its recruitment and examining functions, civil service can and should be replaced by collective bargaining.

This change in the union's emphasis is principally a reflection of changing times. For years, collective bargaining "was at most a slogan for a few crackpots and considered totally impossible for public employees."[8] In 1955, AFL-CIO President George Meany wrote: "It is impossible to bargain collectively with the government."[9] A year earlier the secretary-treasurer of the Illinois Federation of Labor had told the AFSCME convention in Chicago they were "in the peculiar position of labor unions that must depend on legislation to achieve [their] ends."[10] And the president of the Chicago Federation of Labor had told them how lucky employees of

4. *AFSCME Proceedings* (1960), p. 43.

5. Constitution of the American Federation of State, County and Municipal Employees, AFL-CIO (amended, 1972), Art. 2, B.

6. *Proceedings, Special Constitutional Convention, American Federation of State, County and Municipal Employees, AFL-CIO* (1965), p. 25.

7. Jerry Wurf, "Current Issues of State, Local and Municipal Collective Bargaining," in "Proceedings of the Second Labor Relations Symposium on Labor-Management Relations in the Public Sector" (Labor Education Center, University of Kentucky, 1969; processed), p. 49.

8. *AFSCME Proceedings* (1966), p. 13.

9. Quoted in Kramer, *Labor's Paradox*, p. 41.

10. *AFSCME Proceedings* (1954), p. 4.

the city's Park District, Library, and Board of Education were to have union members serving on those agencies' boards.[11] As late as February 1959, the AFL-CIO executive council could concede that "in terms of accepted collective bargaining procedures, government workers have no right beyond the authority to petition Congress— a right available to every citizen."[12] Later that year, however, the AFL-CIO convention passed a resolution supporting collective bargaining legislation for public employees.[13]

President Kennedy's Executive Order 10988 extending collective bargaining rights to federal employees, the Supreme Court's reapportionment decisions of 1962 and 1964 leading to greater representation of urban interests in state legislatures, and aggressive lobbying by AFL-CIO councils and public employee unions sparked the enactment of collective bargaining laws for state and local government employees. By 1970, AFSCME had negotiated more than 1,000 collective bargaining agreements—four times the number in effect in 1958 and almost twice the number in 1964.[14] Agreements had been negotiated in thirty-eight states and the District of Columbia; thus the union had signed contracts in at least seventeen states with no statutory basis for collective bargaining. Eighty percent of these agreements were in counties, municipalities, and school districts. In addition to signed contracts, AFSCME has negotiated many other settlements, generally in jurisdictions without laws, which have been incorporated in memorandums of understanding, city ordinances, and civil service rules and regulations, and in oral agreements.

While preferring comprehensive laws covering both state and local government employees and not prohibiting strikes, AFSCME has been pragmatic in its approach to legislation that falls short of its objectives. In some states it has supported laws that apply only to local governments, excluding state employees, and it has urged legislators to vote for bills even though they prohibited strikes by government workers, as almost all state laws do. AFSCME has continued to press for collective bargaining legislation in states that

11. Ibid., p. 3.

12. Kramer, *Labor's Paradox*, p. 41.

13. *Proceedings of the Third Constitutional Convention of the AFL-CIO* (1959), pp. 191–97.

14. *AFSCME Proceedings* (1970), p. 15; (1960), p. 326; (1964), p. 179.

have none and to support liberalization of existing laws to extend coverage to all public employees, expand the scope for bargaining, permit negotiation of union security, and eliminate no-strike provisions and strike penalties where they exist.

But the union has not been willing to support some legislation extending collective bargaining rights to public employees. In New York State, AFSCME bitterly but unsuccessfully opposed adoption of the Taylor Act, primarily because of its strong penalties against unions and union leaders who violated the act's prohibition against strikes. But AFSCME representatives in upstate New York are more kindly disposed toward the act than those in New York City. One staff member thought that the union was better off under the Taylor Act than having to rely on the support of the labor movement and political officeholders. And the editor of a local union newspaper in Buffalo wrote: "Based on the strides that have been made during the short existence of the Taylor Act, a few more amendments and a continuing sincere effort upon the part of all governments will give it the stature of the Wagner Act."[15]

In Louisiana, AFSCME withdrew its support for a bill that its Council 17 had introduced in 1968 granting collective bargaining rights to public employees but limiting representation to organizations whose primary purpose was to represent public employees. When the bill was amended to permit representation by mixed unions and to exclude all school employees, both instructional and noninstructional, AFSCME lost interest. The director of Council 17, a member of the Louisiana Long family with excellent political connections, withdrew AFSCME support for the bill and later expressed doubt that public employees in Louisiana were ready for collective bargaining.

Until 1970, AFSCME did not favor federal legislation to provide collective bargaining rights to all public employees or to extend coverage to state and local employees under the National Labor Relations Act.[16] Some union leaders, reacting against the Taylor Act's strong penalties for strikes, argued that coverage under a federal law would be preferable to state laws administered by political appointees who favored other unions over AFSCME.[17] The con-

15. *AFSCME News*, Local 264, Vol. 3 (September 1968).
16. Kramer, *Labor's Paradox*, p. 34; *AFSCME Proceedings* (1968), pp. 184–85.
17. *AFSCME Proceedings* (1968), pp. 186–87.

viction that Congress would include punitive antistrike provisions in any law extending collective bargaining rights to public employees was a forceful deterrent, however. In the words of one council director: "We can beat a State act, and we have beaten a State act, but if they put an anti-strike provision in the federal act . . . I would hate like hell to be up against federal troops."[18]

In 1970, AFSCME apparently concluded that the likelihood of obtaining acceptable acts in states that had not already enacted laws was slim. The union drafted a National Public Employees Relations Act which gives to public employees the same rights guaranteed to workers in the private sector. The proposal would establish a five-member National Public Employees Relations Commission, appointed by the President, with responsibilities similar to those of the National Labor Relations Board. It makes no mention of strikes but does provide for fact finding with recommendations.[19]

MIXED UNIONS

The mixed unions have not pressed as hard as AFSCME for collective bargaining in government—undoubtedly because their existence and growth do not depend on success in organizing public employees. Except for the Service Employees International Union (SEIU), these unions had a relatively insignificant number of public employee members until the 1960s. More important, unions like the SEIU, the Laborers' International Union, and the International Brotherhood of Teamsters did not need statutory protection in order to organize public employees in the areas in which they concentrated much of their activity. Close ties with political administrations, especially in large cities, enabled them to gain informal recognition for certain groups of workers. Elected public officials in "union cities" found it in their interest to deal with these unions, which had considerable influence in central labor bodies and were in a position to grant or withhold labor support in political campaigns. Under the circumstances, public employee collective bargaining held little attraction for the mixed unions, and a statute providing machinery for determining bargaining units, election of exclusive representatives, and the right to bargain collectively, far

18. Ibid., p. 192.
19. *AFSCME Proceedings* (1970), pp. 523–25.

from helping them, might serve to disturb what was already a perfectly satisfactory arrangement from their point of view. Their situation was entirely different from that of AFSCME, a union engaged exclusively in organizing public employees, with little or no influence in AFL-CIO central labor bodies or with elected political officials.

While not particularly enthusiastic about collective bargaining legislation, once it was enacted the mixed unions were quick to formalize their claims to representation of public employees and to extend their organizing efforts among government workers. Representation elections have often involved AFSCME, SEIU, Teamsters, other unions, and independent associations, in varying combinations. As more and more states have adopted collective bargaining laws for public employees, the attitude of the mixed unions, and the labor movement generally, has become more favorable to such laws, except in a few states where the building trades have influenced AFL-CIO councils to withhold support from legislation favored by public employee unions.

The mixed unions view civil service with mixed feelings. In jurisdictions that have neither civil service nor collective bargaining legislation, union representatives want the protection of civil service for their members. But where civil service and collective bargaining are both in effect, union officials complain about management control of the system, discriminatory testing procedures, and conflicts between the two methods of regulating wages and conditions of employment. Most union representatives believe that collective bargaining can, and will in time, replace civil service except in recruitment and administration of competitive examinations. While some would like to retain the best features of civil service along with collective bargaining, they see the two approaches as basically in conflict and would not hesitate to give up the benefits of civil service if necessary to obtain collective bargaining.

UNIFORMED SERVICES

National organizations representing fire fighters and policemen have differed in their attitudes toward collective bargaining. The International Association of Fire Fighters (IAFF) has for many years supported and promoted legislation providing collective bargaining for its members and, in some states, has been successful in getting special provisions enacted giving fire fighters privileges not accorded to other public employees. In 1969, nine states had laws providing for organization rights, collective bargaining, or dispute settlement that applied to fire fighters but not to policemen.[20] Four states had compulsory arbitration laws covering fire fighters and policemen, and two had statutes applying only to fire fighters.[21] The two national police organizations—the Fraternal Order of Police (FOP) and the International Conference of Police Associations (ICPA)—have only recently espoused the cause of collective bargaining but have not actively lobbied for legislation.

The IAFF interest in collective bargaining is evident in the lobbying efforts of state and local associations. At the union's biennial conventions the regional vice-presidents stress the progress made in obtaining state legislation and local ordinances providing collective bargaining for fire fighters.[22] The IAFF supports the National Public Employees Relations Act that AFSCME has proposed to extend collective bargaining to all state and local government employees.[23] The FOP and ICPA, on the other hand, are much more concerned with protecting the civil rights of policemen and with "law and order" issues than with collective bargaining. This probably accords with the preferences of many local police associations, which consider themselves capable of representing their members in economic matters but feel frustrated and powerless to deal with Supreme Court decisions and civil rights legislation which they regard as undermining their position as law enforcement officers and endangering their lives in the performance of their duty.

Fire fighter and police organizations tend to prefer written contracts in states where the law permits collective bargaining for public employees. Elsewhere, terms agreed on in negotiations are usually embodied in local ordinances. In some localities, IAFF local unions engaged in negotiations even before collective bargaining

20. "Summary of State Labor Laws," in Bureau of National Affairs, *State and Local*, GERR Reference File 42 (1972), pp. 51:501–51:521.

21. Ibid.; and Bureau of National Affairs, *Government Employment Relations Report (GERR)*, No. 397 (April 19, 1971), p. B-5.

22. *Reports, 30th Convention, International Association of Fire Fighters* (1970), pp. 63–95.

23. Ibid., p. 130.

was sanctioned by law and boast of having had written contracts before other public employees were recognized and bargained with city authorities. Leaders of IAFF locals that have won wage increases and other economic benefits through political action nevertheless prefer collective bargaining. Among the issues that written contracts can include are seniority, transfers, overtime, call-in pay, wash-up time, pay for uniforms, and many others that usually get lost in the shuffle of political deals, where wages, pensions, and hours of work occupy center stage. Local police association leaders generally favor collective bargaining but, perhaps because of the advantageous position that public concern over racial conflict, student unrest, and "law and order" gives them, also stress the importance of politics in determining wages and working conditions. Some police groups have done so well in cities where wages are set by the state legislature or by referendum that they express a disinterest in formal collective bargaining. Both IAFF and police association leaders agree that as long as the final decision resides in the office of the mayor or other elected officeholders, politics cannot be ruled out as a major influence, with or without collective bargaining.

Opinions regarding the relationship between civil service and collective bargaining vary widely among local organizations representing police and fire fighters. While some representatives agree with the overwhelming union belief that collective bargaining could and should replace civil service (with the possible exception of the recruitment and examination functions), others' opinions range from complete satisfaction to acceptance of existing civil service procedures with some modifications. Greatest unhappiness is voiced in cities where the merit system is administered by police and fire commissions, which are usually criticized as being political bodies.

Many police and fire fighter leaders, especially the former, appear to favor civil service as a way of keeping blacks out of the uniformed forces. This is usually put in terms of maintaining high standards and moving toward greater professionalization. Some police and fire fighter leaders prefer merit to seniority as a criterion for promotion because it would advance the cause of professionalization. Opposition to the merit system centers not on the concept but on its operation. The system is often described as merely a front for political decisions made by the mayor, the police and fire commission, or a civil service board appointed and controlled by the city administration.

Those who believe that civil service procedures should be modified most often suggest that the commission perform only the functions of a personnel office, namely recruitment and administering promotion tests; that the discretionary element in civil service be reduced by eliminating or reducing the weight given to oral examinations and performance reviews; that the civil service commission as a final appeals body in disciplinary hearings be replaced with final and binding arbitration; and that civil service procedures be subject to collective bargaining.

Police organizations are inclined toward continuing civil service with modifications, while fire fighters lean more toward the typical union position of replacing civil service by a comprehensive collective bargaining agreement.

ASSOCIATIONS

Prior to 1970, state associations generally opposed collective bargaining for public employees. However, once a collective bargaining law has been enacted, associations almost invariably have adapted to it by presenting themselves for certification as employee representatives, participating in negotiations, and becoming parties to written agreements. This has been true in Oregon, Washington, Massachusetts, New Jersey, and Rhode Island, all states that now have collective bargaining for state employees. Associations have opposed collective bargaining because of a long history of progress through legislation, unfamiliarity with collective bargaining techniques, the close association of collective bargaining with trade unionism, fear of competing with unions for exclusive representation, and opposition to specific provisions of proposed laws. Two associations have, however, taken a positive approach to collective bargaining: the Civil Service Employees Association (CSEA) supported the enactment of the Taylor Act in New York, and the Hawaii Government Employees Association (HGEA), reversing a position taken only two years earlier, testified in 1969 in favor of a state collective bargaining law. In states still without laws, the trend now is toward supporting collective bargaining legislation of some kind.

Independent local associations have assumed a more passive role than state associations on collective bargaining legislation. With limited resources and little influence in state legislatures, they have, for the most part, adopted a posture of watchful waiting and adaptation. They have been more active in trying to influence municipal and county ordinances dealing with collective bargaining. Associations in Baltimore and Los Angeles County vigorously opposed collective bargaining ordinances but, after such laws were enacted, participated in elections to represent public employees. In Michigan, most local associations took no position on the state law covering local government employees when it was under consideration in 1965, but many now represent public employees under the law. Several local associations in states without collective bargaining laws now favor either a state law or a local ordinance; this undoubtedly represents their recognition that legislation is likely to be enacted and their desire to have some influence in shaping laws under which they will have to operate.

Regardless of their position on collective bargaining, state and local associations strongly support the merit system and civil service. The Assembly of Governmental Employees favors "continued unabrogated existence" of the merit system and advocates removal of the merit system concept from the list of negotiable items in collective bargaining.[24] But a number of associations would like to see changes made in civil service practices. Those that have accepted the idea of collective bargaining are more critical of the way in which civil service has operated in their jurisdictions and suggest more drastic changes than associations that continue to oppose collective bargaining. Proposed modifications include greater emphasis on seniority in promotions with a corresponding decrease in importance, though not elimination, of oral examinations and performance ratings; replacement of the "one in three" rule by a requirement that the top man be selected for a vacant position; extension of coverage to employees not presently under civil service, particularly state highway department employees who often are still subject to the "spoils" system; reduction in the number of job classi-

---

24. Advisory Commission on Intergovernmental Relations, *Labor-Management Policies for State and Local Government* (Washington: ACIR, 1969), pp. 125–26.

fications; and replacement of the unilateral authority of the civil service commission in grievance cases with bilateral discussions and possibly by impartial arbitration of grievances.

While they recognize some conflict between collective bargaining and civil service, associations generally do not regard the two approaches as incompatible.

NURSES

The American Nurses' Association (ANA) was, in 1946, the first major professional organization to endorse collective bargaining, urging state and district affiliates to act as exclusive agents on behalf of their memberships in collective bargaining.[25] State associations were under no compulsion to duplicate the ANA Economic Security Program, through which the House of Delegates resolution was to be implemented. However, states were encouraged to follow the ANA lead, and in 1949 an ANA committee published "Criteria for the Evaluation of State Programs in Relation to Official National Policy."[26] In 1954 the ANA House of Delegates passed a resolution urging every state association "to assume active leadership in the organization of local groups for purposes of improving employment conditions."[27]

One of the states that were slow to follow the lead of the ANA in establishing an economic security program was Michigan. Eight years elapsed between the adoption of the national program and the institution of a program in Michigan. Even as late as 1962 the Michigan Nurses' Association (MNA) regarded collective bargaining as a last resort to be used "only where other approaches had failed."[28] The major impetus for change was the enactment of the Michigan Public Employment Relations Act in 1965. It quickly became apparent that if the nurses did not act through their own organization, they would be included in collective bargaining units that also included nonprofessional hospital employees. By the end of 1966 the MNA was fully committed to collective bargaining, and

25. "The ANA Economic Security Program," *American Journal of Nursing*, Vol. 47 (February 1947), pp. 70–73.

26. *American Journal of Nursing*, Vol. 49 (October 1949), pp. 656–57.

27. Ibid., Vol. 54 (June 1954), p. 701.

28. Alice L. Ahmuty, "The Development of the Michigan Nurses' Association's Economic Security Program" (Master's thesis, Michigan State University, 1968), p. 93.

by 1970 over 3,100 Michigan nurses were covered by collective bargaining agreements.[29]

The Michigan association's change of attitude was influenced by a recognition that the organization's very survival might depend on its willingness and ability to represent members effectively under the state law. For if other organizations, including unions, secured the right to speak for nurses on economic matters and elicited dues or other financial support from them, it would not be long before many nurses would question their need to pay dues to two organizations. The MNA might lose the right to represent nurses on professional matters unless they were willing to represent them on economic matters. Nurses' associations in other states have undoubtedly faced the same dilemma. The fear of union competition probably forced many of them to act more quickly and more effectively than they might have without this pressure.

From the outset the ANA has been committed to the principle that the right of all health care employees to organize and bargain collectively should be protected through legislation. It also believes in uniform treatment of employees in public, proprietary, and non-profit hospitals through federal law, with due regard for state laws that contain innovative features worthy of retention. The ANA favors repeal of the National Labor Relations Act section that permits states to prohibit the union shop, and it opposes limitations on union security in state laws.[30]

State nurses' associations have sponsored collective bargaining legislation for registered nurses and have supported comprehensive laws covering all public employees. In New York the state association supported the Taylor Act as well as a special law for nurses in nonprofit hospitals. The Illinois association supported a 1968 public employment collective bargaining bill which was endorsed by most public employee unions but failed of enactment.

In 1968, associations in 47 states engaged in representation activities on behalf of some 74,000 nurses. By the end of the year, 227 contracts, including 85 with state and local governments, were in effect in 18 states covering more than 30,000 nurses. Of the 61 "first-time" agreements negotiated, 33 were in local government, 3 in

29. Ibid., p. 93; and Michigan Nurses' Association, "Membership Comparisons, 1966–70" (memorandum, n.d.).

30. ANA, Economic Security Department, "ANA Statement on Federal and State Labor Relations Laws" (New York: ANA, November 1969; processed).

state government, and 1 at the federal level. While 144 had been negotiated under federal, state, or local ordinances, 83 agreements were negotiated without legal protection, mostly in California and Washington where the earliest collective bargaining agreements were reported by state nurses' associations.[31]

Union Security

The enactment of state collective bargaining laws covering public employees contributed greatly to the security of public employee unions. Exclusive recognition and signed collective bargaining agreements enhanced the attractiveness of union membership and guaranteed a union that it would not have to fight off competing organizations for the right to represent all employees in the unit for which it had been recognized. But the second element of security available to private sector unions—the right to negotiate agreements requiring employees to join or pay a service fee to a union— was denied to those in the public sector in all but a few states. Most state laws give public employees the "right to refrain" from joining organizations designated as collective bargaining representatives, which would appear to make union shop agreements illegal, and a few specifically prohibit the union or agency shop.[32] On the other hand, Hawaii and Rhode Island have laws mandating the agency shop in any exclusive recognition agreement between the state and an employee organization; Wisconsin, New Hampshire, and Massachusetts permit the agency shop to be negotiated;[33] and Pennsylvania authorizes maintenance of membership agreements.[34]

31. ANA, Research and Statistics Department, "Summary of SNA Economic Security Program Activities, 1968" (ANA, 1969; processed).

32. Harry H. Wellington and Ralph K. Winter, Jr., *The Unions and the Cities* (Brookings Institution, 1971), Chap. 2.

33. ACIR, *Labor-Management Policies*, pp. 75–76; *GERR*, Reference File 51:3017; *GERR*, No. 454 (May 29, 1972), p. B-5. In 1972, the Michigan Supreme Court ruled that the agency shop was illegal in public employment. Many such agreements had been negotiated before the decision. (*GERR*, No. 482 [Dec. 11, 1972], pp. B-1–B-3.)

34. *Report of the President and Headquarters Departments, 19th International Convention, AFSCME, AFL-CIO* (1972), p. 91. Union shop agreements require all employees to become members of the union within a certain period of time; agency shop requires all employees in the unit to join or pay a "service fee"; maintenance of membership requires all those who are members as of the date the agreement is effective, or who join thereafter, to continue their membership for the life of the agreement.

TABLE 6-1. *Union Security Provisions in Public Employment Contracts, January 1, 1968*

Security provision	Total		AFSCME[a]		SEIU		Laborers		Teamsters[b]	
	Number	Percent	Number	Percent	Number	Percent	Number	Percent	Number	Percent
Closed shop	7	2	0	0	2	4	4	10	1	2
Union shop	79	27	37	25	11	23	7	18	24	44
Agency shop	10	3	5	3	0	0	0	0	5	9
Maintenance of membership	32	11	25	17	0	0	2	5	5	9
Preferential shop	5	2	1	1	3	6	0	0	1	2
None	156	54	80	54	31	66	26	67	19	35
Total	289	100	148	100	47	100	39	100	55	100

Source: Paul F. Gerhart, "The Scope of Bargaining in Local Government Labor Agreements" (Ph.D. dissertation, University of Chicago, 1973). Based on contracts on file in unions' national offices, except for SEIU at U.S. Bureau of Labor Statistics. Percentages may not total 100 because of rounding.
a. Random sample of one-sixth of all contracts.
b. Random sample of one-half of all contracts.

In view of the restrictions in most states, it is surprising to find that various forms of union security have been negotiated in a substantial number of contracts between unions and government employers. As Table 6-1 shows, almost one-third of the state and local agreements included in a 1968 survey contained closed, union, or agency shop provisions, the first type being illegal even in the private sector. An additional 13 percent contained such lesser forms of union security as maintenance of membership or preferential hiring clauses. Some form of union security was included in two-thirds of the Teamster agreements, half of the AFSCME contracts, and one-third of the SEIU and Laborers agreements. While these percentages are far below the 80 percent of all contracts with union security provisions in private industry,[35] they are much larger than might be expected, given the dubious legality of such provisions in public employment.

Traditional union security agreements are more often negotiated in states without public employee collective bargaining laws than in states with such laws. Thus, at least half the contracts surveyed in Pennsylvania (before its law was enacted), Indiana, Illinois, and Montana contained union or closed shop provisions. On the other hand, such agreements were relatively scarce in Massachusetts, Connecticut, New York, Michigan, and Wisconsin, all states with comprehensive public employment laws.[36] None of the forty agreements surveyed in Wisconsin contained any form of union security.[37] Government employers in states that provide no legal protection for collective bargaining appear to be more prone to grant union security than employers in states with laws that prohibit or are silent with respect to the union or agency shop. Employers in states without laws who engage in collective bargaining do so voluntarily and are probably prepared to grant union security more readily than employers who recognize and bargain with unions only because state laws require them to do so. The latter employers are less likely to agree to provisions that are either unlawful or at least of dubious legality. This would explain the fact that almost

35. U.S. Bureau of Labor Statistics, *Union Security and Checkoff Provisions in Major Union Contracts, 1958–59,* Bulletin 1272 (1960), p. 1.

36. Paul F. Gerhart, "The Scope of Bargaining In Local Government Labor Agreements" (Ph.D. dissertation, University of Chicago, 1973).

37. Wisconsin's law did not permit agency shop agreements prior to November 1971.

two-thirds of the 210 AFSCME contracts in effect in 1959, when there were no state public employment collective bargaining laws, provided for the union shop, while only about one-fourth of the 1,000 agreements in 1968 contained union shop provisions.[38]

The importance of the union or agency shop to a union is indicated by the fact that AFSCME with 550,000 members bargained for twice that number of employees, all of whom would be members or pay dues to AFSCME if the union could negotiate security agreements.[39] In New York City alone, AFSCME Council 37 expected to add 35,000 members to the 90,000 it had in 1971, if the agency shop were authorized by state law. And in Wisconsin the union in 1970 estimated it would grow from 30,000 to 50,000 members, making AFSCME the largest union in that state, if the legislature passed a bill authorizing agency-shop bargaining agreements.[40] While some membership gains resulting from agency shop agreements may be made at the expense of other unions, there is little doubt that legalization of the agency shop in public employment would result in a substantial increase in overall union membership.

Unlike unions of nonuniformed government employees, organizations of fire fighters and police have shown little interest in union security. With close to 100 percent membership among employees they represent, these organizations feel much less need for union security than AFSCME and the mixed unions. Some leaders of the uniformed protective service organizations reject the union or agency shop on principle, saying they would not force membership or dues payment on those who did not join voluntarily.

No statistics are available on union security provisions negotiated by state and local employee associations or by state nurses' associations. Civil service association representatives are generally indifferent or opposed to compulsory membership. Nurses, on the other hand, favor union security and have succeeded in negotiating union shop clauses in contracts in Delaware, Washington, and California. Membership in SNA bargaining units tends to be quite high, and the ANA has advised state associations not to file for exclusive representation unless a majority of nurses in the requested unit have

---

38. Kramer, *Labor's Paradox*, pp. 45–46; *AFSCME Proceedings* (1968), p. 25.
39. *GERR*, No. 455 (June 5, 1972), pp. B-12–B-17.
40. *Public Employee*, Vol. 35 (December 1970), p. 5.

pledged their support. Several states require 75 percent membership in a unit before the association will become involved. Thus expenditures of association resources and funds are limited to units that have demonstrated, through a high proportion of ANA members, their willingness to share the cost of representation.

Arrangements for dues to be deducted from wages or salaries by employers is widespread among all types of public employee organizations. The checkoff has existed for a long time in public employment and is almost universal in units represented by unions. Many state associations also have payroll deduction of dues. Dues checkoff is common but not universal in units represented by state nurses' associations.

Contract Negotiations

The various unions and associations differ little in their formulation of demands, strategy and tactics, and ratification procedures in negotiations. Bargaining unit members are usually consulted in determining which demands to press and the priority to be assigned to each. Negotiations are conducted by teams consisting of local committees, assisted or led by full-time staff members. The final decision on acceptance or rejection of an agreement is almost invariably lodged in the membership of the affected unit.

The degree of nonlocal involvement in negotiations depends on the structure and resources of the organization. The mixed unions, whose locals are likely to be financially independent, rely less on intermediate and national office assistance than AFSCME, the fire fighters, and the nurses. In AFSCME the union spokesman is usually the director or staff member of a council, and the international has developed a computerized system to provide comparative information on wages and other benefits to affiliates in negotiations.[41] IAFF vice-presidents and international representatives are available to assist locals in negotiations, in contrast to the FOP and the ICPA which have neither the resources nor the expertise at the national level to help local police associations. Police bargaining teams are usually led by an attorney who is sometimes the sole negotiator.

41. *AFSCME Proceedings* (1970), pp. 440–46.

This probably reflects relative inexperience in bargaining by police associations, frequent contact with lawyers in their work, and the importance of law and the courts in determining working conditions of policemen. In the American Nurses' Association, responsibility for collective bargaining resides in the state associations which either employ full-time staff or rely on outside consultants to conduct negotiations.[42]

Wage and salary demands dominated negotiations during the late 1960s, often because public employee organizations were negotiating first contracts during a period of inflation. The large proportion of low-income workers in AFSCME and the mixed unions often results in a strong preference for across-the-board wage increases as opposed to percentage increases which yield larger absolute amounts to higher paid workers. Government employers, like their counterparts in private industry, generally favor percentage increases in order to maintain skill differentials and to help in recruitment of skilled employees. Wage comparisons are as important in public employment as in the private sector. Unskilled workers make interdepartmental as well as public–private sector comparisons; skilled workers look to the building trades in setting wage targets; nurses compare their salaries to other professional groups. But the greatest competition occurs among police and fire fighters over the issue of "pay parity."

During the 1960s the traditional parity between salaries of policemen and firemen was questioned in many cities, as policemen faced increased crime and violence, racial tensions, and campus unrest, and the hostility toward them grew among militant blacks and young people. Difficulty in filling police vacancies, coupled with an oversupply of fire fighter recruits, led administrators in some cities to support differential pay scales for the two protective services.[43] Elected officials and a sympathetic public have allowed pay parity to be discontinued in some places.

Fire fighters have reacted by insisting on continuation of traditional pay parity arrangements, or emphasizing professionalization

42. In 1968, twenty state associations employed outside consultants in negotiations (ANA, Research and Statistics Department, "Summary of Annual Reports from State Nurses' Association, March, 1968" [ANA, 1968; processed]).

43. Eugene J. Devine, *Analysis of Manpower Shortages in Local Government: Case Studies of Nurses, Policemen, and Teachers* (Praeger, 1970), p. 77.

of their jobs. They have increased union expenditures on public relations and political action, become more militant, and have more frequently resorted to job actions and strikes. Fire fighters believe that they should be paid more than policemen because their jobs are more hazardous, and they cite statistics to prove their point.[44] IAFF locals often compare fire fighters to skilled tradesmen and demand wages and benefits comparable to those in the building trades. The international claims that "the professional fire fighter must possess a broad knowledge that ranges across the spectrum of many scientific and technical fields," including construction, chemistry, hydraulics, physics, physiology, electronics, law, teaching, radiology, fire suppression technology, and personnel management.[45] City officials do not accept the comparison with skilled tradesmen, and some union officers acknowledge that their strategy is to maintain or restore parity with police by putting forward a far more costly alternative.

Despite the fact that different groups of local government employees are drawn from the same labor market, depend on the same financial resources, and work in close proximity under the same civil service rules and regulations, there is little cooperation between the organizations that represent them in negotiations with their common employer. The competition and conflict that characterized the organizational period have continued to divide unions and associations that would appear to have a common interest in cooperating in collective bargaining. AFSCME is regarded as the most intransigent and uncooperative union by other labor organizations; it does not make a good ally either in organizing or collective bargaining. In a number of cities, other unions have complained that AFSCME was the only union unwilling to agree to a division of employees according to established jurisdictional interests or to engage in joint negotiations. Coordinated organization drives and even joint negotiations have been worked out among

44. A full page advertisement headlined "We Die Nine Years Sooner . . ." noted 294 fire fighters killed on duty as compared with 49 policemen, 8 sanitationmen, 2 transit patrolmen, and no housing or correction officers. Yet, the advertisement charged, New York's "crazy-quilt parity structure equates, to a penny, a fire fighter's salary with police, transit police, correction officers and housing cops." (*New York Times*, April 15, 1971.)

45. Research and Education Department, International Association of Fire Fighters, "Negotiating Information and Statistics, 1969" (IAFF, n.d.; processed), p. 2.

mixed unions in several cities, and, despite their enmity over the parity pay issue, fire fighter and police organizations have also co-operated in bargaining in a number of localities. AFSCME has almost always remained aloof from such arrangements.

Collective bargaining in local government is inextricably intertwined with politics, in a process often referred to as "double-deck bargaining." Mayors, council members, and those aspiring to office are as often responsible for mingling political considerations with collective bargaining as unions that try to improve on what they have won in negotiations by using political pressure or influence with elected officials. Representatives of mixed unions and police and fire fighter organizations more readily acknowledge the political nature of negotiations in public employment than do AFSCME staff members. This is more a reflection of the political influence of the mixed unions, the building trades, and the protective organizations than of the degree of dedication to "pure" collective bargaining of the various organizations. However, representatives of all organizations express a preference for collective bargaining over settlements reached through political accommodations, and there is evidence that politics is playing a less important role in negotiations as professionals take over the representation function on both sides of the bargaining table.

Funding Contract Costs

"Ability to pay" is an important consideration in collective bargaining in both private and public employment. However, in government the union's interest in "ability to pay" often extends to active involvement in helping the employer raise the necessary funds to pay the cost of an agreement. Union assistance of this kind is not only welcomed but is frequently solicited by government employers. This is a unique aspect of public sector bargaining that is not present in labor relations in private industry.

Collective bargaining agreements requiring action by third parties, who are not involved in the negotiations, may take various forms. A contract may be made contingent on the local government's ability to obtain funds from the state legislature to pay the increased costs resulting from a settlement; or legislative approval may be required before certain types of benefits, such as pensions, may be effectuated or changed; or a salary increase may be tied to the outcome of a voter referendum on a millage increase or a favorable vote on a city payroll or income tax. In agreements that commit the employer to increased costs, failure to raise the necessary funds to pay for the increase may cause the employer to take actions unpalatable to the union, such as reducing employment. To avoid such situations, unions usually try to influence the legislature or the voters, including of course their own members, to take favorable action to provide the funds necessary to implement the agreement.

Unions indicate their interest in the government employer's "ability to pay" in a number of ways. In Philadelphia, for instance, the Central Labor Council in 1961 supported an increase in the city wage tax to provide funds to pay for a wage increase for city employees represented by AFSCME. In 1968, city unions again requested AFL-CIO support for a tax increase to pay for their wage demands. The AFL-CIO Council supported the demands of the unions, but disassociated itself from the substantial increase in taxes that followed.[46]

In Youngstown, Ohio, the city in 1967 went to the voters with a request for an increase in the city income tax to pay for wage increases agreed to after a five-day strike of police and fire fighters. The FOP, IAFF, and all unions in Youngstown supplied manpower to campaign for approval of the tax increase. The city permitted employees to take time off with pay from their jobs to work for the increase, which was approved by the voters.

In 1970, Cleveland Mayor Carl Stokes agreed in negotiations with unions representing public employees to add $30 million to the city's prospective labor bill for the next two years, but the voters declined to pay the bill with a higher income tax. Twice, Clevelanders voted down proposed increases in the city income tax, despite strong union support, including cash contributions to pay campaign costs. After the first defeat in November 1970, a thousand city employees were laid off and Mayor Stokes indicated that another thousand would be laid off as a result of the second defeat in February 1971. During the next two years the city tried to reduce wage costs by layoffs, mandatory retirements, pay cuts, and reduc-

46. Letter to the author from AFSCME Area Director, Philadelphia, Pennsylvania, Oct. 23, 1970.

tion in hours of work. The unions resisted by strikes, slowdowns, and court litigation.[47]

In New York City, AFSCME Council 37 negotiated pensions for city employees that would provide half pay at age fifty-five after twenty years employment and full pay after forty years. The union, seeking to convince the state legislature it should implement the pensions, pointed out that they were negotiated after months of "hard bargaining" with "give and take" on both sides and without a strike threat.[48] When the legislature failed to act, Council 37 and Teamsters Local 237, whose members were also affected by the pension settlement, called a strike that trapped several hundred thousand motorists in massive traffic jams by opening twenty-seven of the city's twenty-nine movable bridges. The reaction of the legislature was to kill the pension bill for the 1971 session. After two days, the unions accepted a settlement formula worked out by the city's Office of Collective Bargaining: the plan would be resubmitted to the 1972 legislature; if it was again defeated, the parties would try to agree on a solution; and if that failed, the issue would go to an impartial panel for recommendations of an alternative that would not require legislative approval. When the legislature again withheld approval of the pension increase in 1972, Council 37 proposed to the panel that the pension plan be replaced with severance benefits for employees terminated by death, retirement, layoff, or resignation. As of January 1973, the issue was still unresolved.[49]

The relationship between collective bargaining and funding of agreements is particularly close in independent school districts which must go directly to the electorate to raise funds to finance operations. Teachers' organizations and unions representing non-instructional school workers are usually found in the forefront of those actively supporting and campaigning for a favorable vote in such referendums. Police and fire fighters in many cities are also dependent on the legislature or the voting public for approval of wage increases or increased revenues to finance the cost of collective bargaining agreements. The tie-in between the benefits and costs of collective bargaining for other government employees, while less

47. "When Cities Collide with Unions," *Business Week*, Jan. 2, 1971, p. 24; *New York Times*, Feb. 7, 1971, p. 33; Feb. 13, 1972, p. 62; Feb. 28, 1972, p. 35; Sept. 26, 1972, p. 31.

48. *New York Times*, May 13, 1971, p. 59.

49. Ibid., June 8, 9, and 10, 1971, pp. 1, 1, and 34, respectively, and Jan. 27, 1973, p. 24.

direct, is nonetheless brought to the attention of the public through higher taxes and on election day in a way that has no counterpart in private sector negotiations.

Summary

Collective bargaining for government employees was, until about 1960, considered impracticable, not only by government employers but also by many union leaders. Today it is recognized and accepted, if not necessarily welcomed, by all public employee organizations, including many associations originally opposed to collective bargaining, and by a rapidly growing number of government employers. Unlike the private sector, where union demands for legislation to protect the right to organize and bargain collectively were pressed for many years before the enactment of the Wagner Act, in public employment the espousal of collective bargaining by employee associations, and even by some unions, followed and was a direct result of a federal executive order and state legislation.

The advent of collective bargaining for government workers presages significant modifications in the merit system and civil service, as these concepts have developed during the twentieth century.[50] Leaders of organizations that engage in collective bargaining regard civil service systems as passé, and their own organizations as appropriate successors in all aspects of the employment relationship except recruitment and test administration. Only the Assembly of Governmental Employees and state and local associations that have not espoused collective bargaining remain staunch supporters of civil service systems.

Collective bargaining in government is largely a local and individual organization process. It is time-consuming and lends itself to whipsawing, interorganization competition, and political maneuvering. Joint negotiations, involving representatives of several organizations and bargaining units, are relatively rare, but appear to be a logical way to arrive at settlements among groups that are so closely interrelated. During the coming decade, as organizational disputes over recognition are resolved and bargaining relationships become more stabilized, joint negotiations will undoubtedly increase.

50. See David T. Stanley, *Managing Local Government under Union Pressure* (Brookings Institution, 1972), pp. 9–10, 32–45, 60–64.

CHAPTER SEVEN

Bargaining Units and Representation Elections

One of the most important concepts in the American system of industrial relations is that of the bargaining unit. Under federal and state labor relations laws in both the private and public sectors, a union is recognized as the exclusive representative and bargains for employees in an "appropriate bargaining unit." If the parties cannot agree on what constitutes an appropriate unit, the determination is made by an administrative body such as the National Labor Relations Board under federal law and state labor relations boards or commissions under state laws.

Bargaining units in the private sector may encompass employees in a particular craft, department, plant, company, area, or even an entire industry. Supervisory employees are excluded from coverage under the National Labor Relations Act and under state acts regulating private labor–management relations in intrastate commerce. In public employment, units may include employees in a particular occupation or job title, department or agency, blue collar or white collar jobs, or an entire governmental jurisdiction such as a city, county, or school district. There is, as yet, no counterpart in government to the multiemployer bargaining that is found in the private sector on an industry or area basis, although the president of the American Federation of State, County and Municipal Employees (AFSCME) has indicated he favors consolidation of bargaining among cities on the basis of size, geographic area, or other common attribute.[1]

The treatment of supervisors varies under state laws governing collective bargaining in public employment. Some permit supervisors to bargain collectively in separate units; others have excluded them from coverage; and a few laws are silent on the subject of supervisors, leaving the determination of whether or not they should be covered to the agency administering the act. The Advisory Commission on Intergovernmental Relations has recommended that "managerial and supervisory personnel who have authority to act or recommend action . . . in such matters as hiring, transferring, suspending, laying-off, recalling, promoting, discharging, assigning, rewarding, or disciplining other employees; who have authority to assign; and/or who direct work or who adjust grievances" be denied rights and privileges accorded to other employees under state public labor relations laws.[2]

The scope of the bargaining unit can significantly affect the membership composition of employee organizations, the outcome of representation elections, and the content of collective bargaining agreements. The first two of these matters are discussed here; the third is the subject of a separate Brookings Institution research project devoted to collective bargaining in public employment.

Organization Views on Bargaining Units

For every organization the ideal collective bargaining unit closely resembles the organization's membership structure. Thus, the industrywide AFSCME prefers a unit that covers all city or county employees. The mixed unions, following the lead of their private sector units, usually favor occupational groupings. And the associations in their diversity seem to accept the kind of bargaining unit that local circumstance forces on them. The uniformed services

1. Labor-Management Relations Service, "A Look at Public Employee Unions" (Washington: LMRS, September 1970; processed); see also, Neil M. Gundermann, "Multi-Employer Bargaining: For and Against," *LMRS Newsletter*, Vol. 2 (September 1971), pp. 3–4.

2. Advisory Commission on Intergovernmental Relations, *Labor-Management Policies for State and Local Government* (Washington: ACIR, 1969), p. 95.

resist inclusion with other occupational groups, insisting on their uniqueness. Nurses' associations have only recently recognized the possible advantage of joining with others to win representation rights.

UNIONS

Generally, unions seek to represent employees in the largest possible unit from which they draw their membership, with due regard for the community of interest among employees and the organization's strength in the particular unit. Public employee unions favor bargaining units that reflect the composition of their membership and their strengths and weaknesses among different occupational and functional groups of employees.

For AFSCME, a broadly based industrial union of government employees, the ideal bargaining situation is a city or countywide unit of nonuniformed blue collar workers, with separate units for white collar and supervisory employees. AFSCME has that arrangement in Philadelphia, where the city initiated the idea in 1957, when it first recognized an AFSCME unit as the representative of all blue collar employees. As one Philadelphia official put it: "We have a monster that we love." Other large cities that recognize AFSCME for all blue collar workers have deliberately sought to avoid fragmentation of bargaining units and dealing with a multiplicity of organizations.[3]

While AFSCME does not favor including supervisors in the same bargaining units as employees they supervise, it does hold that they should be permitted to belong to the same unions as other employees and to bargain collectively in separate units.[4] This position is understandable; a 1968 survey showed that 3.6 percent of AFSCME's membership were supervisors, a higher proportion than that of sanitation workers, policemen, park and recreation workers, or most other job categories in the union.[5] While supervisors have occupied a decreasingly important role in recent years, they were

3. See New York City, Office of Collective Bargaining, *Annual Report, 1968*, p. 4, and *1969*, p. 22; LMRS, "The City Prepares for Labor Relations: The Experience in Detroit, Baltimore and Milwaukee" (LMRS, September 1970; processed).

4. ACIR, *Labor-Management Policies*, p. 155.

5. *Proceedings of the 17th International Convention, American Federation of State, County and Municipal Employees, AFL-CIO* (1968), pp. 417–18.

instrumental in organizing the union and some have occupied leadership positions in AFSCME.

The treatment of supervisors in AFSCME is basically a local union decision, subject to the international constitution which contains no prohibition on membership of supervisory employees. Many locals discourage new supervisors from joining but permit employees promoted to supervisory rank to retain membership. Some local unions have tried to bar all supervisors from membership, in violation of the constitution.[6] Others accept supervisors as members, even though they may not be included in the bargaining unit. In some jurisdictions, supervisors belong to separate local unions and have their own bargaining units. On the other hand, some AFSCME locals actively solicit supervisors for membership and try to have them included in the bargaining unit, up to as high a level as the law or the government employer will allow.

The mixed unions are much less likely than AFSCME to be designated as exclusive representatives in city or countywide bargaining units. While they would certainly not be averse to representing all employees in a locality, and do in some places, they have tended to concentrate on functions and occupations that are akin to those they represent in the private sector. Thus, bargaining units represented by the Service Employees International Union (SEIU) are most often composed of custodial workers and janitors, hospital and other institutional workers, and social workers;[7] the Laborers' International Union generally represents relatively unskilled employees in sanitation and in street and highway maintenance; and the International Brotherhood of Teamsters, in most areas outside of New York City, has been interested primarily in representing truck drivers, equipment operators, and equipment maintenance workers. Membership and representation among supervisory public employees appear to be less of an issue in the mixed unions than in AFSCME. Perhaps as a result of their private sector origin and

6. In 1964, Council 77 in Detroit reversed a decision by a member local union declaring a former president of the local ineligible for membership because of his promotion to a supervisory position. (Minutes of the AFSCME International Executive Board, Jan. 25–27, 1965.)

7. The last named group represents a departure from SEIU private sector membership, but is one in which this union has been particularly successful, especially in California.

experience, the mixed unions do not have a large supervisory employee membership, although there is no constitutional exclusion of supervisors and locals are free to determine their own policy with respect to supervisory membership.

ASSOCIATIONS

Given the difference in attitudes among state and local employee associations toward collective bargaining, there can be no clear-cut association position with respect to the scope of the bargaining unit. Appearing before the Advisory Commission on Intergovernmental Relations, the president of the Assembly of Governmental Employees (who, as executive secretary of his state association, has opposed collective bargaining) testified that for "those categories of public personnel with whom public employers must meet and confer and those with whom public employers must bargain collectively . . . exclusive recognition [should] be accorded to organizations representing a majority of the employees in the largest possible bargaining unit."[8] Some associations have conceived of the "largest possible bargaining unit" as encompassing both blue collar and white collar employees, including foremen and supervisors.

A highly publicized dispute involving the size and composition of the appropriate bargaining unit occurred in New York State in 1968 when Governor Nelson Rockefeller entered into negotiations with the Civil Service Employees Association (CSEA) as the representative of a single unit of 124,000 employees. The state Public Employee Relations Board (PERB), which had recommended that state employees be divided into six bargaining units, ordered the governor to discontinue negotiations pending a final determination on the bargaining unit issue, but the courts upheld the state's right to negotiate with the CSEA. In order to force the state to stop negotiating with CSEA, AFSCME Council 50 called strikes against four state mental institutions. The governor finally ceased negotiations with CSEA when PERB ordered elections to be held to determine representation in five bargaining units instead of the single unit preferred by the state and CSEA.[9] Single statewide units have also

8. ACIR, *Labor-Management Policies*, p. 127.
9. *New York Times*, Nov. 28, 1968.

been proposed by other associations without success.[10] Some associations, recognizing that such broad units were not viable, have favored separate units of blue and white collar employees and supervisory and nonsupervisory employees.[11]

The Assembly of Governmental Employees (AGE) has held that inclusion or exclusion of supervisory employees from a particular bargaining unit should be a negotiable issue and not decided by law or administrative determination.[12] For many associations this is a very important issue because of their substantial supervisory membership and leadership.

Membership in associations has usually been open to all government employees with the exception of elected and appointed officials, though even these are eligible in a few state and local associations. Agency and department heads, division chiefs, and lower echelon supervisors are generally eligible for membership, but their participation varies more or less inversely with the level of the position occupied. Top level supervisors who have come up from the ranks are much more likely to continue to belong than are those who would have to join as new members. Some associations that engage in collective bargaining deny full membership privileges to supervisory employees who are not in the bargaining unit. There is an increasing recognition by supervisors in such associations that they are no longer wanted and many have allowed their membership to lapse.

UNIFORMED SERVICES

Organizations of uniformed police and particularly of fire fighters tend to be all-inclusive up to and sometimes including the chief or commissioner. In recent years, the trend in large cities has been toward separate organizations for patrolmen and superior police officers. AFSCME police locals do not usually exclude officers from membership; in Connecticut the director of the AFSCME police council, which has 29 locals and 3,000 members, holds the rank of

10. See Bureau of National Affairs, *Government Employee Relations Report* (GERR), No. 397 (April 19, 1971), p. B-8; No. 315 (Sept. 22, 1969), p. B-16; and No. 323 (Nov. 17, 1969), p. B-9; and LMRS, "The City Prepares for Labor Relations," pp. 8–9.

11. Letter to the author from Executive Director, Oregon State Employees Association, Aug. 16, 1971.

12. ACIR, *Labor-Management Policies*, p. 127.

captain. The Fraternal Order of Police (FOP) adheres to the philosophy of all-inclusive membership, reflecting the view that there is a fraternal bond among all men in blue regardless of rank. The only major city with separate organizations for rank-and-file fire fighters and officers is New York, and even there both locals belong to the International Association of Fire Fighters (IAFF).

The all-inclusive nature of police and fire fighter employee organizations is fostered by a strong in-group feeling which excludes civilian employees, part-time or volunteer personnel, meter maids, and school crossing guards. Both groups regard themselves as professionals, train new recruits in their own academies or on the job, and promote exclusively from the ranks. The hazardous and dangerous nature of the job, regardless of rank, contributes to the bond that exists between the rank-and-file and superior officers. This is particularly true among fire fighters, who work as a team; a man's life may depend on the ability of the men and officers to work together. The firehouse as a home-away-from-home also tends to draw the men together much more than in other occupations, including police work. Many police and fire organizations that started as benevolent, fraternal, burial, or social organizations have continued as all-inclusive organizations even after they have taken on new functions and changed their primary objectives.

The advent of collective bargaining has, however, strained and sometimes broken the bonds. Since, under most state laws, supervisors may not be members of the same bargaining unit as other employees, organizations of uniformed police and fire fighters have sometimes been certified as collective bargaining representatives for units that exclude some of their members. The definition of an appropriate unit varies, but the cut-off rank is usually higher for fire fighters than for policemen.

The strong community of interest between officers and rank-and-file fire fighters has been recognized by law, administrative rulings, and court decisions. Michigan specifically provides that in deciding on appropriate bargaining units "no person subordinate to a fire commission, fire commissioner, safety director, or other similar administrative agency or administrator shall be deemed to be a supervisor."[13] The Connecticut Labor Relations Board has held that

13. Michigan Public Employment Relations Act, Act 336 of the Public Acts of 1947 as amended (1965).

statutory criteria for public employees do not necessarily apply to police and fire departments: "higher supervisory positions shall be included in the unit in police and fire departments than in other departments."[14] In Barre, Vermont, where all fire officers except the chief have been union members since 1946, the state Labor Relations Board found that all officers except the chief were nonsupervisory employees because of "the power of the City Manager over the fire department, the lack of deviation from prescribed policy by these officers, the grievance route that commences with the fire chief and terminates with the City Council."[15] Many major cities recognize fire fighter units that include various levels of superior officers.[16] But there have also been cases in which the courts or boards administering state acts have found that, based on their duties and responsibilities, fire officers were supervisory employees and could not be in the same bargaining unit as other fire fighters.[17]

Bargaining units that include both patrolmen and officers are less common than all-inclusive units in fire departments. This reflects the greater distance between ranks, which in a number of cities has led to different organizations, as well as differences in responsibility in the jobs of police officers. Most police departments have either a single bargaining unit that excludes officers, generally at the rank of lieutenant and above, or two units, one for patrolmen and noncommissioned officers up to or through sergeants and the other for lieutenants, captains, and assistant and deputy chiefs. Sergeants are in some places included in the same unit as patrolmen, in others in the officers' unit. Police chiefs and commissioners are almost always considered part of management and are excluded from any bargaining unit. In some cities, police organizations have succeeded in including officers in the same bargaining unit as patrolmen.

In Michigan a supervisor is defined as "any individual having authority, in the interest of the employer, to hire, transfer, suspend, lay-off, recall, promote, discharge, assign, reward or discipline other

14. "Report of American Bar Association Committee on State Labor Law, 1969–70," in Bureau of National Affairs, *Issue and Techniques,* GERR Reference File 5 (1970), p. 61:204.

15. Ibid.

16. *GERR,* No. 390 (March 1, 1971), pp. B-8, 9.

17. "Report of American Bar Association Committee," p. 61:204; *GERR,* No. 399 (May 3, 1971), p. B-1; and *GERR,* No. 392 (May 15, 1971), p. B-3.

employees, or responsibility to direct them, or to adjust their grievances, or effectively to recommend such action, if in connection with the foregoing the exercise of such authority is not merely of a routine or clerical nature, but requires the use of independent judgement."[18] The state's Employment Relations Commission has held that the final criterion is "how completely the responsibilities of the position in question identify or align the holder with management."[19] In Kalamazoo township the commission noted that corporals "engage for the most part in the same activities as patrolmen." Since corporals' authority to suspend subordinates "is completely reviewed by higher authority," it is unlikely they "would, because of their position, identify or align themselves with management." Sergeants, on the other hand, "have the authority to suspend subordinate employees, review the suspensions made by corporals, process grievances, assign employees, corporals included, to work schedules, and make recommendations on the qualifications of an applicant for employment." The commission concluded that the sergeants had supervisory authority and should be excluded from a unit of corporals and patrolmen.[20]

It appears that whether or not particular ranks will be included or excluded from units of fire fighters or policemen varies with the wishes of the parties, the definition of the term *supervisor* as contained in the law, the interpretation of the law by the administering agency and the courts, and the circumstances in each case. It is also likely that the supervisory level will be set at a higher rank in states that do not extend collective bargaining rights to supervisors than in states that permit such employees to bargain in separate units. In states without collective bargaining laws for public employees, police and fire fighter organizations tend to speak for all members, who often include not only officers but even the chief.

NURSES

As a professional association open only to registered nurses, the American Nurses' Association (ANA) favors statutory protection in both private and public sector labor relations "of the right of a professional group to a separate and autonomous bargaining unit

18. Michigan Public Employment Relations Act, sec. 13.
19. *GERR*, No. 332 (Jan. 19, 1970), p. B-1.
20. Ibid., p. B-2.

composed exclusively of the members of one profession."[21] Some employers and unions have, for different reasons, favored the inclusion of nurses in bargaining units with nonprofessionals or with other professionals in which they represent only a minority of all employees. Thus, in Philadelphia, nurses are included in AFSCME's exclusive recognition rights for all nonuniformed city employees; and in New York State, 4,000 nurses are submerged in a statewide unit of 38,000 professional, scientific, and technical employees and 1,900 job titles.[22]

The ANA also believes that the right of supervisors to organize and bargain collectively should be protected by law. This is an important issue to nurses because many of them occupy what the ANA regards as "middle-management" positions. According to the ANA, only nurses who exercise a decisive voice in institutional policy making, generally carrying the title "director" or "administrator," should be considered part of management and excluded from coverage under collective bargaining laws. The ANA favors laws that permit supervisors and nonsupervisors to be in the same bargaining unit or to be represented in separate units by the same professional association.[23]

The association argues that the educational backgrounds and working values of all registered nurses are much alike. Responsibility to the patient transcends concepts of rank. While supervisors may advise and assist, each nurse "directs" her own practice. Moreover, nurses change jobs frequently, moving up and down in the hierarchy without thought of how their "careers" are being affected. Few possess supervisory authority in the industrial sense, and those alien standards should not be applied in determining appropriate bargaining units for nurses.[24]

The importance of the issue is readily apparent; of the 600,000 employed nurses in 1966, some 166,000 held positions as administrators, supervisors, or head nurses or their assistants. Two-thirds of all registered nurses are employed in hospitals or other institutions—where the issue of collective bargaining is most pressing—

---

21. American Nurses' Association, "Statement on Federal and State Labor Relations Laws" (ANA, Dec. 12, 1969; processed), p. 18.
22. Ibid., p. 19.
23. Ibid., p. 20.
24. Ibid., pp. 20–22.

and of those, 36 percent are in the supervisory categories.[25] The three groups probably represent as large, if not a larger, proportion of the ANA membership as of the profession generally.[26] Nurses holding the titles of "administrator" or "director," and their immediate assistants, whom the ANA considers the only representatives of management, constitute only about 3.5 percent of all nurses.

State nurses' associations have met with considerable success in obtaining bargaining rights for all nurses, except administrators and directors, either in the same unit or in separate units of non-supervisory and supervisory nurses. As in the case of fire fighters and policemen, the cut-off point for supervisors has tended to be higher under laws denying bargaining rights to supervisory employees than under state laws that allow supervisors to bargain in separate units.[27]

Prior to 1970 the ANA sought to restrict representation to units made up exclusively of registered nurses, refusing to represent licensed practical nurses, nurses' aides, and other hospital employees. Delegates to the 1970 convention decided that this policy had "not proved workable," especially with respect to licensed practical nurses. In states that encouraged large units encompassing all hospital employees, associations were put at a disadvantage in competing with unions. The new policy gives state associations the prerogative to assist other groups when joint representation would be advantageous to both groups.[28] Thus far only a few state associations have experimented with this new approach.

Representation Elections

Most comprehensive state laws governing collective bargaining in public employment follow the National Labor Relations Act in their procedures for designating the exclusive bargaining repre-

25. ANA, *Facts About Nursing: A Statistical Summary* (New York: ANA, 1969 edition), p. 18.

26. The Michigan Nurses' Association reported that head nurses and nursing service administrators constituted 31 percent of its 1970 membership, with an additional 10 percent coming from the ranks of educational administrators, consultants, and teachers. Michigan Nurses' Association, "Membership Comparisons, 1966–70" (memorandum, n.d.).

27. Daniel H. Kruger, "The Appropriate Bargaining Unit for Professional Nurses," *Labor Law Journal*, Vol. 19 (January 1968), pp. 3–11.

28. *American Journal of Nursing*, Vol. 70 (June 1970), pp. 1271, 1273–74.

sentative of employees in an appropriate bargaining unit. An organization may be recognized voluntarily by an employer or as a result of a determination made by the agency administering the law. Either an employee organization or an employer may seek such a determination, based on evidence that an organization represents a majority of the employees in the bargaining unit or, if necessary, by a secret ballot election. The results of representation elections provide the best available indications of public employees' attitudes toward collective bargaining, and of the kind of organization they prefer as a bargaining agent. Representation elections in New York, Connecticut, Michigan, and Wisconsin during the 1960s illustrate these points.

ELECTION RESULTS

During the eight-year period 1962–69, a total of 1,284 representation elections, exclusive of elections among school teachers, were conducted at local levels of government in the four states represented in Table 7-1[29] (further information on the elections is given in Tables B-2–B-6 in Appendix B). Michigan has consistently outstripped the other states in number of elections held, and the number conducted each year has been decreasing (as it has in Connecticut). Wisconsin has a long and fairly steady elections history, and New York's experience is too limited to suggest a trend.[30]

Unions or associations have won 88 percent of all elections held in the four states, with only slight variations by state (see Table 7-2). The percentage of victories is much higher than labor organizations' victories under the National Labor Relations Act: unions won 66 percent of all elections conducted by the National Labor Relations Board (NLRB) during the period 1936–69, with a high of 75 percent during 1936–43, and slightly less than 60 percent since 1957.[31] A similar trend toward a decreasing number of vic-

29. With the possible exception of Massachusetts, for which data are not available, these four states have probably conducted more elections than any other states.

30. One-third of all New York elections have been conducted by the Office of Collective Bargaining of New York City, and only two by local public employment relations boards which are permitted to establish their own procedures under the state Taylor Act. The remaining elections were conducted by the state Public Employment Relations Board.

31. National Labor Relations Board (NLRB), *Annual Report,* 1936–69 issues.

TABLE 7-1. *Representation Elections among Local Government Employees in Four States, 1962–69*[a]

Year	Four states	Michigan	Wisconsin	Connecticut	New York
		Number and percent of total in state			
1962	53(*4*)	...	53(*15*)	...	...
1963	46(*4*)	...	46(*13*)	...	...
1964	23(*2*)	...	23(*6*)	...	...
1965	94(*7*)	50(*7*)	34(*9*)	10(*9*)	...
1966	292(*23*)	200(*28*)	49(*13*)	42(*36*)	1(*1*)
1967	252(*20*)	170(*24*)	56(*15*)	24(*21*)	2(*2*)
1968	278(*22*)	161(*22*)	45(*12*)	21(*18*)	51(*59*)
1969	246(*19*)	138(*19*)	57(*16*)	19(*16*)	32(*37*)
Total	1,284(*100*)	719(*100*)	363(*100*)	116(*100*)	86(*100*)

Source: Data supplied by state agencies. Elections under laws governing collective bargaining were instituted in Wisconsin in April 1962, in Connecticut in July 1965, in Michigan in August 1965, and in New York in November 1966. Percentages may not total 100 because of rounding.
a. Excludes representation elections for school teachers.

tories shows up in public employee organizations in Wisconsin, where wins dropped from 91 percent of all elections during 1962–64 to 84 percent in 1967–69, and in Michigan, where they declined from 92 percent initially to 87 percent in 1968–69. The percentage of elections won by employee organizations in Connecticut has held fairly steady at about 90 percent each year since 1965, while the experience in New York has been too limited to show any trend.

An overwhelming proportion of all public employee elections—85 percent—involved a single organization. In New York, the only state that deviated significantly from this norm, half of the elections involved two or more employee organizations competing for exclusive representation, with employees given the option of voting for the organization they preferred or for no representation. The important factor is the Civil Service Employees Association in New York; none of the other three states has a comparable employee association that competes actively with unions for representation rights among local government employees.

A vote in favor of representation is somewhat more likely in elections involving two or more organizations than in single-organization elections—95 percent as opposed to 87 percent. In NLRB elections, by contrast, the difference between single-union and multiple-union results is great, with unions winning about 87 percent of the latter in 1952–69 but only 57 percent of the former.[32] Since the 1955 merger of the AFL and the CIO, NLRB elections involving two or more unions have been about the same proportion as in government elections.

The attitude of government employers toward organization is undoubtedly a major factor in the success of employee organizations in public sector elections. Many private employers have strongly resisted organization of their employees by unions, while government employers have usually not opposed organization, and elected officials have often come out in support of collective bargaining for public employees in their jurisdictions. The relatively small number of charges of unfair labor practices brought by unions against public employers as compared to private further substantiates the difference in employer attitudes.[33]

Most local government elections have been for representation rights among small groups of employees. Almost half the elections have been held in units of 25 or fewer employees, and an additional 22 percent have involved units with 26 to 50 employees. At the other extreme, only 1 percent of the elections were in units of more than 1,000 employees and 14 percent in units with over 100 employees. Election units tended to be larger in New York than in the other three states. The same sorts of distribution by size have been found in NLRB elections conducted since 1952.[34]

A fourth of all the elections in local government jurisdictions have been held in units of nonacademic employees in schools, libraries, and museums, 20 percent in hospitals and health services, 19 percent in public works departments, and 15 percent in administrative services. Police and fire fighters have been involved in 9 percent of the elections, while supervisors, parks and recreation, and welfare and public assistance employees have each participated in 2 percent.

Despite the fact that AFSCME, employee associations, and government employers prefer broad units,[35] all-city and all-county units constituted only 12 percent of the election units in the four

32. Ibid., 1952–69 issues.

33. Ibid.; Michigan Employment Relations Commission, *Annual Report*, 1965–69 issues; and Wisconsin Employment Relations Commission, *Annual Report*, 1962–69 issues.

34. NLRB, *Annual Report*, 1936–69 issues.

35. ACIR, *Labor-Management Policies*, pp. 73–74; see also Derek C. Bok and John T. Dunlop, *Labor and the American Community* (Simon and Schuster, 1970), pp. 324–25.

TABLE 7-2. *Results of Representation Elections among Local Government Employees in Four States, by Number of Organizations Participating, 1962–69*

Type of election	Four states	Michigan	Wisconsin	Connecticut	New York
All elections					
Total number	1,284	719	363	116	86
Number and percent won by organization	1,129(88)	633(88)	318(88)	104(90)	74(86)
Number and percent won by no organization	155(12)	86(12)	45(12)	12(10)	12(14)
Single-organization elections					
Total number and percent of all elections	1,085(85)	615(86)	324(89)	103(89)	43(50)
Number and percent won by organization	939(87)	533(87)	281(87)	91(88)	34(79)
Number and percent won by no organization	146(13)	82(13)	43(13)	12(12)	9(21)
Multiple-organization elections					
Total number and percent of all elections	199(15)	104(14)	39(11)	13(11)	43(50)
Number and percent won by organization	190(95)	100(96)	37(95)	13(100)	40(93)
Number and percent won by no organization	9(5)	4(4)	2(5)	0(0)	3(7)

Source: Data supplied by state agencies. Percentages may not total 100 because of rounding.

states. Both unions and associations have a practice of requesting recognition as soon as they have succeeded in organizing a substantial proportion of employees in a particular department rather than waiting until they have achieved broad enough support throughout a governmental jurisdiction to petition for an election. Relatively narrow election units may also result from determinations by government boards when employee organizations and employers disagree on the appropriate unit. However, election units should not be confused with bargaining units. As in private industry, several election units often combine into one bargaining unit. This is most easily accomplished when a single organization represents employees in several departments, but is also possible when two or more organizations agree to conduct joint negotiations with a government employer.

ORGANIZATION PARTICIPATION

AFSCME participated in more than half of all the elections held in Michigan, Wisconsin, Connecticut, and New York during the years 1962–69 (see Table 7-3). Associations, the Teamsters union,

TABLE 7-3. *Results of Representation Elections among Local Government Employees in Four States, by Organization, 1962–69*

	Elections participated in		Elections won		Elections lost	
	Num-ber	Percent of all elections	Num-ber	Percent of col. 1	Num-ber	Percent of col. 1
Organization	(1)	(2)	(3)	(4)	(5)	(6)
All elections[a]	1,284	100	...	...	...	...
AFSCME	675	53	523	77	152	23
SEIU	111	9	78	70	33	30
Laborers	2	*	1	50	1	50
Teamsters	170	13	124	73	46	27
Building trades	25	2	23	92	2	8
IAFF	23	2	22	96	1	4
FOP	6	*	5	83	1	17
ANA	63	5	55	87	8	13
Other unions	184	14	134	73	50	27
Associations	233	18	164	70	69	30
No organization[b]	1,284	100	155	12	1,129	88

Source: Data supplied by state agencies.
a. Sum of organization figures exceeds total elections because some elections involve two or more organizations.
b . Denotes vote against all organizations on ballot.
*Less than 0.5 percent.

and SEIU have also been fairly frequent contenders. The Laborers' Union has been involved in only two elections and the Fraternal Order of Police in six. AFSCME's participation has been relatively lightest in New York—26 percent of all elections—and heaviest in Wisconsin, where it has been involved in 73 percent of all elections. Associations have been most active in New York, participating in 62 percent of all elections; in Wisconsin they were on the ballot in only 5 percent of the elections. Other organizations' election participation is more consistent among the four states.

The best records in representation elections are held by organizations that have participated relatively infrequently. Those most often involved in elections—AFSCME, SEIU, Teamsters, and associations—have won between 70 percent and 80 percent of the elections in which they participated. Each of the unions has done well in some states and poorly in others; while associations have fared about equally well in all four states.

Most of the organizations have a relatively poor won-lost record in large units, where both unions and associations often compete for representation rights. Thus, SEIU won only 7 out of 19 elections in units of more than 200 employees; the Teamsters won less than half of 23 elections in units of 101 to 1,000 and lost all 3 of its elections in units of more than 1,000 employees. Only AFSCME and employee associations won more elections than they lost in units of more than 200 employees. In 14 elections involving more than 1,000 employees, AFSCME and the associations won 6 each, SEIU was successful in 1, and the employees voted against representation in 1 unit. Conversely, all organizations had favorable won-lost records in elections involving units of less than 100 employees, which usually gave employees a choice of voting for one organization or no representation.

Except for AFSCME, which is active among almost all local government employees, organizations tend to concentrate their efforts in one or a few functions. Thus, the SEIU won most of its elections in hospitals and health services and in educational institutions, the Teamsters in public works and education, the building trades in public utilities, the nurses in hospitals and health services, and employee associations in administrative services, hospitals and health, education, and all-city and all-county units. The FOP and IAFF were active only in elections among police and fire protection employees.

When the various organizations have been in direct competition with one another—in 199 of the 1,284 elections—only the Teamsters have been able to win a majority of a large number of elections. Building trades, IAFF, and the nurses have also won more such elections than they have lost, but their contests have been few. The SEIU has won 46 percent of a fairly small number of contested elections. AFSCME and the employee associations, on the other hand, have either jointly or individually been involved in almost all of the contested elections, AFSCME winning 40 percent of those it entered, and the associations 44 percent of their contests. These two groups summarize fairly well the records of direct confrontations between competing organizations (see Table 7-4). While both have been more extensively involved than other organizations in elections for representation rights in New York, Connecticut, Michigan, and Wisconsin, in contests with those other organizations their opponents have competed effectively for the right to represent particular groups of public employees.

TABLE 7-4. *Winners in Representation Elections among Local Government Employees Involving AFSCME and Associations in Four States, 1962–69*

| | Election won by | | |
Contest	Principal contestant	Opponent	Neither
AFSCME (principal) versus			
Association	27	26	3
SEIU	3	7	0
Teamsters	17	23	1
ANA	2	3	0
Laborers, building trades, IAFF, FOP	1	6	0
Other unions	7	7	2
Association (principal) versus			
AFSCME	26	27	3
SEIU	6	3	0
Teamsters	9	13	0
ANA	3	5	0
Laborers, building trades, IAFF, FOP	2	1	0
Other unions	6	7	1

Source: Data supplied by state agencies.

Summary

Bargaining units in local government tend to be relatively small because they are limited to individual governmental jurisdictions and because each jurisdiction often contains several separate bargaining units. Consolidation of election units into larger bargaining units or multiemployer bargaining beyond the confines of a single city, county, or school district is favored by some unions and government officials. However, enlargement of bargaining units through these approaches may raise legal problems in public employment that do not exist in the private sector. May local governments with different constituencies and separate sources of financing enter into a common agreement? If not, may they bargain jointly but enter into separate agreements with employee organizations? These questions will certainly be raised during the 1970s and their resolution will have a profound effect on collective bargaining in local government. The issue has already been posed with respect to school districts in states that are considering replacing the local property tax with state financing as the major source of income to support public education. If school bargaining goes statewide, for both teaching and noninstructional personnel, it will have an important influence on bargaining in other units of local government.

There is already a discernible trend toward larger units within local governments. The problems of fragmented bargaining units have plagued some cities and counties, and many local governments have tried to minimize the number of units and organizations with which they negotiate. Experience with collective bargaining among state employees is more limited than in local government. However, decisions regarding appropriate units in several states—New York, New Jersey, Pennsylvania, and Hawaii, for example—have favored a small number of statewide units based on broad departmental or agency lines.

A major issue affecting the composition of bargaining units is the status of supervisors. Should supervisors have the right to bargain collectively? Should they be permitted to belong to and be represented by organizations that represent nonsupervisory employees? Should supervisors be permitted to bargain within the same units as nonsupervisory employees?

The answer to the first question, under almost all state laws, is "yes," and all public employee organizations favor collective bargaining for supervisors, a right denied them in private employment under the National Labor Relations Act. Public employee unions and associations are equally insistent on their right to enroll and represent both supervisory and nonsupervisory employees, either in the same or in separate locals or chapters. Employers have reservations about possible conflict of interest of supervisors who belong to the same organization as employees they supervise, but few jurisdictions prohibit such membership.

Employee organizations differ with respect to the question of supervisors and other employees being included in the same bargaining unit. Unions of nonuniformed employees generally favor separate units, but organizations of policemen, fire fighters, and nurses and state and local associations prefer all-inclusive units, arguing that in the uniformed services, nursing, and government employment generally, very few persons are really supervisors in the sense that the term is used in private industry.

The uniformed services and the nurses have had considerable success in persuading state legislatures and boards administering state laws to their view. Some laws and administrative decisions on appropriate bargaining units have included police and fire officers and head nurses and nurse supervisors in units with other employees. All-inclusive units are even more common in jurisdictions without laws, based on voluntary agreements between employee representatives and government employers. But during the last few years, administrative decisions appear to have been directing separate units for police and fire officers, and for supervisory nurses, with increasing frequency.

Separation of supervisory and nonsupervisory employees for bargaining purposes is likely to have a significant effect on the membership of organizations with substantial supervisory membership and leadership. There is already evidence of unions barring, or at least discouraging, supervisors from joining, or prohibiting them from holding office;[36] of local police associations being split into

36. A proposed constitutional amendment to prohibit supervisors from seeking local union office, other than that of trustee, in locals that include both supervisors and nonsupervisors was referred to the executive board by the 1972 AFSCME convention. (*Public Employee,* Vol. 37 [March 1972], p. 13, and letter to the author from AFSCME, Research Department, Aug. 7, 1972.)

separate organizations for patrolmen and officers; and of supervisors withdrawing from membership and leadership of their own accord in organizations that cannot represent them in bargaining. The differentiation between supervisory and nonsupervisory employees will probably become much sharper in all organizations during the 1970s.

Unions and associations have won nine out of every ten elections held in local government units in Wisconsin, Michigan, Connecticut, and New York—a much better record than that of unions during the early years of the Wagner Act or in any subsequent period of several years. The higher proportion of public employee organization victories may have been influenced by: (1) the virtual nonexistence of employer opposition in government elections, as compared with the efforts of many private employers to influence employees to vote against unions in NLRB elections; (2) considerable interorganization competition in public employment, leading to an unusual amount of campaigning by unions and associations; (3) greater employee acceptance of unions and other employee organizations as a result of over thirty-five years of experience under the National Labor Relations Act; (4) a feeling, on the part of public employees, that collective bargaining has been responsible for higher wages and fringe benefits in private industry than in public employment; (5) a fear among public employees, during a period of inflation and high wage settlements, that without collective bargaining they would fall even further behind private industry workers.

Experience in states with the oldest public employee relations laws and under the National Labor Relations Act indicates that the proportion of organization election victories will decline over time. But, given the large number of states that do not yet have such statutes and the recency of enactment of laws in many other states, unions and associations should continue to win a very high percentage of representation elections during the 1970s.

CHAPTER EIGHT

The Strike Issue

The greatest change in public employee relations, as far as the general public is concerned, has been the increased militancy of government workers as manifested in the tremendous increase in strikes. During the thirteen-year period 1958 through 1970 the total number of government strikes, including those called by teachers, rose from 15 to 412 per year, workers involved from 1,720 to 333,500, and man-days of idleness as a result of strikes from 7,510 to 2,023,200 (see Table 8-1). The year 1966 marked the transition from a relatively calm state of government labor relations to the comparative turbulence of recent years. In the years 1958–65 there were, on the average, 31 strikes each year, involving 13,714 workers and 50,501 days' work lost. But from 1966 through 1970 the average rose to 280 strikes each year, involving 186,460 workers and 1,403,-820 working days lost—9 times as many strikes, 14 times as many workers involved, and 28 times as many man-days lost as during the preceding eight years. Public employee strikes have increased at a much more rapid rate than strikes in the private sector. Whereas strikes in government constituted 0.4 percent of all strikes, 0.08 percent of the workers involved, and 0.03 percent of total idleness in 1958, these ratios had risen to 7.2 percent, 10.1 percent, and 3.0 percent, respectively, by 1970.[1]

1. All data in this chapter are from U.S. Bureau of Labor Statistics (BLS), *Work Stoppages in Government, 1958–68*, Report 348 (1970); BLS, "Government Work Stoppages, 1960, 1969, and 1970" (1971; processed); and BLS, "Work Stoppages in 1971" (1972; processed).

TABLE 8-1. *Work Stoppages among Government Employees, 1958–70*

Year	All stoppages			State government stoppages			Local government stoppages		
	Number	Workers involved	Man-days idle	Number	Workers involved	Man-days idle	Number	Workers involved	Man-days idle
1958	15	1,720	7,510	1	30	60	14	1,690	7,450
1959	26	2,240	11,500	4	410	1,650	22	1,830	9,850
1960	36	28,600	58,400	3	970	1,170	33	27,600	57,200
1961	28	6,610	15,300	...	...	...	28	6,610	15,300
1962	28[a]	31,100	79,100	2	1,660	2,260	21	25,300	43,100
1963	29	4,840	15,400	2	280	2,160	27	4,560	13,300
1964	41	22,700	70,800	4	280	3,170	37	22,500	67,700
1965	42	11,900	146,000	...	...	1,280[b]	42	11,900	145,000
1966	142	105,000	455,000	9	3,090	6,010	133	102,000	449,000
1967	181	132,000	1,250,000	12	4,670	16,300	169	127,000	1,239,000
1968	254[c]	201,800	2,545,200	16	9,300	42,800	235	190,900	2,492,800
1969	411[d]	160,000	745,700	37	20,500	152,400	372	139,000	592,200
1970	412[e]	333,500	2,023,200	23	8,800	44,600	386	168,900	1,330,500

Sources: U.S. Bureau of Labor Statistics, *Work Stoppages in Government, 1958–68*, Report 348 (1970), p. 9, and "Government Work Stoppages, 1960, 1969, and 1970" (1971; processed). Based on stoppages lasting a full day or shift or longer and involving 6 workers or more. Data on number of stoppages and workers involved refer to all stoppages beginning in the year; on man-days idle to those in effect during the year. Because of rounding, sums of individual items may not equal totals.
a. Includes 5 stoppages of federal employees, affecting 4,190 workers, and resulting in 33,800 man-days of idleness.
b. Idleness resulting from 2 stoppages that began in 1964.
c. Includes 3 stoppages of federal employees, affecting 1,680 workers, and resulting in 9,600 man-days of idleness.
d. Includes 2 stoppages of federal employees, affecting 600 workers, and resulting in 1,100 man-days of idleness.
e. Includes 3 stoppages of federal employees, affecting 155,800 workers, and resulting in 648,300 man-days of idleness.

Despite these large increases, strike activity among government employees remains low relative to work stoppages in the private sector. In 1966–70 only 1.5 percent of all government employees were involved in work stoppages, while 3.9 percent of all workers were so involved. The more significant comparison, however, is of workers in local government, where most public employee strikes occur; there, 2.1 percent of all employees were involved in work stoppages during this five-year period. Furthermore, the local government percentage has been increasing while the number of workers involved in all strikes, as a percentage of total employment, has remained fairly stable during the last decade.

Government employee strikes tend to be shorter than those in private industry, averaging only 5.5 days of idleness per worker in 1958–70 as compared with 16.8 among all workers. Again, however, the average in government strikes has tended to be longer during the last five years than previously: 7.4 days compared to 4.4 days. There has been no similar trend toward longer strikes in private industry.

Prior to 1966 the average number of workers involved in public employee strikes was generally smaller than in all stoppages. During 1966–70, however, government strikes were, on the average, larger than all strikes in four out of five years. For the five-year period, workers involved averaged 692 in government stoppages as compared with 522 in all strikes.

Geographically, public employee strikes have occurred most frequently in the Midwest, followed by the Northeast, South, and West, in that order. California, with 116 strikes during 1958–70, is the only western state that has experienced any sizable number of stoppages. Only four of the seventeen southern states have had more than 25 strikes during the thirteen-year period: Kentucky and North Carolina 35 each, Florida 34, and West Virginia 33. The three states experiencing the largest number of strikes—Michigan (234), Ohio (198), and Illinois (158)—are all located in the Midwest. In the Northeast, New York with 126 strikes, Pennsylvania with 104, and New Jersey with 82 accounted for almost 75 percent of all strikes in that region.

In numbers of workers involved and man-days lost, New York State—and specifically New York City—makes the Northeast the most active region. The 1968 New York City teachers' strike, which

TABLE 8-2. *Local Government Strikes, by Organization Involved, 1965–69*

Organization	1965–69	Number and percent of year's total strikes				
		1965	1966	1967	1968	1969
AFSCME	187(34)	12(32)	32(32)	25(30)	57(38)	61(33)
SEIU	34(6)	3(8)	10(10)	3(4)	7(5)	11(6)
Teamsters	45(8)	4(11)	5(5)	6(7)	13(9)	17(9)
Laborers	15(3)	1(3)	2(2)	3(4)	4(3)	5(3)
Building trades	32(6)	4(11)	4(4)	3(4)	11(7)	8(4)
IAFF	18(3)	0(0)	2(2)	5(6)	11(7)	11(6)
FOP	9(2)	0(0)	2(2)	2(2)	3(2)	5(3)
PBAs	6(1)	0(0)	0(0)	1(1)	3(2)	3(2)
Associations	44(8)	1(3)	12(12)	8(10)	13(9)	10(5)
Other	50(9)	4(11)	11(11)	11(13)	12(8)	12(7)
No organization	114(21)	8(22)	23(23)	20(24)	23(15)	40(22)
Total	554(100)	37(7[a])	101(18[a])	84(15[a])	149(27[a])	183(33[a])

Source: U.S. Bureau of Labor Statistics, unpublished data. Percentages may not add to 100 because of rounding.
a. Percent of total over 1965–69 period.

involved 47,000 teachers, lasted 55 days, and resulted in the loss of 1,645,000 man-days, represents 65 percent of the time lost due to all strikes that year. States in the South have the dubious distinction of being second only to those in the Northeast when it comes to the intensity of strike activity. Though southern states experienced less than half as many strikes as states in the Midwest during the period under study, these disputes involved more workers and resulted in more man-days of idleness than did those in the Midwest. Not only do strikes in the South tend to be larger, but it appears that government employers in the South put up greater resistance to union demands than employers in the Midwest.

Clearly, there is little relationship between the incidence of government strikes and state laws regulating labor relations in public employment. Michigan, one of the three states with the largest number of strikes, has had a comprehensive law since 1965, while Ohio and Illinois, the other two, have no state statute providing collective bargaining for public employees. Other state patterns are similarly inconclusive. The one effect of laws that can be documented is that they reduce greatly the number of strikes over the issue of union recognition. But other issues, particularly wages, have apparently increased the number of strikes sufficiently to more than compensate for the elimination of union recognition as an important issue in states with public employment laws.

Strikes in Local Government, 1965–69

While federal and state employees have shared in the changes that have been occurring in government labor-management relations, strike action has been heavily concentrated among employees in cities, counties, school districts, and other local government jurisdictions. The organizations involved, functions affected, duration, and issues in dispute in 554 strikes in local government (excluding work stoppages involving only school teachers) during the period 1965–69 are presented in Tables 8-2 through 8-7.

Approximately one-third of all local stoppages during the five-year period, and in each year, involved local unions or councils affiliated with the American Federation of State, County and Municipal Employees (AFSCME), as Table 8-2 indicates. The major

TABLE 8-3. *Local Government Strikes, by Function Affected, 1965–69*

	Strikes in function		Number and percent of strikes affecting	
Function	Number	As percent of all strikes[a]	Single function	Two or more functions
Sanitation	203	37	83(*41*)	120(*59*)
Streets	165	30	22(*13*)	143(*87*)
Water	89	16	8(*9*)	81(*91*)
Sewage	92	17	7(*8*)	85(*92*)
Parks	65	12	5(*8*)	60(*92*)
Housing	13	2	12(*92*)	1(*8*)
Administration	32	6	2(*6*)	30(*94*)
Police	51	9	29(*57*)	22(*43*)
Fire	39	7	17(*44*)	22(*56*)
Hospitals	62	11	57(*92*)	5(*8*)
Social service	22	4	17(*77*)	5(*23*)
Noninstructional education	71	13	70(*99*)	1(*1*)
Other	64	12	47(*73*)	17(*27*)

Source: U.S. Bureau of Labor Statistics, unpublished data.

a. Total of 554 strikes. The number of strikes by function affected exceeds the total because many strikes affect two or more functions.

mixed unions—the Service Employees International Union (SEIU), the International Brotherhood of Teamsters, and the Laborers' International Union—together accounted for 17 percent of the strikes. Associations accounted for 8 percent and the uniformed services— the International Association of Fire Fighters (IAFF), the Fraternal Order of Police (FOP), and various police benevolent associations —for 6 percent of the total. One strike out of five involved no organized group of government employees. The total number of strikes increased each year except 1967, so that by 1969 there were five times as many strikes as in 1965.

Sanitation services and street maintenance were affected by local government strikes far more frequently than other functions. The data in Table 8-3 suggest a relationship between organizational activity and stoppages: those functions that have been the target of organizing efforts and demands for union recognition in recent years have experienced more strikes than those in which employees have been organized for some time (usually by nonunion associations).

Strikes in local government often affect more than one function because the organization calling the strike represents workers in several departments. Employees in sanitation, streets, water supply, sewage, and parks, for instance, often belong to the same union—generally AFSCME—and frequently act together in strikes; 60–90 percent of the strikes in these services shown in Table 8-3 involved two or more functions. Strikes are sometimes called jointly by two or more unions—about half of those in the protective services were joint efforts, usually involving organizations of police and fire fighters. Union strategy is to put pressure on the government employer by involving employees in at least one essential service. Strikes of employees in administration almost always were conducted in concert with other functions, probably because administrative employees do not usually perform services of sufficient urgency to the public to permit them to conduct a successful strike by themselves. Noninstructional employees in schools and employees in hospitals, housing, and social service were most often involved in single-function strikes. Schools and hospitals are sufficiently important to public health and welfare to enable employees to strike without help from other workers, while housing and social service employees often are members of different organizations than those representing other government employees. Employees considered vital to public safety, health, welfare, and convenience were frequently involved in strikes that did not affect other government activities.

The diversity of government activities that the various employee organizations are involved in is reflected in Table 8-4. AFSCME, for example, took part in strikes affecting every governmental function. At least half the AFSCME strikes affected sanitation or street maintenance, and one out of four affected water supply, sewage disposal, and parks and recreation. Strikes by the three mixed unions tend to be concentrated in sanitation and street maintenance and a few other functions. For the employee associations, including nurses, about one-third of all strikes have been in hospitals, and all stoppages involving the IAFF, FOP, and police benevolent associations (PBAs) have been in the protective services. Workers belonging to no union or association have conducted stoppages affecting every type of local government activity except housing.

Public employee strikes usually last only a few days. The mean duration of all local government strikes was about nine days and

TABLE 8-4. *Local Government Strikes, by Function and Organization, 1965–69*

| | All strikes | | Number of strikes and percent of total strikes by | | | | | | | | | | |
Function	Num-ber	Percent of total strikes	AFSCME	SEIU	Team-sters	Laborers	Building trades	IAFF	FOP	PBAs	Associa-tions	Other orga-nization	No orga-nization
Sanitation	203	37	89(48)	8(24)	24(53)	8(53)	5(16)	0(0)	0(0)	0(0)	7(16)	12(24)	50(44)
Streets	165	30	89(48)	6(18)	20(44)	10(67)	6(19)	0(0)	0(0)	0(0)	6(14)	10(20)	18(16)
Water	89	16	50(27)	4(12)	7(16)	4(27)	5(16)	0(0)	0(0)	0(0)	3(7)	7(14)	9(8)
Sewage	92	17	51(27)	2(6)	7(16)	3(20)	7(22)	0(0)	0(0)	0(0)	4(9)	6(12)	12(11)
Parks	65	12	43(23)	1(3)	4(9)	2(13)	2(6)	0(0)	0(0)	0(0)	3(7)	5(10)	5(4)
Housing	13	2	5(3)	3(9)	1(2)	1(7)	3(9)	0(0)	0(0)	0(0)	0(0)	0(0)	0(0)
Administration	32	6	24(13)	0(0)	1(2)	1(7)	0(0)	0(0)	0(0)	0(0)	3(7)	1(2)	2(2)
Police	51	9	3(2)	0(0)	0(0)	2(13)	0(0)	0(0)	9(100)	6(100)	7(16)	5(10)	19(17)
Fire	39	7	1(1)	0(0)	0(0)	2(13)	0(0)	18(100)	1(11)	0(0)	2(5)	7(14)	8(7)
Hospital	62	11	20(11)	8(24)	0(0)	0(0)	0(0)	0(0)	0(0)	0(0)	15(34)	7(14)	12(11)
Social service	22	4	7(4)	4(12)	0(0)	0(0)	1(3)	0(0)	0(0)	0(0)	3(7)	6(12)	1(1)
Noninstructional education	71	13	27(14)	6(18)	6(13)	1(7)	3(9)	0(0)	0(0)	0(0)	9(20)	3(6)	16(14)
Other	64	12	19(10)	3(9)	3(7)	2(13)	15(47)	0(0)	0(0)	0(0)	3(7)	10(20)	9(8)
Total	554	100	187(100)	34(100)	45(100)	15(100)	32(100)	18(100)	9(100)	6(100)	44(100)	50(100)	114(100)

Source: U.S. Bureau of Labor Statistics, unpublished data. Percentages may not add to 100 because many strikes affect two or more functions.

the median four days (see Tables 8-5 and 8-6).[2] One out of every five was settled within one day, and half the stoppages lasted three days or less. About 30 percent of the strikes continued for over a week and one out of twelve lasted more than four weeks. The expected inverse relationship between essentiality of the service affected and strike duration, while fairly close, did not always occur. Thus, while strikes of policemen, fire fighters, and sanitation workers were among the shortest, stoppages affecting housing and parks were equally short. By far the longest strikes have occurred in social services, a relatively nonessential activity for the general public. Strikes affecting "administration" have also been relatively long. Strikes in hospitals and water supply and sewage disposal, usually considered essential services, have been above average in mean duration but relatively short in terms of median duration, reflecting a small number of very long stoppages in each of these functions. The fact that some struck functions lend themselves more easily than others to continued operation, though at a diminished level, due to automation and supervisors or other employees doing strikers' work also explains why some stoppages continue for a long time. The Laborers appear to have a predilection for long strikes, while organizations in the protective services rarely engage in strikes that last more than a week. In general, strike duration appears to be more closely related to the function affected than to the organization involved.

The point has often been made that strikes in public employment occur frequently over the issue of union recognition because many states do not have laws governing collective bargaining in government.[3] Table 8-7 shows that recognition is indeed an important issue, involved in almost one out of every four strikes. Sixty percent of the Laborers' Union strikes were over the issue of recognition, and one-third of AFSCME and Teamster strikes. Only two IAFF and no police stoppages were over this issue, reflecting their longer existence and greater acceptance by municipal authorities. The number of recognition strikes has decreased substantially

2. The mean duration of strikes varies between Table 8-5 (8.9 days) and Table 8-6 (9.5 days) because each strike is counted once by organization but frequently more than once by function. The lower mean in Table 8-5 indicates that multifunction strikes tend to be shorter than single-function strikes.

3. Advisory Commission on Intergovernmental Relations, *Labor-Management Policies for State and Local Government* (Washington: ACIR, 1969), pp. 94, 96, 145.

TABLE 8-5. *Local Government Strikes, by Function and Duration, 1965–69*

Function	All strikes	Number of strikes and percent of strikes in that function lasting								Mean number of days	Median number of days
		1 day	*2 days*	*3 days*	*4–7 days*	*8–14 days*	*15–28 days*	*29–42 days*	*More than 42 days*		
Sanitation	203	37(18)	37(18)	30(15)	49(24)	25(12)	19(9)	1(0)	5(2)	7.1	3.0
Streets	165	27(16)	22(13)	24(15)	39(24)	27(16)	19(12)	3(2)	4(2)	8.5	4.0
Water	89	9(10)	17(19)	14(16)	16(18)	10(11)	15(17)	1(1)	7(8)	11.8	4.0
Sewage	92	12(13)	14(15)	18(20)	19(21)	13(14)	13(14)	0(0)	3(3)	9.2	4.0
Parks	65	9(14)	10(15)	18(28)	11(17)	7(11)	9(14)	0(0)	1(2)	6.9	3.0
Housing	13	5(38)	2(15)	2(15)	1(8)	1(8)	2(15)	0(0)	0(0)	5.0	2.0
Administration	32	2(6)	2(6)	6(19)	9(28)	6(19)	6(19)	1(3)	0(0)	8.6	6.0
Police	51	14(27)	9(18)	7(14)	12(24)	6(12)	2(4)	1(2)	0(0)	4.9	3.0
Fire	39	8(21)	7(18)	7(18)	9(23)	2(5)	4(10)	2(5)	0(0)	6.5	3.0
Hospitals	62	13(21)	8(13)	10(16)	8(13)	8(13)	4(6)	5(8)	6(10)	14.8	3.5
Social service	22	2(9)	1(5)	1(5)	2(9)	4(18)	5(23)	1(5)	6(27)	29.4	15.5
Noninstructional education	71	18(25)	13(18)	3(4)	19(27)	4(6)	8(11)	3(4)	3(4)	8.4	4.0
Other	64	12(19)	13(20)	11(17)	9(14)	9(14)	5(8)	5(8)	0(0)	6.7	3.0
Total	968	168(17)	155(16)	151(16)	203(21)	122(13)	111(11)	23(2)	35(4)	8.9	4.0

Source: U.S. Bureau of Labor Statistics, unpublished data. Percentages may not add to 100 because of rounding.

TABLE 8-6. *Local Government Strikes, by Organization and Duration, 1965–69*

Organization	All strikes	Number of strikes and percent of strikes by that organization lasting								Mean number of days	Median number of days
		1 day	2 days	3 days	4–7 days	8–14 days	15–28 days	29–42 days	More than 42 days		
AFSCME	187	40(21)	20(11)	25(13)	42(22)	25(13)	22(12)	5(3)	8(4)	9.4	4.0
SEIU	34	10(29)	7(21)	5(15)	4(12)	1(3)	1(3)	3(9)	3(9)	14.5	3.0
Teamsters	45	11(24)	11(24)	5(11)	9(20)	5(11)	3(7)	0(0)	1(2)	7.8	3.0
Laborers	15	0(0)	2(13)	1(7)	3(20)	4(27)	2(13)	1(7)	2(13)	18.1	8.0
Building trades	32	4(12)	5(16)	3(9)	3(9)	8(25)	5(16)	1(3)	3(9)	13.4	3.0
IAFF	18	3(17)	4(22)	4(22)	5(28)	0(0)	1(6)	1(6)	0(0)	6.2	4.0
FOP	9	3(33)	0(0)	1(11)	3(33)	1(11)	1(11)	0(0)	0(0)	4.0	4.0
PBAs	6	4(67)	0(0)	0(0)	2(33)	0(0)	0(0)	0(0)	0(0)	3.0	1.0
Associations	44	12(27)	9(20)	5(11)	9(20)	3(7)	3(7)	1(2)	2(5)	7.0	3.0
Other	50	4(8)	8(16)	8(16)	8(16)	11(22)	4(8)	2(4)	5(10)	15.4	8.0
No organization	114	25(22)	24(21)	22(19)	23(20)	10(9)	5(4)	2(2)	3(3)	6.6	3.0
Total	554	116(21)	90(16)	79(14)	111(20)	68(12)	47(8)	16(3)	27(5)	9.5	4.0

Source: U.S. Bureau of Labor Statistics, unpublished data. Percentages may not add to 100 because of rounding.

TABLE 8-7. *Local Government Strikes, by Issue and Organization, 1965–69*

Organization	All strikes	Recognition	Wages	Paid time off	Fringe benefits	Union security	Work rules	Written contract	Contract enforcement	Other
		Number of strikes and percent of strikes by that organization involving								
AFSCME	187	59(32)	126(67)	19(10)	35(19)	22(12)	26(14)	20(11)	9(5)	40(21)
SEIU	34	7(21)	21(62)	3(9)	4(12)	2(6)	10(29)	1(3)	4(12)	6(18)
Teamsters	45	14(31)	30(67)	4(9)	9(20)	1(2)	6(13)	1(2)	1(2)	7(16)
Laborers	15	9(60)	10(67)	1(7)	3(20)	2(13)	1(7)	2(13)	1(7)	2(13)
Building trades	32	5(16)	21(66)	3(9)	8(25)	2(6)	4(12)	1(3)	1(3)	6(19)
IAFF	18	2(11)	18(100)	1(6)	1(6)	0(0)	0(0)	2(11)	0(0)	7(39)
FOP	9	0(0)	8(89)	0(0)	0(0)	0(0)	0(0)	0(0)	0(0)	0(0)
PBAs	6	0(0)	6(100)	0(0)	0(0)	0(0)	2(22)	0(0)	1(11)	1(17)
Associations	44	9(20)	37(84)	5(11)	6(14)	1(2)	2(5)	1(2)	0(0)	12(27)
Other	50	17(34)	34(68)	3(6)	4(8)	3(6)	7(14)	4(8)	3(6)	12(24)
No organization	114	8(7)	85(75)	7(6)	9(8)	0(0)	13(11)	0(0)	2(2)	18(16)
Total	554	130(23[a])	396(71[a])	46(8[a])	79(14[a])	33(6[a])	71(13[a])	32(6[a])	22(4[a])	111(20[a])

Source: U.S. Bureau of Labor Statistics, unpublished data.
a. Percentage of all strikes in which this is an issue.

as states have enacted public employment relations laws; these strikes could be practically eliminated if a federal statute were enacted.

Most strikes in both private and public employment involve wages either exclusively or as one of the issues in dispute. In 1965–69, 71 percent of all local government stoppages were, at least in part, over wages. Other issues were far less recurrent, some of them appearing to be important only in strikes of specific organizations.

The data on local government strikes indicate that work stoppages by public employees are becoming more like those in private industry. The number and types of organizations willing to engage in concerted action is growing, as are the functions and services affected by strikes and the issues over which stoppages are called. There are still, however, two significant differences between strikes in the public and private sectors, one of which is expected to be transitory and the other more permanent.

A sizable number of strikes in government involve unorganized workers, a phenomenon that rarely occurs in private industry. This probably reflects the newness of organization, the poor contact between workers ripe for organization and public employee unions, and the absence of legislation and procedures for recognition and bargaining in many states and local governments. Spontaneous strikes by unorganized workers were also common in private industry before the passage and during the early years of the Wagner Act when unions could not move rapidly enough to reach the many workers wanting to be organized. Strikes by unorganized groups of workers can be expected to decrease in government just as they have in private industry.

Strikes in public employment, though they have been lengthening over the years, are still of much shorter duration than those in the private sector. This difference reflects a combination of factors: practically all government strikes are unlawful and are often stopped by court injunctions; public pressures for early settlement are much greater than in private industry; government employers put up less resistance to union demands than private employers because elected officials are loath to risk the political consequences of long strikes; and union leaders and workers in essential services exercise self-restraint in calling and continuing strikes because they recognize the serious consequences that may result. These inhibiting factors are likely to continue and therefore public employee strikes should also continue, on the average, to be much shorter than strikes in the private sector.

Organizational Attitudes toward Strikes

All public employee organizations have had to deal with the strike issue. For unions, the legal prohibition on strikes against the government has conflicted with the traditional trade union belief that the right to strike is an essential element of collective bargaining. In addition to the legal prohibition, which applies to all government employees, the danger to the public inherent in strike action has placed severe moral restraints on police and fire fighter organizations. For civil service employee associations, the presumption that the protection and security provided by civil service made strikes, or even collective bargaining, unnecessary ruled out, until recently, serious consideration of the strike issue. And until the mid-1960s, strikes were regarded by associations as a form of behavior that might be appropriate for blue collar workers but not for professionals.

The increase in organization among public employees and the advent of collective bargaining in government have been accompanied by increased militancy and a change in the attitudes of public employee organizations. Constitutional prohibitions against strikes have been eliminated and organizations have engaged in work stoppages and a wide range of pressure tactics that varied according to the kinds of employees involved and the nature of the work performed.

The official attitudes of unions of nonuniformed government employees have changed less than those of other public employee organizations. The only restriction the AFSCME constitution has ever contained on strikes—applying only to police and other law enforcement officers—was removed in 1970.[4] Of the major mixed unions, only the Teamsters has a constitutional prohibition on

4. *Convention Proceedings, 18th International Convention, American Federation of State, County and Municipal Employees, AFL-CIO (AFSCME Proceedings)* (1970), pp. 287–88.

strikes against government employers.[5] It reportedly was inserted in the constitution in 1961 to satisfy a legal requirement in some states and localities that only unions that prohibited public employee strikes could be recognized for purposes of collective bargaining. This provision has obviously not inhibited the Teamsters from striking against government employers, for during the period 1965–69, Teamster public employee locals were involved in more strikes than locals of any other union except AFSCME (see Table 8-2). The two unions with the largest membership among state and local government employees—AFSCME and SEIU—have publicly opposed legislation prohibiting public employee strikes and penalizing those who engage in or lead such strikes, and have favored specific recognition by law of the right of government workers to strike.[6]

AFSCME

While AFSCME has always insisted on the right to strike, its attitude on the strike issue has changed considerably over the years. The union's early leaders supported local strikes against employers who refused to bargain or meet with union representatives but discouraged strikes for economic objectives.[7] Prior to 1966, the number of strikes called by AFSCME and other all-public employee unions, including the teachers' union, was exceeded in every year by strikes conducted by mixed unions.[8] This situation changed during the last half of the 1960s. Not only did the leaders of the all-public employee unions start talking tougher, but they also started to behave in a more militant manner.

In AFSCME, the authority to call a strike or to accept an agreement to end a strike resides in the local union, not in the international.[9] In every year since 1966, AFSCME locals have engaged in more public employee strikes than all the major mixed unions,

5. Constitution, International Brotherhood of Teamsters, Chauffeurs, Warehousemen, and Helpers of America (1971), Art. 12, sec. 13.

6. ACIR, *Labor-Management Policies*, pp. 121–23, 151–58.

7. Leo Kramer, *Labor's Paradox—The American Federation of State, County, and Municipal Employees, AFL-CIO* (Wiley, 1962), p. 51.

8. BLS, *Work Stoppages in Government, 1958–68*, pp. 6–7, 13–14.

9. *AFSCME Proceedings* (1968), p. 383. However, some councils require council approval before a strike may be called.

including the building trades, combined. Approximately half of the forty AFSCME council and local union representatives interviewed for this study were involved in at least one government strike during the 1960s, and those who were not said that they would not hesitate to recommend such action to their members if the occasion called for it. Only leaders of AFSCME police locals and a few staff members in the South and West expressed reservations about the use of the strike weapon. The director of a southern council was opposed to strikes because of their potential for stirring up racial conflict. In the state of Washington, both councils require local unions to obtain council approval before engaging in any kind of job action, and one director said: "The day of the strike is over because the public is fed up with public employee stoppages." An Oregon representative considered his locals too weak to carry out an effective strike and therefore preferred other pressure tactics such as slowdowns, informational picketing, and sick calls.

AFSCME local unions have engaged in many long strikes in all parts of the country. The most famous was the 1968 Memphis strike over union recognition which lasted nine weeks and was settled only after the assassination of Martin Luther King, who had come to Memphis to address the strikers. In Akron, Ohio, 750 nonprofessional hospital employees struck for 65 days to force a representation election;[10] in Cincinnati a one-month strike was triggered by a lower wage increase offered to 2,000 nonuniformed workers than had been granted to police and fire fighters;[11] a stoppage over dismissal of a local union chapter chairman in Little Rock, Arkansas, lasted eight months;[12] and, in what may be the longest strike in public employment, 130 Garrett County, Maryland, road workers won recognition for their union after a stoppage lasting 207 days.[13]

10. Bureau of National Affairs, *Government Employee Relations Report (GERR)*, No. 317 (Oct. 6, 1969), p. B-10; No. 318 (Oct. 13, 1969), p. B-13.

11. *New York Times*, Jan. 31, 1970; *GERR*, No. 331 (Jan. 12, 1970), p. B-10; No. 335 (Feb. 9, 1970), p. B-2; and No. 337 (Feb. 23, 1970), p. B-15; *Public Employee*, Vol. 36 (July 1971), p. 14. A local lawyer filed a taxpayer's suit to block agreed upon pay raises to the strikers, on the ground that the increases violated Ohio's Ferguson Act, which prohibits strikes and specifies that striking workers who are rehired must receive prestrike wages for one year. His suit was upheld in the lower courts, but the Supreme Court of Ohio ruled in favor of the union.

12. *GERR*, No. 366 (Sept. 14, 1970), p. B-15; *GERR*, No. 470 (Sept. 18, 1972), pp. B-4–B-6.

13. *GERR*, No. 349 (May 18, 1970), p. B-15; No. 364 (Aug. 31, 1970), p. B-12; *Public Employee*, Vol. 35 (November 1970), p. 3.

MIXED UNIONS

The national officers of mixed unions have been less vocal in support of public employee strikes than the AFSCME leadership. This probably is a reflection of their lack of preoccupation with government employees rather than of a basic difference in attitude toward strikes against the government. The greater decentralization in the structure of the mixed unions and differences in leadership style may also account for the different public image they project on the subject of public employee strikes. Regardless of these differences, local unions affiliated with the SEIU, Laborers, Teamsters, and the building trades accounted for 23 percent of all local stoppages during the five-year period 1965–69 (see Table 8-2).

Strike activity by SEIU local unions has been concentrated in California, where representatives of every one of the seven locals interviewed for this study have been involved in one or more strikes. Among the important strikes conducted by California SEIU locals were two in Los Angeles, involving some 2,000 social service employees in a dispute over wages, that lasted a total of 23 days and led to the enactment of the County Employee Relations Ordinance of 1968.[14] A Sacramento strike of 217 County Welfare Department employees over salary demands and union recognition resulted in the discharge of the workers involved.[15] Three SEIU locals as well as a few other unions and the California Nurses' Association accounting for about half of San Francisco's 14,000 employees struck for four days in 1970 over pay and the right to engage in collective bargaining.[16]

In Pittsburgh, both strikes and strike threats were deemed too risky by SEIU leaders because most of their members were not protected by civil service and feared for their jobs. The importance of civil service protection as a contributing factor to employee militancy was also underscored by the representative of a Boston SEIU local. Locals in New York, Chicago, Seattle, and Portland, Oregon, reported no strike action.

The Laborers' Union, which has fewer state and local government members than either of the other mixed unions, has also had

14. Paul D. Staudohar, "Strikes and Rights of Public Employees in California," *California Public Employee Relations,* No. 7 (November 1970), pp. 7–8.
15. Ibid., p. 6.
16. Ibid., p. 8.

fewer strikes. During the period 1965–69, public employee locals affiliated with the Laborers took part in only fifteen strikes (see Table 8-2). Perhaps the most publicized, though unsuccessful, Laborers' strike involved 3,400 state road maintenance workers in West Virginia, appointed under a patronage system, who demanded union recognition and job security when the Republicans took office after eight years of Democratic rule. After a blizzard caused mammoth traffic tie-ups and accidents, the governor appeared on television and announced that he was firing all the strikers.[17]

Laborers' Union business agents have been cautious in calling strikes. Several favor compulsory arbitration and would prefer to use other tactics that would not be in violation of the law. For example, in October 1969, members of a Laborers' local in Milwaukee representing 300 street and engineering department employees refused to work overtime in order to enforce demands for a $75 biweekly wage increase. A union official explained the strategy: "We figure this is our only weapon. We can't strike according to state statute. When the snow flies, we'll just work our eight hours and go home, like everybody else does."[18] In Providence, Rhode Island, the Laborers representative reasoned that if he had to call a strike to force the city to live up to its contract, he should wait until spring, when he could find jobs for strikers in private construction. The Seattle business agent of a Laborers local who would choose more "subtle ways" to bring pressure on politicians than strikes, which involve risks of court action, refuses to specify what they are.

The most famous recent strike of a Teamster government local was the February 1968, nine-day stoppage by 10,000 New York City sanitation workers which brought the mayor and governor into an angry confrontation and resulted in a fifteen-day jail sentence for the local union president and an $80,000 fine for the union. Cancellation of the checkoff of union dues, an additional penalty invoked at the time of the strike and affirmed by the United States Supreme Court, was never enforced by the city. In July 1970,

---

17. *Business Week*, Sept. 27, 1969, p. 54. The union's suit for reinstatement of the strikers, back pay, recognition, and job security rights was denied by district and circuit courts and was appealed to the United States Supreme Court.

18. *GERR*, No. 320 (Oct. 27, 1969), p. B-11.

Mayor Lindsay agreed not to cancel the checkoff if the union did not engage in any strike action before April 1, 1973.[19]

INTERNATIONAL ASSOCIATION OF FIRE FIGHTERS

The strike issue has been a perennial subject of debate at IAFF conventions throughout the fifty-year history of the union. The original IAFF constitution, adopted in 1918, asserted that strikes by fire fighters were "inadvisable" and made financial assistance to strikers dependent on prior sanction of the strike by the international. Since the international had only limited financial resources and no strike fund, this amounted to minimal control over strikes.

Immediately after the IAFF was organized, strikes occurred in a number of cities.[20] The Boston police strike in the summer of 1919, however, dealt a blow to fire fighters as well as policemen. IAFF locals in Boston, Washington, D.C., and some fifty other cities were dissolved in the year following the strike.[21] In the wake of the Boston strike and a strike of Memphis fire fighters shortly thereafter, the IAFF president sought authority that would have required locals to surrender their charters if they took strike action without submitting disputes for international consideration. The 1920 convention, however, voted to forbid locals to issue an "ultimatum" to city officials or take other "decisive action" until they had received replies from the international executive committee to requests for permission to take strike action.[22] The entire provision was deleted in 1930 when the convention voted an outright prohibition on strikes.[23] In 1936 the international showed it meant business when it revoked the charter of the Vancouver, British Columbia, local union for voting strike action, even though it did not actually strike.[24]

During the next thirty years, several efforts were made at IAFF

19. *New York Times,* Feb. 2–10, 1968, and July 2, 1970; *GERR,* No. 234 (March 4, 1968), p. B-1.
20. Rudolph A. Oswald, "Is Compulsory Arbitration a Proper Tool of Public Policy? A Case Study" (Ph.D. dissertation, Georgetown University, 1965), p. 41.
21. Ibid., p. 44.
22. *Convention Proceedings of the Third Annual Convention of the International Association of Fire Fighters (IAFF Proceedings)* (1920), p. 108.
23. *IAFF Proceedings* (1930), p. 61.
24. Oswald, "Compulsory Arbitration," p. 48.

conventions to delete or weaken the constitutional prohibition on strikes, all without success. In 1964 the convention reaffirmed the "no strike" provision by an almost unanimous vote.[25] However, two years later, opposition to the "no strike" policy had become so strong that the IAFF leadership agreed to appoint a commission "to review, reappraise, reaffirm, modify or reject" the constitutional prohibition on strikes.[26]

The commission was chaired by the president of the Railway Clerks, who was also a vice-president of the AFL-CIO; its members were a Catholic priest, the general counsel and two vice-presidents of the IAFF, one local union president, and, rather surprisingly, four employer members.[27] The commission recommended unanimously that the "no strike" provision in the constitution be replaced by an agreement not to withhold fire protection services, but where procedures for resolving disputes were not available, to "refer the matter to the International President and the International Executive Board for such further handling as may be available or necessary to secure an acceptable settlement of the dispute."[28]

Delegates to the 1968 convention, however, were in no mood for halfway measures. By a six-to-one vote, they adopted an amendment to delete from the constitution any reference to strikes.[29] Only locals from the South were generally opposed to the deletion. By its action on the strike issue the IAFF returned decision making on this important matter to the locals, where it was fifty years ago when the international was organized.[30]

The sharp reversal in attitude by convention delegates between 1964 and 1968 was influenced in part by recent fire fighter strikes in a number of cities—Atlanta, Youngstown, St. Louis, Kansas City,

25. *IAFF Proceedings* (1964), pp. 270–72.

26. "Report and Recommendations of the International Association of Fire Fighters' Fact Finding and Review Commission," Jan. 10, 1968, p. 1.

27. The employer representatives were the general manager of the National Fire Protection Association, the executive director of the League of Wisconsin Municipalities, and two city managers.

28. "Report of the IAFF's Review Commission," pp. 15–16.

29. "Resolutions as Adopted by 1968 Convention," IAFF Resolution No. 18.

30. Another attempt to give the international some measure of control over strikes by locals failed at the 1972 convention when a constitutional amendment to establish guidelines that would have to be met by locals seeking assistance from the union's Emergency Disputes Fund was defeated. (Leon E. Lunden, "International Association of Fire Fighters Convention," *Monthly Labor Review*, October 1972, pp. 54–55.)

Lansing—that had won major gains and had not been met by repressive legislation. Strikes by other public employee unions and associations—teachers, nurses, sanitation workers, even police—encouraged a "why not us, too" feeling among fire fighters. Another factor was the membership's unhappiness with the IAFF leadership, particularly the president, whose support of the commission's recommendation did not help and may even have contributed to its defeat.

During the two years before the 1970 convention, fire fighter local unions engaged in approximately a hundred "strike situations." These included not only actual work stoppages but also strike threats, slowdowns, mass sickness, and other job actions.[31] In 1969 there were 11 strikes by IAFF locals, more than twice as many as during the previous two years (see Table 8-2). Strikes occurred in all parts of the country, but were concentrated in the Midwest.

Membership participation in strikes has been very high and, generally, only the very top fire officers and probationary employees have remained on the job. Wages, often coupled with parity pay with police, were the major issue in almost every dispute. The strikes have almost always been of short duration, lasting from a few hours to a few days, and rarely more than a week. Many IAFF locals that have not struck have threatened to do so during the course of negotiations. Others have engaged in demonstrations or used other pressure tactics in support of their demands.

Despite the increased militancy among fire fighters, many union leaders are fearful of strikes and wish to avoid strike action if at all possible. Removal of the constitutional prohibition on strikes has enabled IAFF locals to bargain more aggressively for pay and other benefits even though they have no intention of striking. A number of local unions have retained no-strike provisions in their local constitutions, and many favor binding arbitration either by law or by contractual agreement.

POLICE ORGANIZATIONS

Until 1970, all police organizations had constitutional prohibitions against participation in strikes. In 1970, AFSCME removed its ban on stoppages by police locals, and in 1971 the International Conference of Police Associations took similar action. The Frater-

31. *Reports, 30th Convention, IAFF* (1970), p. 7.

nal Order of Police and the SEIU National Union of Police Officers (NUPO) continue to prohibit strikes by their members.

The FOP penalty is "immediate expulsion" for any member or lodge engaging in strike action.[32] However, in 1968 the FOP president, in a widely publicized statement after three Cleveland policemen were killed by black militants, suggested that a "two-day holiday" might be in order to call attention to the policeman's problems. The FOP executive board shortly thereafter reiterated disapproval of "any walkout or cessation of duties" and stated that "it would be disastrous for any community to be unprotected, particularly during these critical times when crime on the streets is one of the major issues facing the country." The board urged police to bring their grievances before the public through civil, fraternal, and other organizations and through the news media, rather than by engaging in strikes.[33]

Despite the strong constitutional bar against strikes, nine stoppages by FOP lodges were reported in 1967–69 (see Table 8-2). There is no record of an FOP lodge being expelled for engaging in strike action in violation of the FOP constitution.

The NUPO (formerly the International Brotherhood of Police Officers) stated in its first constitution, adopted in May 1970, that it "is opposed to strikes by police officers and will not engage in such strikes."[34] The no-strike clause, according to the union's president, "proves that we realize that policemen cannot be put in the position of undermining the things that we stand for and represent."[35] However, the president does not equate "job action," such as picketing, demonstrations, and slowdowns, with strikes.[36]

The ICPA has changed its policy on strikes twice during the past five years. The original constitution, adopted in 1954, was silent on the subject of strikes. In 1967 it was amended to read: "This Conference shall not engage in, condone, or support strikes against any government, and does not advocate the overthrow of any government."[37] Four years later the antistrike section was omitted from

32. Constitution and By-Laws, Fraternal Order of Police (1967), Art. 2, sec. 2.
33. *National Police Journal,* Autumn 1968, p. 8.
34. *GERR* No. 341 (March 23, 1970), p. B-1; and No. 351 (June 1, 1970), p. B-13.
35. *GERR,* No. 351 (June 1, 1970), p. B-14.
36. *GERR,* No. 341 (March 23, 1970), p. B-2.
37. By-Laws, International Conference of Police Associations (1967), Art. 3, sec. 4.

the revised constitution, and the ICPA adopted a "policy statement" which said: "We believe in the collective bargaining processes for police officers and do not encourage strikes against government."[38]

Until 1970, AFSCME's position against strikes by police and other law enforcement officers was unequivocal. While insisting on the right of all other public employees to strike, AFSCME asserted in the charter of every local union that included police a proviso that the charter would "be revoked immediately if the members . . . who are employed as law enforcement, police, or penal officers call or participate in a strike or refuse in concert to perform their duties."[39] The international showed that it took this language seriously when, in 1967, it expelled a police local in Lockport, Illinois, for striking.

AFSCME police locals tried to get rid of the strike prohibition at the 1965 and 1968 conventions. Police delegates argued that they were entitled "to the same rights and benefits as the rest of the members."[40] But the union's president took the floor to "plead" with the delegates to retain the no-strike provision, however "obnoxious to trade unionists," and warned that the union would be "seriously jeopardized" without it.[41] The secretary-treasurer put his position more bluntly: "We prefer not to see another Calvin Coolidge in the White House."[42] Convention delegates supported the administration on each occasion.

It thus came as a surprise when the administration proposed and the 1970 convention voted, without debate, to eliminate the section of the constitution restricting the charters of locals with police officers.[43] Reportedly, pressure had come from locals in state penal institutions, which had been included in the strike prohibition and were growing increasingly restive and prone to take strike action, regardless of international policy. Also, competition from the newly formed International Brotherhood of Police Officers, which was

---

38. Ibid. (revised July 1971).
39. *AFSCME Proceedings* (1968), p. 384.
40. *Proceedings, Special Constitution Convention, AFSCME, AFL-CIO* (1965), p. 88; *AFSCME Proceedings* (1968), p. 241.
41. *Proceedings, Constitution Convention, AFSCME* (1965), p. 89; *AFSCME Proceedings* (1968), p. 242.
42. *AFSCME Proceedings* (1965), p. 88.
43. Ibid. (1970), p. 288.

seeking an AFL-CIO charter, forced the attitude of the AFSCME to change.

The union's executive board had been open to the idea of a national police union when it was proposed in 1969. But as time elapsed, the IBPO proved unable to muster substantial support among police officers and AFSCME leaders decided to fight to retain the union's police and law enforcement locals and their 10,000 members. Meantime, the bargaining position of police locals within AFSCME had strengthened sufficiently for them to obtain elimination of the prohibition on strikes and chartering of additional police councils, which they had previously sought unsuccessfully from the international.

Policemen have shared the increased militancy of other municipal employees. While they have been much more loath to engage in strike action, police in many cities have participated in an endless variety of 'job actions"—slowdowns, mass sick calls, blue flu epidemics, moratoriums on writing traffic tickets, stepped-up issuance of summonses, mass resignations, marathon professional meetings, and mass demonstrations. In one of the more ingenious proposed "job actions," the Knoxville, Tennessee, FOP threatened to conduct a "pray-in" by attending Evangelist Billy Graham's Crusade every night, unless the city council took positive action on its proposal for a 40-hour week with 48 hours' pay. The FOP president said: "I cannot advocate work stoppages, strikes, or sick call-ins, but I am a firm believer in prayer."[44] By the late 1960s, policemen in some cities were willing to drop euphemistic titles and engage in work stoppages that they admitted were strikes. Fifty-one police strikes were reported in the five-year period 1965–69 (see Table 8-3).

The largest stoppage of policemen occurred in January 1971, when about 85 percent of the 27,400 members of the ICPA-affiliated Patrolmen's Benevolent Association (PBA) of New York City engaged in a six-day wildcat strike. The strike was attributed to "frustration," "humiliation," and "anger" that had been building up for years. The final "injustice" was the court's refusal to act on a PBA lawsuit over the proper relationship between the pay of patrolmen and sergeants. There was no breakdown in law and order similar to the crime waves and riots that had occurred during police

44. *GERR*, No. 350 (May 25, 1970), p. B-13.

strikes in Montreal a year earlier and in Boston in 1919. Cold weather and the assignment of nonstriking patrolmen, along with detectives, sergeants, lieutenants, and captains, to locations where they would be visible to large numbers of people were credited with bringing the city through the crisis in good condition. Six months after the strike, the city, acting under the mandates of the Taylor Act, started action to fine 21,000 patrolmen, who had participated in the strike, two days' pay for each day of absence from their jobs and to place them on probation for one year.[45]

ASSOCIATIONS

Of all public employee organizations, state and local employee associations are the least prone to strike or to threaten strike action. Yet, even among these organizations, there has been a discernible movement toward greater militancy, as evidenced by removal of constitutional strike prohibitions in several associations, unsuccessful efforts to change the no-strike policy in a few others, and a number of strikes or other forms of job action.

For many years the idea of striking was so alien to the very nature of civil service employee associations that many of them had never even officially considered the matter. As a result, several associations, though strongly opposed to strikes, do not expressly prohibit strike action in their constitutions. The leaders claim that such provisions are unnecessary, given the stated objectives of the organizations. These associations have pledged their allegiance to the merit system and civil service procedures designed to promote that system, and have stated, in positive terms, the methods to be used to achieve their objectives. For example, the Connecticut State Employees Association, whose constitution is silent on the strike issue, states that it will employ such methods as petitioning, creating and fostering public sentiment favorable to proposed reforms, cooperating with state officials, promoting legislation, and other "ethical lawful means."[46]

Several state and local association constitutions do prohibit strikes. Representatives of a number of associations have indicated that their organizations were opposed to strikes and the membership

45. *New York Times*, Jan. 20, 1971, pp. 1, 19; June 10, 1971, p. 1.
46. Constitution, Connecticut State Employees Association (1969), Art. 2.

was unlikely to resort to such action. On the other hand, a few leaders of associations with no-strike provisions believe that their members are growing more militant and would strike if necessary. The changing attitude toward strikes among civil service employees is best illustrated by associations that have repealed or are considering repeal of provisions in their constitutions prohibiting strikes.

The New York Civil Service Employees Association (CSEA) requires local chapters to secure authorization from the board of directors before engaging in strikes or other job actions. Chapters in the New York City area, whose members are more militant than those upstate, have initiated action to eliminate the no-strike provision from the constitution. In 1971 the CSEA board scheduled a statewide strike of 150,000 members to save the jobs of 8,250 state employees slated to be eliminated because of budget cuts. The strike was called off the day it was to begin, with the CSEA claiming, and the state denying, that it had won significant concessions.[47] The following year the CSEA did shut down mental hospitals, juvenile training schools, prisons, and other state institutions on Easter weekend. The strike, involving 7,000 employees in a pay dispute, was settled when the state offered new concessions. Striking employees were penalized two days' pay for each day off the job, as mandated by the Taylor Act.[48]

The California State Employees Association removed a ten-year-old strike prohibition from its constitution in 1969, after two previous tries in 1967 and 1968 had failed. The action was triggered by the legislature's enactment of a law permitting cities and counties to bargain collectively with their employees but denying this privilege to state employees.[49] Strikes must be authorized by a two-thirds vote of the California association's board of directors and approved by a majority of the members employed in the state facility involved.[50]

The Oregon State Employees Association in 1970 went on record as favoring an amendment to the state law that prohibits public employee strikes. It favored a statute, similar to laws in Hawaii and Pennsylvania, that "hits at the core of the strike question, by pro-

47. *New York Times*, May 19, 1971, p. 26; June 17, 1971, p. 46.
48. *GERR*, No. 447 (April 10, 1972), p. B-17; No. 452 (May 15, 1972), pp. B-12, 13.
49. *California State Employee*, Vol. 40 (Oct. 17, 1969), p. 3.
50. *GERR*, No. 357 (July 13, 1970), p. B-16.

tecting the public health and safety while removing unworkable, second-class citizen types of restriction on public employees whose activities are similar to those of workers in private industry."[51]

The Maryland Classified Employees Association (MCEA) repealed its no-strike policy in 1971 after rejecting such a move in 1968.[52] The reversal reflected increased membership militancy and pressures of competition between MCEA and AFSCME. Two years earlier, the Baltimore Classified Municipal Employees Association had removed a no-strike provision from its by-laws in order to improve its position in a representation election against AFSCME and the Laborers' Union. In the election, AFSCME won the right to represent blue collar workers, while the association was victorious among white collar employees.

The Hawaii Government Employees Association withdrew its no-strike pledge in June 1970, before voting to affiliate with AFSCME. The action was explained as necessary to prepare the association for collective bargaining, under the new state law, and to accommodate to the admission of private sector employees, under a proposed reorganization that was voted on and approved at the same time.

Official positions on the strike issue are not necessarily reliable predictors of what association members will do in the heat of negotiations or in response to alleged unfair treatment by government employers. Associations have engaged in at least forty-four strikes against local government employers during the period 1965–69 (see Table 8-2).

AMERICAN NURSES' ASSOCIATION

In 1968 the American Nurses' Association rescinded the no-strike policy it had adopted eighteen years earlier. The 1950 policy reaffirmed the nurses' "voluntary relinquishment of the exercise of the right to strike" and asserted their employers' "increased obligation to recognize and deal justly with nurses."[53] The 1950 convention also adopted a policy of neutrality in disputes involving other

51. *GERR*, No. 373 (Nov. 2, 1970), p. B-16.
52. *GERR*, No. 421 (Oct. 4, 1971), p. B-19.
53. *Proceedings, House of Delegates, Division on Practice, 46th Convention, American Nurses' Association (ANA Proceedings)* (1968), p. 25.

hospital employees. ANA members were advised that "they should neither, as partisans to non-nurse employees, refuse or fail to carry out their proper and necessary nursing duties; nor, as partisans of management, accept the assignment of duties normally discharged by the non-nurse personnel unless a clear and present danger to patients exists."[54]

The 1968 action arose from a charge by the ANA Commission on Economic and General Welfare that employers had not been behaving "justly" in their dealings with nurses.[55] The commission, recommending elimination of the no-strike policy, had concluded that it could not be enforced at the national level. State associations, which ultimately had to make the final decision, held differing positions with respect to strikes, mass resignations, and other forms of job action. Some had no policy, some had repudiated the ANA no-strike policy, while others endorsed the policy in principle but departed from it in practice, and still others had modified or reinterpreted the ANA policy statement. To accommodate these variations, the commission recommended that policy on the strike issue be left to individual state associations.[56]

The motion to withdraw the no-strike policy was adopted by a two-to-one majority vote.[57] This action was followed by adoption of a resolution that supported steps taken by state associations serving as bargaining agents, "including concerted economic pressures which are lawful and consistent with the nurse's professional responsibilities and with the public welfare."[58] Since the resolution supported only "lawful" actions, it would appear to rule out support of strikes in public hospitals or government departments employing nurses, where such action is prohibited by law. However, no distinction was made between public and nonpublic employment in the discussion, either on the withdrawal of the no-strike policy or the resolution to support actions taken by state associations. Between the 1968 and 1970 ANA conventions, thirteen state associations rescinded their no-strike policy (five others had done

54. ANA, Economic Security Department, "Policy for Guidance of Nurses During Employer-Employee Negotiations or Disputes" (June 27, 1969, processed); "If a Hospital Strike Occurs," *American Journal of Nursing,* Vol. 60 (March 1960), pp. 344–52.

55. *ANA Proceedings* (1968), p. 25.

56. Ibid., p. 25.

57. Ibid., p. 28.

58. Ibid., pp. 28–31.

so before the 1968 convention), and eight associations reaffirmed their no-strike policy.[59]

The changing attitude of nurses toward strikes was again evidenced in 1970 when the "neutrality" policy in disputes involving nonnurses was rescinded in favor of a policy that let each state association determine its own position in stoppages involving other employees.[60] The mood of some nurses was expressed by a delegate from New York who said: "Neutrality has never produced radical change, and radical change is what is needed now in our health care system."[61]

According to ANA's executive director, the two-year period following withdrawal of the no-strike policy was marked by an increase in economic security activity in the states, without an accompanying rise in strikes. In fact, it appears that strike activity had already started to decline before the ANA policy change in May 1968. In 1966, state associations reported 32 cases of "strikes, mass resignations, sick calls and other instances in which withdrawal of services [was] either threatened or carried out."[62] The incidence of such actions declined to 20 in 1967 and 15 in 1968. In one hospital, nurses took part in a "nurse-in" by reporting to work during off-duty hours to demonstrate the need for additional staff.[63]

The year 1966 marked a high point in the use of economic pressure tactics by nurses and started a series of moves that eventually ended with the rescinding of the ANA no-strike policy. In that year, 11,500 nurses in 13 states—about 23 percent of the 50,000 represented by state associations at the time—were involved in various forms of job action,[64] including strikes. In 1968 only 700 nurses—about 1 percent of the 70,000 involved in representation activity—engaged in such action. By far the most popular form of job action among nurses is mass resignation. Job actions have also included strike threats, "spontaneous" walkouts lasting a few hours to a few days, picketing of city hall, reporting sick or taking sick leave, sign-

59. *House of Delegates Reports, 1968–70, 47th Convention, American Nurses' Association* (1970), p. 25.
60. *American Journal of Nursing*, Vol. 70 (June 1970), p. 1271.
61. Ibid., p. 1274.
62. *ANA, House of Delegates Reports, 1968–70*, p. 25.
63. ANA, Research and Statistics Department, "Summary of SNA Economic Security Program Activities" (ANA, Nov. 7, 1969; processed).
64. ANA, *House of Delegates Reports, 1968–70*, p. 25.

ing post-dated letter of "intent" to resign, and other ingenious ways of putting pressure on hospital administrators and public authorities.[65] The severe shortage of registered nurses in almost all parts of the country and widespread recognition of their underpaid status have contributed to significant gains following job actions by nurses. Contrary to experience of other public employees, nurses have almost never been discharged or disciplined for withdrawing their services.

Arbitration

The sharp increase in public employee strikes and elimination or disregard of constitutional prohibitions against work stoppages have revived interest in compulsory arbitration of labor disputes. Several states have made arbitration compulsory in police and fire fighter disputes and a number of municipalities require that all unresolved issues in government negotiations be submitted to final and binding arbitration.

Union attitudes toward the arbitration of contractual issues generally depend on the union's strength and its ability to conduct a successful strike. Historically, unions have favored arbitration when they were weak, when collective bargaining was not protected by law, or when employers refused to recognize, let alone negotiate, with unions. At such times, employers were of course unalterably opposed to arbitration. With the Wagner Act's protection of the right of workers to organize and to bargain collectively, unions lost interest in arbitration. After 1935 the view that arbitration, especially if it were compulsory or agreed on in advance of negotiations, undermines collective bargaining took hold and still prevails among both union and management representatives.[66]

Voluntary arbitration has always been more acceptable to unions and employers than compulsory arbitration. In his 1970 Labor Day

65. For examples of strikes and other job actions, see *New York Times*, May 26, 1966, p. 1, Aug. 3, 1968, p. 26; *GERR*, No. 157 (Sept. 12, 1966), p. B-9; No. 158 (Sept. 19, 1966), p. B-5; No. 138 (May 2, 1966), p. B-6; No. 165 (Nov. 7, 1966), p. B-7; No. 179 (Feb. 13, 1967), p. B-1; No. 181 (Feb. 27, 1967), p. B-8; No. 282 (Feb. 3, 1969), p. B-10; and No. 346 (April 27, 1970), p. B-15; and Archie Kleingartner, "Nurses, Collective Bargaining and Labor Legislation," *Labor Law Journal*, Vol. 18 (April 1967), p. 238.

66. Jack Stieber, "Voluntary Arbitration of Contract Terms," in *Arbitration and the Expanding Role of Neutrals*, Proceedings of the 23rd Annual Meeting, National Academy of Arbitrators (Bureau of National Affairs, 1970), pp. 71–124.

statement, AFL-CIO President George Meany espoused voluntary arbitration and even suggested that contracts might provide for arbitration of unresolved issues in forthcoming negotiations.[67] In a 1968 survey, two-thirds of the union leaders and 42 percent of the management representatives contacted were willing to consider voluntary arbitration of contract issues. Both groups heavily preferred arbitration decided on during negotiations in order to avoid a strike to arbitration by prior agreement, on the ground that the latter arrangement would discourage good faith bargaining.[68]

Until recently, public sector unions were much more favorably disposed toward arbitration, including compulsory arbitration, than those in private industry. Except in a few governmental jurisdictions, collective bargaining for public employees did not exist, strikes were prohibited by law, and, in any event, public employee unions were too weak to carry out a successful strike. Before 1960, it would have been unusual for a union leader to refuse the opportunity to arbitrate a dispute with a government employer, and just as unusual to find a government official willing to submit differences with his employees to arbitration.

Today, most leaders of public employee unions take the same position as those in the private sector; they oppose compulsory arbitration but favor voluntary arbitration of contract issues that cannot be resolved by collective bargaining. AFSCME's president has recommended that locals and councils experiment with voluntary mechanisms for arbitrating disputes and suggested that, unless other impasse procedures were developed, unions might be driven to support compulsory arbitration.[69] In January 1972, New York became the first major city to enact a compulsory arbitration statute for all deadlocked municipal labor disputes except those involving teachers and transit employees. Victor Gotbaum, director of AFSCME District Council 37, supported the new law, saying that "State law gave us no alternative but to come up with a final and binding procedure."[70] But John DeLury, leader of New York's

67. *John Herling's Labor Letter*, Aug. 29–Sept. 5, 1970.

68. Stieber, "Voluntary Arbitration."

69. Labor-Management Relations Service, "A Look at Public Employee Unions," Report No. 4 (Washington: LMRS, September 1970; processed); also *Public Employee*, Vol. 36 (December 1971), p. 5.

70. *New York Times*, Jan. 13, 1972, p. 50. Only two other small cities, Vallejo, Calif., and Eugene, Oreg., have compulsory arbitration of all municipal employee disputes.

Uniformed Sanitationmen's Association, affiliated with the Teamsters, said his union would continue to follow a policy of "no contract, no work."[71]

The New York City statute represents a notable breakthrough for compulsory arbitration which previously had little support among either unions or government employers. At the state and local level a large majority of the representatives of the four unions most active among nonuniformed public employees—AFSCME, Service Employees, Laborers, and Teamsters—express strong opposition to compulsory arbitration. However, officers and staff members of some locals of policemen, fire fighters, hospital employees, social workers, and of unions in states without collective bargaining laws, tend to favor compulsory arbitration or are willing to give it a try. A few union leaders see compulsory arbitration as the only way to avoid strikes in public employment.

The strongest support for compulsory arbitration comes from fire fighter and police organization representatives. Even those who believe that their organizations are strong enough to conduct a successful strike recognize the severe moral constraints that would usually keep their members from engaging in strike action that might endanger the community. Police and fire fighter representatives claim credit for the compulsory arbitration laws in disputes involving protective service employees in Rhode Island, Pennsylvania, and Michigan. A few representatives in each service oppose compulsory arbitration because they believe it would discourage collective bargaining or prove too costly, or they prefer to rely on the strike as a more effective way of attaining their objectives. However, delegates to the 1972 convention of the International Association of Fire Fighters endorsed compulsory arbitration for jurisdictions with no-strike laws.[72]

The American Nurses' Association and most state nurses' associations favor compulsory arbitration for much the same reason as police and fire fighters: strikes in hospitals are not acceptable to the public, and nurses also have a strong professional commitment to their patients which would make them most reluctant to strike. State nurses' associations have supported compulsory arbitration

71. Ibid.
72. Lunden, "IAFF Convention," p. 54.

laws for hospitals, whether public or nonpublic, and such legislation has been passed in several states.[73]

State and local employee associations have given less thought to compulsory arbitration than other public employee organizations. Indeed, some have still not decided whether they favor grievance arbitration. Those association representatives who have an opinion on the issue favor compulsory arbitration over strikes. But for most associations, arbitration is not considered an important issue.

Summary

There has been a significant change in policies of public employee organizations and in the attitudes of their members toward the use of the strike weapon. Unions that have never prohibited strikes but discouraged their members from engaging in stoppages now espouse the strike as an essential element in collective bargaining and do not hesitate to utilize it under favorable circumstances. Many employee organizations have repealed constitutional prohibitions against strikes, and those that have retained their no-strike policy do not enforce it against local units that violate official policy. While there is some evidence that repeal of a strike prohibition is followed by an increase in strike activity—the fire fighters are a case in point—more often organization action to reverse a long-standing no-strike policy represents a recognition that the policy is inoperative in the face of increasing militancy among members who refuse to abide by it. In many instances, union and association leaders have been pushed into strikes by members who have taken matters into their own hands or indicated that they would stop work with or without authorization by the leadership. The trend toward repeal of no-strike policies is quickened by competition for members among public employee organizations. It is virtually impossible to suspend a local unit or its members who violate an organizational prohibition against strikes when other organizations stand ready to welcome them into their fold.

All types of employee organizations have participated in strikes.

73. Estelle Hepton, "Battle for the Hospitals," Bulletin 49 (New York State School of Industrial and Labor Relations, Cornell University, 1963); and Judith P. Vladeck, "Collective Bargaining in Voluntary Hospitals and Other Non-Profit Operations," *Proceedings of New York University 19th Annual Conference on Labor* (1966), pp. 221–34.

While AFSCME has called more strikes than any other organization—a reflection of the size and distribution of its public employee membership—the mixed unions, uniformed protective service organizations, state and local employee associations, and professional associations have all contributed to the upsurge in public employee strikes. In addition, unorganized employees have been involved in one out of every five strikes in local government during 1965–69. Job actions short of strikes, resulting in significant reductions in public services, are probably more numerous than actual stoppages.

Contrary to the widespread belief that strikes against government are invariably successful, such strikes are often lost or settled with little gain to the employees involved. In addition, many strikers have been discharged or otherwise punished for engaging in illegal activity. The fact that penalties or the threat of punishment have not deterred workers from striking reflects the intensity of feeling by government employees against laws they consider unfair and discriminatory.

One of the sharpest divisions among public employee organizations occurs over the issue of compulsory arbitration. Organization attitudes toward arbitration vary according to the essentiality of the service performed by their members. Thus, unions and associations of police, fire fighters, and nurses tend to favor compulsory arbitration, while those representing other employees are generally opposed to this method of resolving disputes over the terms of new agreements. The distinction is between employees who, though they may assert their right to strike, are under great pressure not to endanger the safety and health of the community by withdrawing services, and other employees on whom the legal prohibition against strikes weighs less heavily. The major objection to compulsory arbitration is that it interferes with and undermines free collective bargaining. But, then, so do laws prohibiting strikes.

The problem of enforcement of no-strike laws and a growing unease about the fairness and necessity of blanket prohibitions against all strikes by public employees have led to compulsory arbitration in a few government jurisdictions and the enactment of laws in Pennsylvania and Hawaii that permit some strikes by government employees. Undoubtedly, new laws and amendments to existing laws will increasingly utilize one or both of these approaches to the strike problem.

CHAPTER NINE

Political Action

Unions have long recognized the importance of supplementing their activity at the bargaining table with political action. They have raised funds, endorsed candidates, provided manpower to register voters and campaign, and exhorted their members to "reward our friends and punish our enemies" in elections at all levels of government. Through political action, labor hopes to influence legislation favorable to workers generally and to elect officeholders whose policies and programs coincide with those of the labor movement.

For public employee organizations there are additional reasons for engaging in political activity. The men and women elected to executive and legislative office have the power to decide their members' salaries, pensions, and other fringe benefits; to appoint department heads and commissioners who will determine policies under which their members will work; and to select the people who will sit across the bargaining table from them. In some states and localities, the outcome of an election may affect hundreds or even thousands of jobs that are still filled through the spoils system. Under the circumstances, it is not surprising to find that public employee organizations are intensely interested in politics and heavily involved in political activity.

But public employees are limited in the extent to which they may become personally involved in politics. Federal employees are prohibited by the Hatch Act, passed in 1939, from engaging in political

193

campaigns.[1] In 1940, Congress extended this restriction to state and local government employees whose salaries are paid from federal funds. Many states and cities have also enacted "little Hatch acts." These laws, intended to protect government employees from being forced to contribute to political campaigns or to work on behalf of politicians who control their jobs, have also been interpreted to prohibit government employees from running for public office and otherwise becoming actively involved in politics. Despite these restrictions on the political activity of their members, some public employee organizations have managed to develop vigorous and effective political action programs.

AFSCME

The American Federation of State, County and Municipal Employees (AFSCME) opposed the enactment of the Hatch Act and has also opposed state acts restricting political activity of government employees.[2] When the union was relatively small and weak, it coupled resolutions urging repeal of the Hatch Act with demands for continued protection of civil service and job security.[3] More recently its position has become more unequivocal. Thus, a 1970 convention resolution called such legislation "an affront and indignity which the community-conscious public employees should not be required to suffer" and affirmed the right of all public employees to participate in all political processes.[4]

The major vehicle for AFSCME's political action is its PEOPLE (Public Employees Organized to Promote Legislative Equality) program. This program, adopted by the 1968 convention, provides for coordinated and interrelated activities at the international,

1. V. O. Key, Jr., *Politics, Parties, and Pressure Groups* (4th ed., Crowell, 1958), p. 391. However, on July 31, 1972, the U.S. District Court for the District of Columbia ruled that the Hatch Act is unconstitutional because it is "impermissibly vague and overbroad when measured against the requirements of the First Amendment." The court stayed enforcement of an injunction against application of the act pending final determination by the Supreme Court. (*Daily Labor Report*, No. 148, July 31, 1972.)

2. *Proceedings of the Eleventh International Convention, American Federation of State, County and Municipal Employees, AFL-CIO* (*AFSCME Proceedings*) (1958), p. 252.

3. Ibid., pp. 252–53.

4. *AFSCME Proceedings* (1970), pp. 608–9.

council, and local union levels, participation in the AFL-CIO Committee on Political Education (COPE), intensive lobbying in Congress and in state legislatures, education programs, and work to end restrictions on political activities by public employees.[5] The union's 1968–70 legislative program encompassed a broad range of subjects of direct interest to its members, including extension of the federal Social Security Act and state unemployment and workmen's compensation acts to all public employees; federal revenue help for cities and states; promotion of a Federal Public Employee Relations Act; and provision of life and health insurance to noncitizen employees of the U.S. government in the Panama Canal Zone, many of whom are AFSCME members.[6]

But, AFSCME's interest in the political arena extends beyond the economic interests of its members. The 1970 convention also adopted resolutions on poverty and civil disorder; civil rights; extension of the 1965 voting rights act to increase the number of black voters; declaration of a national holiday to commemorate the birthday of Martin Luther King, Jr.; home rule for the District of Columbia; opposition to nominations of Clement F. Haynsworth and G. Harrold Carswell to the United States Supreme Court; consumer protection; abuses in automobile insurance practices; safer cities; national health insurance; contamination of the natural environment; mental health; the use of wire tapping by the Department of Justice; and the use of force to quell demonstrations.[7]

AFSCME was the first AFL-CIO union to depart from the official AFL-CIO position on the Vietnam war. It began by refusing to oppose the war in 1966 and arrived at outright and complete repudiation of U.S. involvement in 1970.[8] Coming only a few days after AFL-CIO President Meany had issued a statement supporting the dispatch of American troops into Cambodia, the 1970 action was interpreted by the press as a repudiation of the AFL-CIO and George Meany.[9] AFSCME's president held that it was simply exercising its right as an autonomous union to "make decisions that we see fit."[10]

5. Ibid., pp. 458–70.
6. Ibid., pp. 462–66.
7. Ibid., pp. 579–658.
8. *AFSCME Proceedings* (1966), p. 254; (1970), p. 264.
9. *John Herling's Labor Letter*, May 9, 1970.
10. *AFSCME Proceedings* (1970), p. 272.

During the 1970 mid-term election campaign, the director of New York Council 37 was reported to have called for a revolt against the AFL-CIO hierarchy, declaring: "We need a progressive coalition in the labor movement to oppose the building trades and Meany."[11] His statement came in the midst of a bitter dispute among New York unions in which the state AFL-CIO endorsed Republican Governor Nelson Rockefeller against the Democratic party's candidate, Arthur Goldberg, former Steelworkers' general counsel.

In the 1972 presidential race, AFSCME President Jerry Wurf was one of only three members of the thirty-five-member AFL-CIO executive council to vote against the federation's taking a neutral stance in the contest between President Nixon and Democratic candidate George McGovern. Unlike other union leaders who endorsed McGovern but chose not to take public issue with AFL-CIO President George Meany, Wurf was outspoken in his disagreement with the council's position, which was regarded as a personal triumph for Meany.[12]

These differences with the AFL-CIO hierarchy illustrate the new independence of the AFSCME leadership which the union could not afford as long as it was small, weak, and dependent on the AFL-CIO and other unions for support. Now as leaders of one of the largest and fastest growing AFL-CIO unions, whose president sits on the AFL-CIO executive council, AFSCME officers feel secure enough to speak out on issues on which they previously might have remained silent. The union has established a reputation for taking positions on political, social, and economic issues independently of the AFL-CIO.

The heart of AFSCME's political activities is at the state and local level. In most states, AFSCME has separate councils of state and local government employees and can thus mobilize its members to support or oppose political candidates and issues on which they have an identity of interest. The union can bring to bear greater pressure on individual politicians and legislative bodies than organizations that must speak for members with many different employers in diverse industries whose interests often do not coincide.

11. *New York Times,* Sept. 28, 1970, p. 11.
12. See, for example, Jerry Wurf, "Running Without George Meany: What Labor Has Against McGovern," *New Republic,* Aug. 5 and 12, 1972.

One of the best organized and most effective political action programs is conducted by Council 28 which, in 1968, had some 60 locals with 8,700 members in the state of Washington. The council's director is convinced of the importance of political action to Washington state employees. "We have to obtain enabling legislation before we can even negotiate in a number of areas, and . . . the extent we can even negotiate with State Agencies, in a number of areas, must come from the Legislative Body itself. So, this is not a game. It is strictly business—of a life and death nature."[13] In pursuit of this "business," local union officers, executive board members, and chief stewards follow carefully drawn rules:

1. We mind our own cotton-picking business, that is, we deal with Legislators only on those matters that are a part and parcel of the program of the Washington Federation of State Employees, AFL-CIO. . . .
2. We support, regardless of political party, the incumbent Legislators who supported us. We do this even when it is unpopular with the rest of the labor movement.
3. We make damn sure we are fully prepared in dealing with the Legislature, and we have had a reasonably good program in keeping our own membership currently informed.
4. Fortunately for us, the record . . . clearly indicates . . . that we have political know-how, and on several occasions, against some rather heavy odds, have delivered the goods.[14]

The council keeps a card file of members by legislative district, and each local has a duplicate file of its membership. A quick mailing can thus be made to any district.

The council also keeps detailed voting records for each legislator. For incumbents with favorable records, a letter signed by the council director is sent to each union member, noting that the legislator has supported the union's program and has voted right on appropriations for state employee pay raises. The letter states that, although the union does not make official endorsements, the legislator deserves to be supported. Copies of the letters are sent to the legislator, "so that you will have some idea of what we are attempting to do further in your behalf." Legislators have used the union's letters in newspaper advertisements in their reelection campaigns.

Council 28 maintains a separate earmarked Legislative and De-

13. Letter from Norm Schut, Director, Council 28, to AFSCME Secretary-Treasurer Joseph Ames, Oct. 23, 1968.
14. Ibid.

fense Fund, financed by $0.20 per member per month out of the council's regular per capita tax of $2. Additional costs of the program are paid for by individual local unions. Legislators have noted their appreciation of the council's efforts and indicated that its approach is more effective than COPE endorsements. During legislative sessions, the council's executive director works full time as a lobbyist, cooperating with other AFL-CIO lobbyists but putting his major effort on bills directly affecting state employees.[15]

Other AFSCME councils have similar, if less elaborate, political action programs. Ohio has a unique arrangement, whereby the seven district councils and two unaffiliated locals all belong to Council 8, whose primary function is to coordinate legislative activities, endorse and support candidates, and lobby in the state legislature; the council is supported by a per capita tax of $0.25 a month paid by members of the affiliated councils. One of the most extensive lobbying programs is carried on by Council 17 in Louisiana where AFSCME has 7,500 members, despite the fact that this state has no collective bargaining law for public employees. During sessions of the state legislature, the council keeps a minimum of four full-time representatives at the state capital, working under the direction of Willie Long, a member of the family that has been influential in Louisiana politics since the 1930s. Council 50 in New York State has found it helpful to bring large numbers of its members to the state capital at a crucial moment during the legislative session; each member is provided with a colorful hat, which identifies him as a Council 50 member, and groups are expected to contact their senator or assemblyman to let him know how they want him to vote. Council 2 of Washington provides its members with oversized postcards printed on salmon-colored stock with the union insignia on the upper left-hand corner; space is available for each member to fill in his place of employment and address and to write an individual message to his representative or senator.[16]

All AFSCME councils engage in political action. Among their most common activities are the endorsement of candidates, distribution of voting records, contributions of manpower and occasionally funds in election campaigns, and invitations to candidates to address union meetings. All councils engage in some form of

15. *AFSCME Proceedings* (1968), pp. 499–502.
16. Ibid., pp. 502–11.

lobbying and testify before legislative committees and similar bodies. Some refrain from endorsing candidates for fear of backing a "loser" and incurring the enmity of the victorious candidate. Others prefer to work through COPE or the central labor body rather than take a position that can be identified with one union.

In several localities, AFSCME claims credit for the election of the mayor or members of the city council or county board of supervisors; the officials are expected to recognize their debt to the union. For example, in Philadelphia the union backed Mayor Tate for reelection in 1967, even though he did not have the support of his own party in the primary election. Tate won by only 11,000 votes, making him beholden to the union without whose support he would have been defeated. In New York, Mayor Lindsay has shown his appreciation for the support he received from Council 37 in 1969, when the AFL-CIO central labor council endorsed his opponent. In Baltimore, AFSCME supported the successful candidates for mayor, city council president, and controller in 1967, despite COPE endorsement of their opponents. This record did not prove harmful when AFSCME became embroiled in a dispute with the Laborers' Union and an association over representation of city employees the following year. In Wayne County, Michigan, the director of Council 23 boasted that he had done favors for almost every member of the board of supervisors and could expect some consideration from them in return. AFSCME's political activities reflect a widespread belief that employee representation in government, with or without collective bargaining, cannot be divorced from politics. In the words of one council director: "We have a natural that no other union has. We can elect our employers."

Mixed Unions

Unions in which public employees constitute a minority of the membership concentrate their political activity on behalf of government workers where public employee membership is significant. Except for civil rights, which are regularly supported in convention resolutions, the mixed unions rarely stray far from subjects directly related to the economic interests of their members. Political action is carried on through the AFL-CIO Committee on Political Education, the Laborers' Political Action League, and the Teamsters' DRIVE program.[17]

At the local level the mixed unions actively support candidates and legislative measures designed to benefit their public employee members. In New York City, SEIU Local 300 acknowledged that the major reason it affiliated with the Service Employees International Union was to benefit from its "political muscle." SEIU Machinist Local 264 in New York, whose members' wages are governed by determinations of the city controller, has always supported the incumbent controller with money and manpower in elections. In Pittsburgh, politics is important in getting jobs that are controlled by elected city officials, and Local 192B conducts its political activities through the SEIU joint district council and central labor bodies. On election day—a holiday for Pittsburgh city employees— union members are expected to get out the vote for the Democratic party in addition to contributing to the party coffers.

SEIU local unions in California, a state with only minimal restrictions on political involvement by government employees, are very active in politics. Social Worker Local 535 led the fight to obtain COPE endorsement for Thomas Bradley, unsuccessful Negro candidate for mayor of Los Angeles in 1969. Welfare ranks with law and order as a sensitive political issue in California, and Local 535 lobbies on behalf of welfare recipients as well as its members. Local 347, which represents public works employees in Los Angeles, makes direct contributions to candidates and supplies manpower in election campaigns. In 1969 eight out of fifteen city council members were considered sympathetic to the union. In San Francisco, SEIU Local 400 negotiates with a board of supervisors whose members have received campaign contributions from unions and are regarded as prolabor. All SEIU public employee locals recognize the importance of political action and engage in politics at the state and local level to the extent permitted by their financial resources.

Laborers local unions in Providence, Cleveland, and Portland, Oregon, have been active politically on behalf of public employee members. In Rhode Island the district council has formed the Laborers' Political League to shore up the AFL-CIO. In 1969 six of the twenty-two Providence council members, a majority of whom received union support in their election campaigns, were reported

17. DRIVE stands for Democratic, Republican, Independent Voter Education.

to be members of the Laborers' Union. In Cleveland, Local 1099 and the AFL-CIO council supported the incumbent mayor against Negro challenger Carl B. Stokes in the Democratic party primary election of 1967, but backed Stokes against Republican Seth Taft when he was elected the first black mayor of a major U.S. city. In Portland, Laborers public employee Local 283 believes that as long as government workers are denied the right to strike, "dealing in public employment is dealing in politics." Acting on this belief, the local has supported candidates with money, manpower, and endorsements and in 1969 counted three of the five city council members as "friends." Seattle Local 1239 follows a policy of "keeping the lines open to both parties."

The political influence of John J. DeLury, president of the New York City Uniformed Sanitationmen's Association, Teamster Local 831, is well known to natives of that city. A former leader of Tammany Hall considers the local to have "the best political machine left in town," and the political power of the sanitation workers is considered on a par with policemen and fire fighters in New York City.[18] In 1969, when the union endorsed Mayor Lindsay for reelection, DeLury, referring to his fifteen-day jail sentence during the 1968 garbage strike, explained: "That was a shameful episode in John Lindsay's life. But we all make mistakes and he has worked hard to remove that blight from his record. He has more than evened the score." He predicted that he would deliver the vote of a majority of his 10,500 members.[19] Lindsay also had the support of most other city employee organizations.

Less in the limelight, but larger and more diverse in membership than the sanitation workers, is Teamster Local 237 in New York City. This 13,000-member union, the fifth largest Teamster local in the country, prefers to work through the Teamsters' Joint Council in political matters, though it does not hesitate to take a different position on political issues or endorsement of candidates, when the interests of its members differ from those of the council.

In Pittsburgh, Teamster Locals 609 and 249 work in concert with the dominant Democratic party. The president of Local 249, which includes both private and public employees, is a member of the city council as was his father before him. He says he would prefer

18. Edward N. Costikyan, "Who Runs New York?" *New York,* Dec. 23, 1968.
19. *New York Times,* Oct. 18, 1969, pp. 1, 21.

to have "straight" collective bargaining but, being realistic, uses political influence as an "insurance policy." Despite its Democratic party ties, Local 249, in keeping with the traditional labor policy of rewarding its friends, supported two Republican state assemblymen in the 1968 election. Teamster Local 609, a mixed private–public union, which represents city sanitation workers, has a black president and a predominantly black membership, but endorsed a white congressman with a perfect prolabor record over a black challenger in 1968. Teamster local unions in other cities all accept, as a fact of life, the interrelatedness of politics and collective bargaining in public employment. For most of them, public employees represent a minority of their membership and do not warrant independent political activity. These locals prefer to channel their political contributions and efforts through DRIVE, the political arm of the Teamsters union.

Uniformed Services

The three major national organizations representing the uniformed protective services differ considerably in their political activities. The International Association of Fire Fighters (IAFF) behaves pretty much like a typical AFL-CIO craft union, adhering closely to economic issues directly related to the fire fighter's job. At its 1968 convention, for example, the IAFF commended Congress for excluding fire fighters from coverage under the Social Security Act and for passing the Fire Research and Safety Act of 1968; supported a fire fighters minimum standards and education bill; supported exemption of fire fighters' pensions from federal income tax; and endorsed a thirty-five-hour week for fire fighters, criminal penalties for attacks on fire fighters in performance of their duties, automatic cost-of-living adjustments in fire fighters' pensions, federal aid to fire departments, a federal minimum wage for fire fighters, establishment of a National Fire Fighters' Academy, and a federal collective bargaining law covering fire fighters.[20] IAFF conventions rarely discuss social legislation, civil rights, or political issues not directly related to the occupational interests of their members.

20. *Resolutions, 29th Biennial Convention, International Association of Fire Fighters, AFL-CIO and CLC* (1968).

In contrast, the Fraternal Order of Police (FOP) devoted its 1969 national conference almost entirely to discussion of "law and order." Relatively little time was spent considering legislation affecting the economic status of police, and there was no discussion of the possible effect on the FOP of the effort, then underway, to form a national union of police officers. The legislative chairman reported on petitions "urging action by the President, Congress and the Judiciary to offset the effects of certain decisions by the Supreme Court (Miranda, Escobedo, etc.)."[21] He also noted with approval the appointment of Chief Justice Warren Burger, remarking that it would help correct "the imbalance in the Court in favor of individual rights as opposed to the rights of the public where crime is concerned."[22]

The convention adopted resolutions citing George C. Wallace for his strong law and order stand in the 1968 presidential campaign; condemning the Black Panthers, Students for a Democratic Society, and "any other groups which through their actions, statements or intimidations have led this assault on the nation's police forces," and requesting that the attorney general "conduct a full investigation" of such groups; and commending the American Legion, Veterans of Foreign Wars, and Fraternal Order of Eagles for their support of "the Police and Law and Order throughout the United States."[23] It refused to support legislation providing federal subsidies to police pension systems on the rationale that "federal control always follows federal money." Throughout the five-day meeting, delegates exhibited a distinct lack of interest in subjects relating to economic matters, but were most enthusiastic and attentive to discussions of law and order, Supreme Court decisions, and civilian review boards.

The International Conference of Police Associations (ICPA) in 1969, while including law enforcement and efforts to combat subversive organizations on its conference agenda, was preoccupied with such matters as professionalization of the police function; improving the image of police officers; collective bargaining, group insurance, and retirement programs; and ways to improve police per-

21. *FOP National Lodge, Reports, Officers and Committees, 39th National Conference* (1969), p. 110.

22. Ibid., p. 111.

23. National Lodge, Fraternal Order of Police, "Proposed Resolutions," 39th Biennial Convention (1969).

formance. In response to a debate on the question "Should police officers belong to a labor union?" delegates voted overwhelmingly against the idea of a national police union.

The president elected at the 1970 convention promised a more active political role for the ICPA. "We shall actually support candidates and legislatures supporting law enforcement, and shall work against candidates . . . which are anti–good law enforcement. We shall let the public know who the judges are that are letting criminals go free." Noting that the first amendment of the constitution regarding free speech includes policemen, he declared that the ICPA "will take to task any court or department" that prohibits a police association from criticizing its department or politicians.[24]

LOCAL POLITICAL ACTIVITY

Fire fighters as a group are generally acknowledged, by representatives of other unions and politicians, to be the most effective political activists among municipal employees. Their success is variously ascribed to the favorable image they project to the public; the nature of the job, which allows ample time to indulge in political discussions and to plan strategy while on duty; willingness to turn out in large numbers for door-to-door canvassing or electioneering; and a general gregariousness which leads fire fighters to enjoy rubbing elbows with politicians and the eating, drinking, and talking that is so integral a part of the lobbying process in American politics. Whatever the reasons, fire fighters, through their IAFF locals and state associations, exercise much greater political influence than numbers alone can explain. IAFF local unions are very active in the AFL-CIO Committee on Political Education, supply manpower and occasionally money in election campaigns, and often endorse candidates, without regard to party, on the principle of rewarding friends and punishing enemies.

Local police associations, whether independent or affiliated with the FOP, ICPA, or unions, are less active politically than fire fighter organizations. Partially, this is so because "little Hatch acts" are much more stringently enforced against them than against other public employee organizations. Moreover, police believe the public

24. Bureau of National Affairs, *Government Employee Relations Report*, No. 365 (Sept. 7, 1970), p. B-14.

would view their overt involvement in politics with greater apprehension than they do that of other organizations.

Police organizations are less formally structured, relatively poorly
financed, and less experienced than IAFF locals in the political
arena. And they are less dependent on political action because so
much power, political and otherwise, resides in the job itself. Police
officers are in a position to do small and sometimes large favors for
people generally and politicians in particular. They often have access to information about political figures that could prove harmful or embarrassing in a campaign. In short, politicians have reason
to court the favor of police organizations without the promise of
financial contributions, manpower, and the other usual kinds of
help that they need to get elected. Recently the political influence
of police organizations has increased, with little effort on their part,
as public concern over crime, violence, student unrest, and law enforcement has increased.

Evidence of the political influence exercised by fire fighter and
police organizations came from almost every city canvassed for this
study. The Patrolmen's Benevolent Association of New York City
mounted a major campaign in 1966 to block the establishment of a
civilian police review board proposed by Mayor Lindsay. Supported
by massive expenditures of funds and police manpower, it was instrumental in defeating the review board proposal by almost a two-
to-one vote in a voter referendum.[25]

The fire fighters of Boston in 1958 won a wage referendum in
which they carried every ward but one. An English language weekly
newspaper read by the Italian community described the victory:

The firemen have representatives of their union who are outspoken
and unafraid of who is Boston's Mayor. They got themselves a substantial wage increase by decision of the voters after their requests for such a
raise had been refused by former Mayor Hynes. There are many astute
politicians among the firemen and their successes stress their ability to
play politics with a professional touch.[26]

In Detroit the IAFF supported Jerome Cavanaugh for mayor in
1961, when he defeated the incumbent who had the backing of the

25. *New York Times,* numerous issues in 1966.
26. *Gazetta del Massachusetts,* quoted in Edward C. Banfield and Martha Derthick
(eds.), *A Report on the Politics of Boston* (Cambridge: Joint Center for Urban Studies
of the Massachusetts Institute of Technology and Harvard University, 1960), pp. III-1,
III-2.

AFL-CIO and the Detroit Police Officers Association. In that campaign the union turned out three hundred men to ring doorbells on three consecutive days before the election. The union also endorsed Republician George Romney for Governor, when the AFL-CIO backed his Democratic opponent. In 1970 the Detroit Police Officers Association endorsed Sheriff Roman Gribbs of Wayne County in his successful race for mayor against a black opponent.

Fire fighters in Denver have been successful in winning all but two pay increase referendums during the past twenty years, police all but one in twelve years (the police defeat came in 1962, when many policemen were found to have been involved in a burglary ring operating in Denver). The local IAFF president and a police detective are given leave from their jobs to engage in lobbying activity when the state legislature is in session. Police and fire fighters joined together to defeat an attempt to put them under the same career service board as other city employees, which would have decreased their pensions and other benefits. The Police Protective Association also successfully opposed a model cities bill because, according to an organization representative, it was a "giveaway to the nigger" and antipolice in its outlook.

In Portland, Oregon, fire fighters and their wives engage in telephone and door-to-door canvassing in campaigns for election of city commissioners. The local union also contributes money to candidates. The IAFF has been instrumental in defeating attempts to change to a city manager or strong-mayor form of government, preferring commissioners who are subject to reelection every two years and thus politically sensitive. The Portland police, affiliated with AFSCME, are also heavily involved in political action, although they stopped endorsing candidates a few years ago. In 1969 the local sent over 5,000 letters, individually typed by policemen's wives, to residents asking them to get their councilmen to vote for a wage increase formula favored by the union.

Both fire fighters and police in Houston maintain legislative representatives at the state capital who are on leave from their duties under a "tacit" agreement with city officials. In 1968 a bond issue to provide funds for a new fire station and new fire-fighting equipment was the only proposition approved by voters out of thirteen on the ballot. A similar bond issue for the police department was defeated. The IAFF claims credit for helping the mayor, who was elected with their support, obtain legislative approval for a city sales tax. Union representatives boast that they have never failed to deliver the entire bloc of Houston votes in the state legislature. The IAFF has not hesitated to break with the AFL-CIO to support conservative candidates friendly to fire fighters.

Associations

Employee associations are much less active politically than other organizations of public employees. They rarely endorse candidates for elective office, contribute funds to political campaigns, provide manpower to help get out the vote, mail campaign literature, or perform the many other tasks that are important in elections. The Assembly of Governmental Employees' constitution prohibits it from participating in election campaigns or "partisan political matters."[27]

The Connecticut State Employees Association has, however, endorsed candidates for state office on a few occasions. The Hawaii Government Employees Association endorses candidates for political office, and two of its staff members have been elected to the state legislature. On the other hand, the constitutions of associations in Massachusetts, Ohio, and Washington prohibit endorsements of candidates. Only a few local associations appear to endorse candidates and contribute directly to their campaigns.

While associations rarely make direct financial contributions, many contribute indirectly to campaigns by purchasing tickets to dinners honoring candidates and conducting special fund-raising affairs. In California the Employees Political Information Committee (EPIC) accepts political contributions from association members in much the same way as COPE does for the AFL-CIO. Financial contributions of any kind are more common among associations in California and other western states than in other parts of the country.

Associations' political action usually consists of providing voting records of legislators on selected bills, giving favorable and frequent mention to friendly legislators and council members in their publications, inviting them to address meetings, and extending hos-

27. Constitution and By Laws, Assembly of Governmental Employees (1971), Art. 7.

pitality at luncheons and cocktail parties. State associations are more apt than local to publish voting records since state legislators have more direct impact on their wages and other conditions of employment. Many associations encourage members to let their state legislators and city council members know how they feel on particular issues of interest to public employees, and they claim that such informal campaigns are very effective.

The most common form of political activity, engaged in by practically all state associations, is lobbying in the state legislature, presenting testimony at legislative hearings and committee meetings, and trying to influence votes on specific bills that affect their members. The Michigan State Employees Association estimates that 80 percent of its staff time is spent in lobbying activity. The California association has a large committee drawn from the membership—one member assigned to each state legislator—which is called on for lobbying activity as the occasion demands. Association lobbying is carried on by staff, officers, and members, rather than by professional full-time lobbyists.

Local associations are much less active in trying to influence city or county officeholders. Those affiliated with state organizations depend on the parent organization to look out for their interests in the state legislature. The greatest amount of political involvement is found among local associations in California, particularly in the San Francisco and Los Angeles areas.

Association political activity, in addition to being much more limited than that of unions, is also less partisan. When candidates are supported, they are as likely to be Republicans as Democrats. Association political action, conducted with very limited financial resources, is oriented more to issues and specific legislation than to political officeholders or candidates. Associations also adhere closely to issues that directly affect their members and rarely take positions on broader social and political issues.

Nurses

The American Nurses' Association and its state affiliates actively promote and support legislation to advance the economic status of nurses and the health needs of the nation, but they do not engage in political action designed to influence the election of individual candidates. The responsibility for conducting the ANA's lobbying activities resides with the Governmental Relations Department, whose function is "to promote desirable social, health and economic legislation."[28] The department in 1971 had four professional staff members working out of the Washington office and one in the New York headquarters of the association.[29]

At the 1970 convention the ANA executive director, assessing the 1968 elections, noted a "more conservative" administration and a Congress that gave "less attention to health problems, more concern with economy in government, with law and order, with more restrictive labor policy."[30] During 1968 and 1969 the association had contacted congressmen and congressional committees regarding aid to nursing education, labor legislation, nurse officers in the armed services, standards of nursing care under social security, health insurance, the exchange visitor program, civil rights, appointments to the Department of Health, Education, and Welfare, occupational health and safety, and unemployment insurance.[31] ANA representatives had also appeared before the Republican and Democratic platform committees in 1968.

The Governmental Relations Department of ANA also reviews and comments on state legislative proposals in response to requests from state associations. State nurses' associations generally do not endorse candidates for office, contribute directly to campaigns, or supply workers to help office-seekers. (The Oregon association does provide its members with the voting records of state legislators.) Commonly, associations lobby and present testimony on behalf of proposed legislation affecting nurses, such as bills providing for collective bargaining for public employees and for proprietary and nonprofit hospitals, licensing laws regulating nursing practice, public funds for nursing education, scholarships for students of nursing, and appropriations for state health, mental health, and welfare agencies.[32] In a number of states, associations have used publicity as a potent political weapon in exposing the pay and working condi-

28. American Nurses' Association, *House of Delegates Reports, 1968–70, 47th Convention* (1970), p. 37.
29. ANA, "Headquarters Staff List" (ANA, Oct. 1, 1971; processed).
30. ANA, *House of Delegates Reports, 1968–70*, p. 37.
31. Ibid., pp. 37–39.
32. Ibid., p. 94.

tions of nurses. It is particularly effective in bringing public opinion to bear on officeholders during negotiations and when an impasse in bargaining poses the threat of a strike or other kinds of job action.

Because of their diverse professional, social, and economic interests, the ANA and its state affiliates cooperate with a broad spectrum of organizations which have little in common with one another. Staff members and officers attend meetings and conferences of the American Medical Association, American Hospital Association, and National Alliance of Businessmen, while also maintaining close contacts with the AFL-CIO, individual labor unions, Civil Liberties Clearing House, Legal Defense Fund Institute, and Urban Coalition for Health. On the whole, however, the ANA and most state associations have much more in common with labor and liberal-oriented organizations than with conservative organizations and work more closely with them in trying to influence legislation in Congress and in state legislatures.

Summary

Before collective bargaining in public employment was widely accepted, government employees were entirely dependent on the political process for the determination of their wages and working conditions. Now, even in jurisdictions that practice collective bargaining, elected officials still must vote the necessary funds before negotiated wage increases and other economic benefits can be made effective. Under the circumstances, public employee organizations have had more reason than unions in private industry to engage in political activity in state and local governments.

All unions work through the AFL-CIO Committee on Political Education (COPE) or similar conduits for raising campaign funds. But at the state and local level, public employee unions have their own programs to elect friendly legislators, members of city councils, and county boards of supervisors. Many of them claim they can identify officeholders who owe their election to votes of union members. While it would be unfair and an oversimplification to say that unions control the politicians whom they were instrumental in electing to office, they expect and do receive a more sympathetic hearing and more favorable voting behavior from them than from other officeholders.

Of the public employee unions, AFSCME has the most elaborate political action program at the national and council levels. Its interests are wide-ranging, with emphasis on issues that are important to its substantial minority group membership. In state and local elections, AFSCME councils often support different candidates than those endorsed by AFL-CIO city and state central bodies. AFSCME has recently taken the leadership in forming a coalition at the national level with the National Education Association and the International Association of Fire Fighters to increase the political influence of public employees.

The IAFF is the most influential union with city and state legislators and with the general public. Many IAFF locals and state associations claim credit for the enactment of state laws and local ordinances of direct benefit to fire fighters. Fire fighters also have an enviable record on referendums on wage increases, pensions, and the issue of parity pay with policemen. Their success appears to be due to their very favorable public image and their willingness to spend money and work hard. Police organizations neither work as hard nor spend as much money as the IAFF, but they too have considerable influence with legislators and voters. But when police and fire fighters are on opposite sides of an issue, like parity pay, the odds are usually on the latter to win.

State and local employee associations confine their political activity to issues of direct benefit to their members. They almost never take positions on social issues such as the Vietnam war, civil rights, or the environment. The associations rarely endorse candidates for office or contribute funds or manpower to political campaigns, as do the unions. Most of their political effort is devoted to lobbying for bills benefiting their members and promoting measures to strengthen the merit system and civil service.

The American Nurses' Association and its state affiliates are active in lobbying and presenting testimony and in other ways trying to influence legislation reflecting their views on social, economic, and professional issues. They cooperate with both conservative and liberal organizations, usually joining with the former on professional matters and the latter on social and economic issues.

CHAPTER TEN

Emerging Patterns

During the 1960s, public sector collective bargaining generally followed the private sector pattern. This study, however, has focused on the distinctive aspects of organization and bargaining in public employment. Moreover, recent developments indicate that, on some issues, the public sector may set the pattern for private industry. Changes in unions and associations, in the attitudes of public employees and employers, and in state statutes suggest the direction that organization and collective bargaining will take in the 1970s.

Organization

Already, employee organization is proportionately larger in state and local government than in private industry. However, the division of organized public employees between unions and associations dilutes their impact as a pressure group and diminishes their influence within the labor movement. The membership distribution has been changing during the last few years in favor of the unions and this trend is likely to continue.

In states that have public employee collective bargaining laws or choose to enact them, organization of public employees should proceed at a rapid pace. All functions and all occupational groups, including supervisors, who are now covered by most state laws, will be included. The pace of organization will probably decrease by

212

the mid-1970s as a hard core of states refuses to enact legislation. However, support for a federal law guaranteeing collective bargaining rights to all public employees will increase as the number of states without such laws grows smaller. By the end of the 1970s, all state and local government employees probably will be protected in their right to organize and bargain collectively.

Unions have grown stronger than associations in local government and there is no reason to expect a reversal of this trend, though associations will continue to be dominant among such occupational groups as policemen, supervisors, and professional employees. Associations have a better chance to withstand the union challenge among state employees where they have existed for many years and have the semblance of a national organization—the Assembly of Governmental Employees (AGE). But policy differences among state associations appear to be greater than their mutual interests, and there is little likelihood that the AGE will evolve into a strong national organization. By the end of the 1970s, most state associations will undoubtedly have merged or affiliated with unions, adapted to the union model while remaining outside the labor movement, or ceased to exist. The traditional type of employee association, oriented to selling group insurance and other consumer services and functioning primarily as a legislative lobbying and political pressure group rather than as a collective bargaining agent, seems to have little future.

Among the unions the American Federation of State, County and Municipal Employees (AFSCME) should continue as the dominant industrial union and the International Association of Fire Fighters (IAFF) as the major craft union in state and local government. The Service Employees International Union (SEIU) and the International Brotherhood of Teamsters will continue to make gains, but the trend toward larger bargaining units and the desire of employers to avoid fragmentation will favor AFSCME because it already has a foothold in many more communities than any other union. The Laborers' International Union appears more interested in federal employment than in state and local government and is unlikely to present a long-range challenge to the major unions. AFSCME, now the seventh largest and the fastest growing union in the AFL-CIO, has the potential to become the largest union in the federation and a major power in the labor movement.

Structure

A number of private sector unions have, over the years, adjusted their internal structures to accommodate to the special problems of skilled workers, white collar employees, and other groups of members. Thus far, only the Laborers' Union, which has established a Federal–Public Service Employees' Division, has made structural arrangements to recognize the special organizational and representation problems of public employees. The recent spate of affiliations of employee associations with unions may result in demands for formal recognition of public employees in the structure and leadership of these unions. The union most likely to be affected is the Service Employees, some one-third of whose membership consists of public employees, including several former associations and the National Union of Police Officers which are considered autonomous units within the SEIU. The American Nurses' Association and its state affiliates may face similar problems of accommodating to the needs of nurses subject to public employee collective bargaining laws.

Professional associations have a special problem of maintaining their professional orientation while engaging in collective bargaining. Collective bargaining has not yet become paramount in the American Nurses' Association, but it has introduced visible strains in some state nurses' associations. A number of professional associations, forced to espouse collective bargaining or risk having their members represented by unions, have chosen the former alternative. The cost and time-consuming demand on exclusive bargaining representatives threaten to push professional objectives aside, yet chapters that have lost representation elections have had difficulty retaining their members. The coming decade will determine whether the ANA and other professional associations can develop structures that will permit them to engage in collective bargaining without significantly diluting the professional commitment of their organizations.

One of the areas in which the public sector may serve as an example for the private is minority group representation. Government, especially at the local level, is the first major employment sector in which blacks and other minority group members have been sufficiently numerous to achieve significant leadership in unions. Many local unions have a majority of black members and black leadership. In a relatively short period of time, blacks have had more success in being elected or appointed to office and staff positions at national and intermediate levels of public employee unions than they have achieved in private sector unions. Except for the uniformed services and more recently in nursing,[1] black caucuses or separate organizations have not appeared as they have in some private sector unions, although race has been an issue in some local union elections. There is no need for such separate groups in organizations where blacks are a majority or a large enough minority to compete for leadership and control within the existing system. Black, and in some areas Puerto Rican and Mexican-American, leadership will grow at all levels in unions during the 1970s.

State associations, because of the preponderance of white collar members and the smaller proportion of blacks in state government, have less minority group membership and leadership than unions. This will be an obstacle in their competition with unions as blacks are hired in greater numbers and in a wider range of occupations. In some areas, associations may represent a white alternative to unions with substantial or majority black membership and leadership.

The relatively small minority group membership in protective service organizations reflects the low employment of blacks and other nonwhites in police and fire departments. Nonwhite leadership in these organizations is almost nonexistent. The uniformed service organizations have generally opposed any relaxation of standards and other measures designed to increase the number of minority group personnel. There is little evidence that unions differ significantly from associations in their approach to race relations. It will be interesting to observe the effect of close and continuous association between large numbers of policemen and blacks if AFSCME or the SEIU National Union of Police Officers succeeds in organizing policemen on a national scale.

1. American Nurses' Association, *House of Delegates Reports, 1970–72, 48th Convention* (1972), p. 25.

Interunion Conflict

The labor movement has never before experienced the intensity of conflict *within* the major federation that currently exists in public employment. In the early 1930s, when industrial unions challenged the craft union orientation of the American Federation of Labor (AFL), the movement split, and for twenty years unions organized into the Congress of Industrial Organizations (CIO) fought AFL unions for the right to represent workers in collective bargaining. When the costs of this warfare became prohibitive and the leaders of the rival federations had died, the two groups merged. After 1955, unions continued to compete with each other, but most large employers had been organized by them and bilateral no-raiding agreements and the AFL-CIO Internal Disputes Plan helped to mute conflicts. Mergers of unions with conflicting or contiguous jurisdictions were consummated and are continuing to be negotiated.

Not so in public employment which presented virgin territory with literally millions of unorganized workers. Cloudy jurisdictions dating from the admission of AFSCME into the AFL afforded no useful guide for resolving conflicting organization claims. Bilateral pacts were unfeasible, given the almost complete overlapping of jurisdictional claims, and the Internal Disputes Plan was ineffective in situations in which there were few established collective bargaining relationships. The result has been sharp and often bitter and vitriolic interunion conflict.

AFSCME, as the only all-public industrial union in state and local government, feels that it has been the target of the mixed unions which, in its view, have no business in public employment. The mixed unions consider AFSCME's jurisdictional claims monopolistic and completely unreasonable. Now, after several years of organizational warfare, AFSCME has called on the AFL-CIO to allocate and if necessary reallocate jurisdictions in the public employment field,[2] a gigantic task filled with what appear to be insurmountable obstacles. On another front, AFSCME has organized a

2. "Selected Constitutional Amendments and Resolutions Adopted by the 19th International AFSCME Convention," Bureau of National Affairs, *Government Employee Relations Report,* No. 455 (June 5, 1972), p. G-3.

Coalition of Public Employee Organizations with the National Education Association and the International Association of Fire Fighters, thus drawing a line between all-public employee organizations, both inside and outside the labor movement, and the mixed unions. Other exclusively public employee organizations have been invited to join. In taking this action, AFSCME appears to be laying the foundation for a grouping of organizations with common interests in preparation for challenges and opportunities it may encounter in the 1970s.

Supervisors

Although state public employee collective bargaining laws are generally more restrictive than the National Labor Relations Act, most of them go beyond the federal law governing private sector labor relations in extending coverage to supervisory employees. Foremen and supervisors were covered under the original Wagner Act in 1935 but were explicitly excluded by the Taft-Hartley Act of 1947.[3] The rationale for including supervisors in public employment is grounded in the strong community of interest between supervisors and nonsupervisory employees in many government functions and the inapplicability of the traditional private sector definitions of *management* and *employee* to the more complex personnel systems that exist in state and local government.[4] Traditionally, supervisors have been members and often officers of the same employee associations and unions as nonsupervisory employees in government.

Regardless of the merits of the issue, units of supervisors have been recognized and bargain collectively in many states and localities. Despite a 1969 recommendation of the Advisory Commission on Intergovernmental Relations that supervisors be denied bargaining rights, there has been no trend in this direction.[5] Thus far there has been no agitation for amending the Taft-Hartley Act to include supervisors, probably because they are not usually enrolled

3. Labor Management Relations Act, 1947, secs. 2(3) and 2(11).
4. Advisory Commission on Intergovernmental Relations, *Labor-Management Policies for State and Local Government* (Washington: ACIR, 1969), pp. 95–96.
5. Ibid., pp. 95–96.

by private sector unions and their few separate organizations disappeared after the Taft-Hartley Act removed their statutory protection. However, it is likely that supervisors in private industry will eventually demand the same rights and privileges extended to their counterparts in public employment. They will be supported by unions eager for a new source of members and the opportunity to extend collective bargaining to this large and growing group of strategically placed employees. Management will undoubtedly strongly oppose turning the clock back from Taft-Hartley to Wagner Act principles, setting the stage for a major controversy in the law of labor-management relations.

Union Security

Another controversial, though more limited, example of public sector trail-blazing is found in the area of union security. Most state public employment laws are much more restrictive than the Taft-Hartley Act. The recent trend to permit agency shop agreements still falls short of the union shop which may be negotiated under federal law except where state laws prohibit such agreements.[6] But Hawaii and Rhode Island have gone beyond merely authorizing agency shop agreements by mandating the payment of a service charge from all nonmembers in a unit for which an employee organization has been accorded exclusive representation. The rationale for such a statutory requirement is that since public policy requires the organization to represent members and nonmembers alike, all employees should be required to contribute to the cost of representation. These laws essentially accept the union argument against "free riders" advanced on behalf of the union shop in private industry.

Public employee unions will certainly press for this automatic service fee payment in other states. As a practical matter, the very high proportion of union shop agreements in the private sector makes mandatory union security less important there. Nonetheless, the principle embodied in the Hawaii and Rhode Island statutes represents a significant development in labor law. This, along with collective bargaining rights for supervisors, is an area in which public sector experience may influence private sector labor relations.

6. Labor Management Relations Act, 1947, sec. 14(b).

The Strike Issue

The year 1970 was the first since 1965 that government statistics did not show a large increase in strikes over the previous year, and in 1971 the number of public employee strikes actually declined.[7] It is interesting that this leveling off in strikes should have occurred during a period when a number of public employee organizations repealed the no-strike provisions in their constitutions. This suggests that organization prohibitions against strikes were not a serious impediment to stoppages and that their repeal was a reflection of strong membership sentiment rather than an inducement to strike action.

Despite the leveling off, strikes in government are still sufficiently numerous and significant in their effect on essential public service to constitute a major issue. The trend appears to be away from blanket legal prohibition of all strikes. Hawaii and Pennsylvania now permit strikes that do not endanger public health and safety; several courts have refused to issue injunctions against public employee strikes;[8] and tripartite conferences of labor, management, and neutral representatives have endorsed at least a limited right to strike by government employees.[9] There has also been an increase in laws providing for compulsory arbitration in disputes affecting police and fire protection and a few statutes require arbitration of all impasses. Unions, which have traditionally been adamantly opposed to compulsory arbitration, appear to have softened their opposition, while many municipal employers, outraged by what they regard as overly generous arbitration awards, have taken a strong position against compulsory arbitration. The strongest support for arbitration, preferably voluntary but compulsory if necessary, comes from the public which prefers almost any resolution of a labor dispute to being harmed or inconvenienced by interruption of public services.

7. U.S. Bureau of Labor Statistics, "Work Stoppages in 1971" (1972; processed), p. 3.

8. AFSCME, *Report of the President and Headquarters' Departments, 19th International Convention* (1972), pp. 91–93.

9. "Collective Bargaining in American Government," Report of the 40th American Assembly, Oct. 28–31, 1971, Arden House, Harriman, N.Y.; "Collective Bargaining in American Government," Report of the Western Assembly, May 11–14, 1972, Highlands Inn, Carmel, Calif.

The next decade will provide extensive experience with a variety of approaches to dealing with strikes in public employment. However, collective bargaining assisted by mediation, conciliation, and fact-finding will prove in public employment, as in the private sector, the best avenue to resolving differences. Strike prohibitions, without an alternative method of resolving disputes, do not deter strikes. Arbitration, while useful and perhaps necessary in some disputes, cannot satisfy the parties in the long run. Furthermore, the supply of qualified arbitrators is much too limited to meet the demand that generalized compulsory arbitration of impasses in public employee disputes would create. A most hopeful development is recognition of the need for extensive training of professional negotiators on both sides and the increasing efforts by unions, government employers, universities, and professional organizations of practitioners to improve the skills of collective bargaining representatives.

Political Activity

One of the presumed benefits of collective bargaining in public employment is a reduction in settlements arrived at through political deals. Experience indicates that even with collective bargaining, politics will continue to be an important element in government labor relations. Unions will not readily forgo opportunities to improve on negotiated settlements through political "end runs" and "double-deck" bargaining, and public officials will continue to make political capital out of their power to approve or vote the funds necessary to implement negotiated agreements. But experienced and sophisticated representatives on both sides recognize the hazards of mixing politics and collective bargaining and are making efforts to minimize this practice.

Politics in collective bargaining should not be confused, however, with political activity in legislative lobbying and election campaigns. In these areas, strong public employee unions and associations will mean more rather than less activity. A willingness to forgo double-deck bargaining does not mean abstaining from trying to elect friendly executives and legislators who appoint department heads, allocate funds, and enact laws that can have significant effects on public employees. A major barrier to political activity by public employees has been the Hatch Act and state acts patterned after it. These statutes have not prevented public employee unions and associations from developing political action programs of varying scope and intensity. Now, public employees and their organizations are challenging these restrictions on individual political activity just as they have successfully challenged restrictions on their right to organize and engage in collective bargaining. Congress is considering proposals to reform the Hatch Act, and a 1972 district court decision holding the act unconstitutional[10] has been appealed to the Supreme Court. The outcome of these deliberations on federal employees' activities will have important implications for state and local government employees.

Convergence of Unions and Associations

When research for this study began in 1968, state and local government employees appeared to be organized into two distinctly different types of organizations: unions and associations. Unions were organizations of workers as distinct from managers, executives, and elected officials (the line between management and workers was blurred, however, and supervisory employees were accorded full membership rights). Associations, in contrast, were open to all employees within specified government jurisdictions, occupations, or professions without regard to hierarchical status.

Unions generally were national or international (including Canada), vertical type organizations with direct lines of authority between local, intermediate, and national bodies; all unions considered themselves part of a "labor movement," grounded not in any formal organization such as the AFL-CIO, but in a mutuality of interest that transcended their differences on specific issues. Associations, whether local, state, or national, strongly emphasized independence and autonomy, with little or no control of lower by higher echelons. They did not regard themselves as part of the

10. In the United States District Court for the District of Columbia, *National Association of Letter Carriers, et al.* v. *United States Civil Service Commission, et al.* (July 31, 1972).

"labor movement" and some were antiunion in origin and philosophy.

Unions were dedicated to collective bargaining as the principal method for determining wages, hours, and conditions of employment, with union security and the right to strike essential elements of the process. Some unions prohibited strikes, especially by police and fire fighters, and even those without antistrike constitutional provisions discouraged work stoppages. Associations opposed collective bargaining, strikes, and compulsory membership. They preferred to use persuasion rather than direct action in pursuit of their objectives.

By the end of 1972, many of the distinguishing features of unions and associations in state and local government had blurred or disappeared. The distinction between supervisory and nonsupervisory employees had sharpened as a result of state public employee bargaining laws, and the role of supervisors had been reduced in both unions and associations. They were less likely to be officers or play a dominant role in associations, as they often had before the advent of collective bargaining.

Associations have tended to strengthen their national offices, improve staff services, and increase dues in order to function more effectively in collective bargaining and other representational activities. Their antiunion philosophy has been toned down and some associations characterize themselves as "like unions," but without ties to the "labor movement" and the national control that they regard as inherent in unionism. Unions, on their part, have reduced their anti-association attitudes and epithets. In some instances, unions and associations have cooperated in legislative lobbying, political activity, and even collective bargaining and strikes.

The most important changes have occurred in the use of collective bargaining, which is now espoused and practiced by many associations. Union security in the form of dues checkoff and the agency shop is recognized as an important adjunct of collective bargaining by almost all employee organizations. Strike prohibitions have been repealed, and strikes and other forms of direct action are utilized by associations and unions alike.

Despite similarities between the two kinds of public employee organizations, unions and associations are still significantly different. It is misleading and an oversimplification to call all public employee organizations unions, as the general public and the mass media commonly do. A union is a continuous organization of workers, whose primary purpose is to improve wages, hours, and working conditions of its members through collective bargaining. Organizations that behave like unions in some respects, but whose primary purpose is social and fraternal interaction, advancing civil service and the merit system, professional improvement, or something else, are not unions, any more than unions are fraternal, civil service, or professional organizations simply because they serve one or more of these purposes for some members or engage in these activities at some time. The Fraternal Order of Police, International Conference of Police Associations, Assembly of Governmental Employees, most state and local employee associations, and the American Nurses' Association are not unions, because collective bargaining to improve wages, hours, and working conditions is not the primary purpose of these organizations.

On the other hand, some organizations that call themselves associations are really unions in everything but name. It matters not that their leaders insist or that their constitutions proclaim that they are not unions, nor that unions refuse to accept them as bona fide labor organizations. If they engage in collective bargaining and devote a major portion of their resources to representing employees in negotiations and grievances, they are unions. It is clear from this study that some associations have already made the transition to unionism and others are in the process of doing so.

The transition is bound to continue during the 1970s. Collective bargaining is not an activity that can be pursued effectively as a sideline. Once adopted, it has a way of pushing other organization objectives into a subordinate role. Given the growing acceptance of collective bargaining in public employment, variations in public employee organization will by the end of this decade be occurring within the confines of unionism.

APPENDIX A

Municipal Employee Representation

In July 1968 a questionnaire concerning their dealings with unions or associations representing city employees with respect to wages and conditions of employment was sent to 2,072 cities with 10,000 or more population.[1] Responses came from 1,530 cities, 74 percent of all cities queried, and was consistently high by size of city, region, census type, and form of government.

The largest proportions of responses came from cities with 250,000–500,000 population, cities located in the West, those classified by the U.S. Census Bureau as central cities, and cities with a council-manager form of government. Geographically all regions of the United States were well represented. The response rate from cities contacted was at least 50 percent in all states except Louisiana (20 percent), Montana (22 percent), and Mississippi (45 percent).

Comparison of total employment in the responding cities with 1968 census figures indicates that the responses covered over 60 percent of all municipal employment in the United States, exclusive of instructional personnel in education. In all nine functional categories the responses covered at least half of all employees, and in five over 60 percent.

Local Employee Representation

Perhaps the most surprising finding of the survey was that more than 60 percent of all employees in the reporting cities were represented by unions or associations with which public officials dealt, "either formally

---

1. The U.S. Bureau of Labor Statistics cooperated with Jack Stieber in the development of the questionnaire. The International City Managers Association distributed the questionnaire.

or informally, on such subjects as wages, working conditions, promotions, grievances or other personnel matters."[2] (See Table A-1.[3]) That figure decreases to 50 percent of all employees if New York City is excluded. With 254,746 employees, exclusive of instructional education personnel, 98 percent of whom were represented by employee organizations, New York City inflates employee representation in every group in which it is included. Thus employee representation without New York City drops from 77 percent to 59 percent in cities with over 500,000 population, from 90 percent to 68 percent for cities in the Middle Atlantic region, from 68 percent to 55 percent in central cities, and from 71 percent to 57 percent in cities with a mayor-council form of government. Tables A-2 and A-3 analyzing employee representation in various municipal functions take account of the influence of New York City by showing the extent of employee organization with and without the most populous and the most highly organized city in the nation.

Employee Representation and Union Membership

Leaders of public employee unions suggest that the organization of employees in municipal government can be influenced significantly by the strength and support of the labor movement generally. They believe that public employees are more likely to join unions in cities where labor has succeeded in organizing workers in the private sector than in nonunion cities. Public employee unions have had difficulty in organizing and in engaging in collective bargaining in some cities where they have not had the support of private sector unions.[4]

Table A-4 indicates the positive relationship between general union membership and public employee representation. Cities in the Middle

2. Language used in questionnaire.
3. The high percentage of employee representation in cities of a quarter of a million or more is probably due primarily to the influence of population. All cities with 250,000 or more people are classified as central cities, and almost all cities with a population of over 500,000 have the mayor-council form of government. Detailed analysis of the survey data yields no evidence that either city type or form of government has any independent influence on extent of employee representation.
4. Chicago is such a city. See Arnold R. Weber, "Paradise Lost; or Whatever Happened to the Chicago Social Workers?" *Industrial and Labor Relations Review*, Vol. 22 (April 1969), pp. 323–38. The correlation of union membership as a proportion of all employees in nonagricultural establishments, by state, and percent of public employees represented by unions or associations, by state, as reported in the survey of cities, was 0.62. This correlation is consistent with the hypothesis that public employee representation is closely related to union membership generally in the various states. (Union membership by city is not generally available. State employment data are from U.S. Bureau of Labor Statistics, *Directory of National and International Labor Unions in the United States, 1969*, Bulletin 1665 [1970], p. 76.)

TABLE A-1. Total Municipal Employees Represented by Unions or Associations, by Size of City, Region, City Type, and Form of Government, 1968

Characteristic	Total cities	Employees		Percent of cities in group with						
		Total	Percent represented	No representation	1–24 percent representation	25–49 percent representation	50–79 percent representation	80–89 percent representation	90–99 percent representation	100 percent representation
Total, all cities	1,530	1,110,826	61	33	13	19	19	6	5	3
Population group										
Over 500,000	23	545,914	77	0	13	35	30	13	4	4
250,000–500,000	24	86,949	63	4	4	25	33	4	17	13
100,000–250,000	78	143,873	47	19	9	18	35	10	8	1
50,000–100,000	193	118,091	53	14	11	18	25	15	8	8
25,000–50,000	364	110,490	42	22	13	21	25	7	8	3
10,000–25,000	848	106,509	25	46	15	18	13	4	2	2
Geographic region										
New England	130	78,540	64	8	17	19	36	10	8	2
Middle Atlantic	239	348,162	90	23	11	28	18	7	6	6
East North Central	336	159,251	60	25	10	24	27	9	4	1
West North Central	149	55,604	46	41	17	21	15	1	3	2
South Atlantic	182	177,532	31	67	14	10	7	1	1	1
East South Central	56	27,694	33	41	23	21	11	1	2	0
West South Central	135	79,272	26	60	17	16	6	0	1	1
Mountain	73	34,510	31	44	25	16	8	4	0	3
Pacific	230	159,261	64	19	9	13	26	13	10	10

City type									
Central	238	830,129	68	16	12	23	29	10	7	4
Suburban	755	167,351	50	31	13	20	20	8	5	4
Independent	537	113,346	27	45	15	17	15	3	3	2
Form of government									
Mayor-council	538	722,002	71	30	12	23	22	7	4	3
Council-manager	888	350,400	42	37	13	17	18	7	5	4
Commission	68	28,606	45	25	21	24	18	3	9	1
Town meeting	23	4,304	45	9	26	22	35	9	0	0
Representative town meeting	13	5,514	51	15	31	23	15	0	15	0

Source: Responses to questionnaire prepared by Jack Stieber with cooperation of the U.S. Bureau of Labor Statistics for International City Managers Association, July 1968. Various characteristics are those on which U.S. census data are based. Percentages may not add to 100 because of rounding.

TABLE A-2. *Percent of Municipal Employees Represented in Various Functions, by Size of City, 1968*

Function	All cities[a]	City population, in thousands					
		Over 500[a]	250– 500	100– 250	50– 100	25– 50	10– 25
Police protection	67(73)	79(87)	82	63	69	58	38
Fire protection	80(82)	95(97)	93	79	80	71	43
Public works	49(55)	66(77)	53	39	52	45	26
Public utilities	36(55)	39(70)	61	43	33	29	16
Public health and hospitals	38(57)	46(71)	38	48	23	23	12
Noninstructional education	40(61)	41(75)	72	36	60	29	28
Parks and recreation	38(46)	47(66)	57	33	38	28	14
Public welfare	31(69)	31(77)	50	25	38	26	4
All others	36(53)	47(73)	42	35	36	22	11
All functions	50(61)	59(77)	63	47	53	42	25

Source: Same as Table A-1.

a. Percentages in parentheses include New York City; it is excluded from principal percentages because its size distorts averages.

Atlantic (without New York City), New England, Pacific, and East North Central regions, all areas of high union organization, show higher percentages of employee representation than the other five regions within almost every population group.

The influence of population on public employee representation is apparent. It is particularly significant in the smallest cities, with 10,000–25,000 population, which rank lowest in representation by sizable amounts in every geographic region, and in cities with 25,000–50,000 people. In cities with over 50,000 population it becomes a much less reliable indicator. The population factors hold true in the various municipal functions also.

There may be a "critical size" factor at work in the organization of public employees. In the private sector, small plants and employers with relatively few employees are among the last to be organized by unions. In part, the closer relationship between employers and their workers is responsible, but many unions do not want to be bothered with signing up a few workers who are more difficult to organize and will almost certainly be relatively expensive to service and satisfy.

It is hardly surprising that cities with only a few hundred employees, spread among a variety of municipal functions and many more occupations, both blue collar and white collar, have relatively small proportions of their employees organized or represented by unions or associa-

TABLE A-3. *Percent of Municipal Employees Represented in Various Functions, by Geographic Region, 1968*

Function	All regions[a]	New England	Middle Atlantic[b]	East North Central	West North Central	South Atlantic	East South Central	West South Central	Mountain	Pacific
Police protection	67	77	89(95)	77	45	33	60	54	55	79
Fire protection	80	89	93(96)	85	79	55	70	66	68	91
Public works	49	71	59(81)	68	54	27	11	18	26	69
Public utilities	36	67	51(95)	54	43	27	41	10	20	36
Public health and hospitals	38	41	53(90)	52	18	29	0	3	5	79
Noninstructional education	40	54	58(89)	15	55	28	57	0	0	62
Parks and recreation	38	60	47(80)	43	51	15	5	7	23	55
Public welfare	31	47	54(97)	33	69	18	10	0	0	82
All others	36	51	36(86)	40	27	31	23	6	10	55
All functions	50	64	68(90)	60	46	31	33	26	31	64

Source: Same as Table A-1.

a. Excludes New York City because its size distorts averages.

b. Percentages in parentheses include New York City; it is excluded from principal percentages because its size distorts averages.

TABLE A-4. *Percent of Municipal Employees Represented in Various Regions, by Size of City, 1968*[a]

		City population, in thousands					
Region	All cities	Over 500	250– 500	100– 250	50– 100	25– 50	10– 25
New England	64	65[b]	c	78	74	54	36
Middle Atlantic	68	91	64	84	63	55	36
East North Central	60	71	71	70	55	48	31
West North Central	46	31[b]	94	44	48	33	16
South Atlantic	31	50	21	20	20	16	6
East South Central	33	c	36	52	42	22	11
West South Central	26	34	49	20	19	12	8
Mountain	31	27	c	56	25	25	11
Pacific	64	61	70	59	81	63	48
All regions	50	59	63	47	53	42	25

Source: Same as Table A-1.
a. Excludes New York City.
b. One city in this category.
c. No city in this category.

tions (see Table A-5). It would appear that the critical size at which public employees are likely to see the benefits of having an organization represent them and, at the same time, attract union or association interest is about 50,000 population. This cutoff point holds generally, though organizations of fire fighters and police tend to be much more successful in smaller cities than unions and associations that are active among other groups of employees.[5]

Employee Representation and State Legislation

There appears to be a close relationship between state collective bargaining legislation for public employees and the extent of employee representation. Of the 14 states that, in summer 1970, had laws requiring municipal employers to bargain collectively with organizations representing a majority of their employees in a bargaining unit, only 2 reported less than 50 percent employee representation. Most states with "permissive" statutes or laws requiring government employers to "meet and confer" with employee organizations also reported relatively high percentages of representation. On the other hand, of the 28 states with

5. The critical size may vary also with the degree of union organization generally and the existence of legislation protecting the right of government employees to organize and bargain collectively.

TABLE A-5. *Average Number of Municipal Employees in Various Functions, by Size of City, 1968*[a]

Function	All cities	*City population, in thousands*					
		Over 500	250– 500	100– 250	50– 100	25– 50	10– 25
All functions	560	13,235	3,623	1,832	612	304	126
Police protection	101	2,336	692	278	117	56	25
Fire protection	86	1,353	562	248	106	53	20
Public works	115	2,132	939	372	137	69	29
Public utilities	103	2,673	326	259	106	49	26
Public health and hospitals	112	1,778	299	209	41	52	25
Noninstructional education	234	1,828	723	595	138	124	44
Parks and recreation	41	693	340	135	45	21	9
Public welfare	47	1,069	174	56	28	11	3
All others	122	3,293	792	339	138	63	27

Source: Same as Table A-1.
a. Excludes New York City.

no legislation dealing with collective bargaining for public employees only 4 reported more than 50 percent representation while 19 had less than 40 percent represented by unions or associations. The labor movement is relatively weak in most of these states and 16 have "right to work" laws that prohibit the union shop.

Legislation undoubtedly facilitates and probably encourages municipal employees to join unions and associations. But it is also likely that organizations that have been successful in attracting large numbers of public employees have influenced the enactment of collective bargaining legislation. Several states with relatively high percentages of employee representation, for example, have enacted collective bargaining laws for public employees since 1970. This suggests an interaction between state laws and extent of public employee organization rather than a one-way relationship.

Some states in which unions and associations have been able to organize substantial proportions of public employees have no state law providing for collective bargaining in public employment. In these states, municipal ordinances, help from the labor movement, geographical location, and other factors all undoubtedly contributed to employee organization.

Michigan illustrates the interaction between legislation and public employee organization. Its Public Employment Relations Act, a comprehensive law providing collective bargaining rights to all public employees, except state employees covered by civil service, was enacted in the summer of 1965. However, unions and associations had already had considerable success in organizing public employees, and unions, working through the Michigan AFL-CIO, were influential in getting legislation enacted. The differences in union organization just before the law was passed and four and a half years later are shown in Table A-6. By 1969 the proportion of cities with organized employees had increased significantly in every employee group. The largest increases were in cities with less than 50,000 population.

The effect of Michigan's law is more clearly indicated by the percent of cities with written agreements in the two years:[6]

	Percent, by population group			
Year	*Over 50,000*	*25,000–50,000*	*10,000–25,000*	*4,000–10,000*
1965	5	25	17	6
1969	75	90	58	45

Since it is an unfair labor practice for a party to refuse to put into writing an agreement reached in negotiations, this upsurge in written agreements must be directly credited to the Michigan Public Employment Relations Act.

It is doubtful that the Michigan act would have been passed in 1965 had unions not been sufficiently strong to exert pressure on the state legislature. Reapportionment of the state legislature in 1964, which increased representation from urban areas where unions are more influential, also made passage more likely. Once passed, the law helped unions and associations organize public employees, especially in medium-sized and small cities where they had not been as successful as in the larger cities.

Public Employee Organizations

Cities in the survey identified the organizations to which their employees belonged according to the function in which they were employed (not, however, by the number of employees belonging to each organization). Tables A-7, A-8, and A-9 show the number of different organizations representing municipal employees and the strength of specific organizations. The American Federation of State, County and Municipal Employees (AFSCME) is the only organization that has substantial membership in all municipal functions (exclusive of fire protection).

6. Michigan Municipal League, *Annual Information Bulletin*, 1965, 1969.

TABLE A-6. *Percent of Municipal Employees Represented in Various Occupations in Michigan, by Size of City, 1965 and 1969*

| | City population, in thousands | | | | | | | | | |
| | Over 50 | | 25–50 | | 10–25 | | 4–10 | | All cities | |
Employees	1965	1969	1965	1969	1965	1969	1965	1969	1965	1969
Clerical and office workers	52	70	30	50	17	27	0	1	17	26
Unskilled and semiskilled laborers	94	95	80	95	45	66	22	37	46	61
Trade and craft workers	52	65	20	30	28	41	5	13	20	31
Policemen	78	80	40	80	54	61	3	20	33	49
Fire fighters	84	90	70	85	57	75	5	16	41	53
Others	5	20	5	20	3	11	3	5	4	11
Number of cities responding to survey	19	20	20	20	35	36	58	59	132	135

Source: Michigan Municipal League, *Annual Information Bulletin*, 1965, 1969.

TABLE A-7. *Number of Organizations Representing Municipal Employees, by Function, 1968*

| | Cities | | | Number of cities and percent of col. 2 reporting employees in | | | |
| | Number reporting employees (1) | Reporting representation | | One organization (4) | Two organizations (5) | Three organizations (6) | Four or more organizations (7) |
Function		Number (2)	Percent of col. 1 (3)				
Police protection	1,498	848	57	759(90)	80(9)	8(1)	1(*)
Fire protection	1,321	781	59	702(90)	76(10)	2(*)	1(*)
Public works	1,432	621	43	537(86)	57(9)	12(2)	15(2)
Public utilities	896	347	39	281(81)	52(15)	6(2)	8(2)
Public health and hospitals	512	128	25	100(78)	17(13)	8(6)	3(2)
Noninstructional education	207	103	50	82(80)	15(15)	4(4)	2(2)
Parks and recreation	1,235	422	34	365(86)	43(10)	6(1)	8(2)
Public welfare	267	76	28	67(88)	6(8)	1(1)	2(3)
All others	1,461	399	27	348(87)	30(8)	12(3)	9(2)
All functions	1,530	1,027	67	351(34)	329(32)	241(23)	106(10)
All functions except police and fire protection	1,530	697	46	506(73)	128(18)	35(5)	28(4)

Source: Same as Table A-1.
* Less than 0.5 percent.

TABLE A-8. *Strength of Various Employee Organizations in Municipalities, by Function, 1968*

Function	Cities — Number reporting employees (1)	Reporting employee organizations — Number (2)	Percent of col. 1 (3)	Number of cities and percent of col. 2 reporting employees belonging to								
				AFSCME (4)	SEIU (5)	Laborers (6)	Building trades (7)	Teamsters (8)	IAFF (9)	FOP (10)	Other union (11)	Local association (12)
Police protection	1,498	848	57	74(9)	3(*)	3(*)	3(*)	15(2)	5(1)	381(45)	118(14)	347(41)
Fire protection	1,321	781	59	21(3)	2(*)	2(*)	1(*)	7(1)	569(73)	2(*)	58(7)	204(26)
Public works	1,432	621	43	301(48)	26(4)	34(5)	34(5)	75(12)	0(0)	1(*)	88(14)	200(32)
Public utilities	896	347	39	153(44)	13(4)	12(3)	28(8)	30(9)	0(0)	0(0)	89(26)	113(33)
Public health and hospitals	512	128	25	51(40)	8(6)	3(2)	4(3)	9(7)	0(0)	1(1)	41(32)	58(45)
Noninstructional education	207	103	50	51(50)	7(7)	3(3)	5(5)	4(4)	0(0)	0(0)	22(21)	42(41)
Parks and recreation	1,235	422	34	202(48)	17(4)	10(2)	15(4)	33(8)	0(0)	1(*)	55(13)	171(41)
Public welfare	267	76	28	29(38)	1(1)	1(1)	2(3)	6(8)	0(0)	0(0)	15(20)	38(50)
All others	1,461	399	27	148(37)	17(4)	12(3)	17(4)	23(6)	0(0)	2(1)	70(18)	200(50)
All functions	1,530	1,027	67	343(33)	40(4)	43(4)	50(5)	104(10)	572(56)	383(37)	268(26)	433(42)

Source: Same as Table A-1.
* Less than 0.5 percent.

TABLE A-9. *Strength of Various Employee Organizations in Cities, by Size of City, Region, City Type, and Form of Government, 1968*

	Number of cities reporting (1)	Cities reporting organizations		Percent of col. 1 and percent of col. 2 reporting employees belonging to								
Characteristic		Number of col. 1 (2)	Percent of col. 1 (3)	AFSCME (4)	SEIU (5)	Laborers (6)	Building trades (7)	Team- sters (8)	IAFF (9)	FOP (10)	Other union (11)	Local association (12)
Population group												
Over 500,000	23	23	100	78 – 78	48 – 48	35 – 35	39 – 39	48 – 48	96 – 96	43 – 43	57 – 57	57 – 57
250,000–500,000	24	23	96	63 – 65	4 – 4	8 – 9	37 – 39	29 – 30	88 – 91	50 – 52	42 – 43	58 – 61
100,000–250,000	78	62	79	35 – 44	9 – 11	6 – 8	10 – 13	18 – 23	67 – 84	35 – 44	42 – 53	36 – 45
50,000–100,000	193	165	85	35 – 41	3 – 4	1 – 1	4 – 4	7 – 8	59 – 69	33 – 39	19 – 22	41 – 48
25,000–50,000	364	283	78	27 – 35	1 – 2	2 – 3	1 – 1	7 – 9	46 – 60	26 – 34	19 – 25	36 – 46
10,000–25,000	848	471	56	14 – 25	1 – 2	2 – 4	2 – 3	4 – 7	23 – 41	21 – 37	12 – 22	20 – 36
Geographic region												
New England	130	115	88	64 – 72	5 – 6	4 – 4	1 – 1	5 – 5	55 – 63	9 – 10	20 – 23	50 – 57
Middle Atlantic	239	186	78	13 – 17	3 – 4	3 – 4	3 – 4	6 – 8	22 – 28	41 – 53	27 – 35	29 – 37
East North Central	336	257	76	34 – 44	3 – 4	4 – 5	5 – 6	13 – 17	57 – 75	44 – 58	20 – 26	22 – 28
West North Central	149	89	60	15 – 25	3 – 6	7 – 11	5 – 9	11 – 18	38 – 64	9 – 16	23 – 38	13 – 22
South Atlantic	182	58	32	8 – 26	0 – 0	1 – 2	0 – 0	1 – 2	21 – 66	23 – 71	5 – 16	9 – 29
East South Central	56	35	62	9 – 14	0 – 0	0 – 0	2 – 3	4 – 6	37 – 60	48 – 77	13 – 20	13 – 20
West South Central	135	60	44	10 – 22	0 – 0	1 – 3	0 – 0	2 – 5	26 – 58	17 – 38	10 – 23	18 – 40
Mountain	73	43	59	16 – 28	0 – 0	0 – 0	1 – 2	3 – 5	40 – 67	18 – 30	11 – 19	26 – 44
Pacific	230	184	80	21 – 26	4 – 5	3 – 3	7 – 9	7 – 9	33 – 41	2 – 3	17 – 21	60 – 76

City type												
Central	238	202	85	43–51	9–11	7–8	12–14	16–18	73–86	40–47	34–40	37–43
Suburban	755	518	69	21–31	2–2	3–4	2–3	7–10	28–40	22–32	16–24	32–47
Independent	537	307	57	15–26	1–2	1–3	1–3	3–5	35–62	23–40	12–21	19–34
Form of government												
Mayor-council	538	384	71	26–37	3–5	4–5	4–5	10–14	42–59	36–51	22–30	22–31
Council-manager	888	561	63	19–30	2–3	2–3	3–5	4–7	33–53	18–28	16–25	32–50
Commission	68	52	76	25–33	3–4	6–8	6–8	9–12	53–69	40–52	12–15	19–25
Town meeting	23	20	87	52–60	4–5	13–15	0–0	9–10	13–15	9–10	17–20	39–45
Representative town meeting	13	10	77	31–40	0–0	8–10	0–0	15–20	62–80	0–0	15–20	69–90
All cities	1,530	1,027	67	22–33	3–4	3–4	3–5	7–10	37–56	25–37	18–26	28–42

Source: Same as Table A-I.

TABLE A-10. *Strength of Various Organizations in Cities, by Number of Organizations Representing Employees, 1968*[a]

Organization	Total cities	Number of cities and percent of total cities with representation by			
		One organization	Two organizations	Three organizations	Four or more organizations
AFSCME	332	207(*62*)	76(*23*)	26(*8*)	23(*7*)
SEIU	39	12(*31*)	7(*18*)	6(*15*)	14(*36*)
Laborers	43	14(*33*)	13(*30*)	3(*7*)	13(*30*)
Teamsters	92	40(*43*)	19(*21*)	12(*13*)	21(*23*)
Building trades	49	5(*10*)	14(*29*)	6(*12*)	24(*49*)
Local associations	262	143(*55*)	74(*28*)	27(*10*)	18(*7*)
Other	186	85(*46*)	53(*28*)	25(*13*)	23(*12*)

Source: Same as Table A-1.
a. Excludes police and fire protection.

TABLE A-11. *Number of Functions Represented by Various Organizations in Cities with One Employee Organization, 1968*[a]

Organization	Total cities	Number of cities and percent of total cities with representation in		
		One function	Two functions	Three or more functions
Total	506	133(*26*)	107(*21*)	266(*53*)
AFSCME	207	41(*20*)	52(*25*)	114(*55*)
SEIU	12	3(*25*)	5(*42*)	4(*33*)
Laborers	14	11(*79*)	2(*14*)	1(*7*)
Teamsters	40	23(*58*)	8(*20*)	9(*22*)
Building trades	5	3(*60*)	1(*20*)	1(*20*)
Local associations	143	17(*12*)	21(*15*)	105(*73*)
Other	85	35(*41*)	18(*21*)	32(*38*)

Source: Same as Table A-1.
a. Excludes police and fire protection.

Tables A-10 and A-11 show that AFSCME is the dominant organization in single-union cities, whereas other unions are more commonly found in cities recognizing several employee organizations. Thus, as organization spreads from employees in represented to nonrepresented functions, AFSCME will be in the most favorable position to be recognized and to increase its membership. For example, if AFSCME were to be recognized for all nonuniformed employees in the 207 cities that reported dealing only with AFSCME, it would stand to gain over 43,000 members. Other unions can expect to gain, at most, a few thousand additional members each from an extension of their influence in single-union cities in which they represent employees. (While local associations often represent employees in several functions, their influence is limited because, like their membership, it is confined to individual cities.)

APPENDIX B

Statistical Tables

TABLE B-I. *Membership of State Public Employee Associations, 1961, 1964, 1967, 1969*

Association	Number of members				Percent change, 1961–69[a]
	1961	*1964*	*1967*	*1969*	
Alaska State Employees Association	400	1,100	1,600	1,600[b]	300
California State Employees Association	89,086	101,439	115,053	120,000	35
Colorado State Civil Service Employees Association	5,152	7,675	10,309	12,000	133
Connecticut State Employees Association	11,374	12,300	17,310	22,000	93
Florida State Employees Association	600	900	450	450[b]	−25
Hawaii Government Employees Association	9,342	10,849	12,436	14,614	56
Idaho State Employees Association	1,226	2,424	3,346	3,346[b]	173
Illinois State Employees Association	10,276	9,478	8,560	10,000	−3
Civil Service Employees Association of Illinois	10,000	10,000	10,000	10,000	0
Indiana State Employees Association	2,000	842	1,780	2,000	0
Kansas Highway Employees Council	4,000	4,000[b]	4,000[b]	4,000[b]	0
Kentucky State Government Employees	...	...	...	2,000	...
Louisiana Society of Public Employees	...	...	1,200	2,000	67
Maine State Employees Association	6,000	7,100	8,500	8,700	45
Maryland Classified Employees Association	12,000	13,220	16,960	18,000	50
Massachusetts State Employees Association	18,000	18,000[b]	18,000[b]	18,000	0
Michigan State Employees Association	13,400	13,000	17,000	18,400	37
Montana Public Employees Association	3,500	4,285	3,883	3,883[b]	11
State of Nevada Employees Association	690	600	1,600	1,600[b]	132
New Hampshire State Employees Association	3,400	3,242	3,356	3,600	6
New Jersey Civil Service Association	20,000	20,000[b]	20,000[b]	20,000	0
New Jersey State Employees Association	5,000	5,000[b]	5,000[b]	5,000	0
New York Civil Service Employees Association	96,000	118,399	153,104	174,090	81
North Carolina State Employees Association	10,083	11,345	12,864	12,864[b]	28

North Carolina Highway and Corrections Association	8,396	9,338	9,984	9,984[b]	19
North Dakota State Employees Association	...	1,000	1,375	1,111	11
Ohio Civil Service Employees Association	15,440	17,654	24,737	25,000	62
Ohio Association of Public School Employees	15,385	17,188	22,555	24,000	56
Oregon State Employees Association	11,128	12,000	15,748	16,000	44
Rhode Island State Employees Association	3,600	3,700	4,300	4,500	25
South Carolina Employees Association	6,200	6,200	8,302	10,000	61
Texas Public Employees Association	22,016	21,886	20,488	25,000	14
Utah State Employees Association	2,563	3,450	4,700	4,700[b]	83
Vermont State Employees Association	2,491	3,500	3,900	4,000	61
Washington State Employees Association	2,000	2,700	3,500	4,000	100
Wyoming State Employees Association	...	403	1,644	1,644[b]	308
All associations	420,748	474,217	567,544	618,086	47

Sources: For 1961, Joseph Krislov, "The Independent Public Employee Association: Characteristics and Functions," *Industrial and Labor Relations Review*, Vol. 15 (July 1962), p. 512, supplemented by correspondence; for 1964 and 1967, Bureau of National Affairs, *Government Employee Relations Report*, No. 227 (Jan. 15, 1968), pp. B-1, B-2, supplemented by correspondence; for 1969, interviews and correspondence.
a. For associations not in existence in 1961, increase is from first year for which figures are available.
b. Information not available; figure same as previous given year.

TABLE B-2. *Distribution of Representation Elections among Local Government Employees in Four States, by Size of Bargaining Unit, 1962–69*

| | Four states | | Number of elections and percent of state's total elections in | | | |
Size of bargaining unit	Total elections	Per-cent won	Michigan[a]	Wisconsin	Connecticut	New York
All units	1,284	88[b]	719(*100*)	363(*100*)	116(*100*)	86(*100*)
1–25 employees	624	49	374(*52*)	161(*44*)	61(*53*)	28(*33*)
26–50 employees	280	22	170(*24*)	68(*19*)	23(*20*)	19(*22*)
51–100 employees	201	16	94(*13*)	75(*21*)	19(*16*)	13(*15*)
101–200 employees	99	8	42(*6*)	40(*11*)	4(*3*)	13(*15*)
201–1,000 employees	66	5	33(*5*)	17(*5*)	7(*6*)	9(*10*)
Over 1,000 employees	14	1	6(*1*)	2(*1*)	2(*2*)	4(*5*)

Source: Data supplied by state agencies. Percentages may not total 100 because of rounding.

a. Size of bargaining unit based on total votes cast which, according to staff of Michigan Employment Relations Commission, has usually been about 90 percent of eligible employees.

b. In Michigan 88 percent, Wisconsin 88 percent, Connecticut 90 percent, and New York 86 percent.

TABLE B-3. *Results of Representation Elections among Local Government Employees in Four States, by Function, 1962–69*

| | Elections in four states[a] | | Number of elections and percent of state's total elections in | | | |
Function	Number	Percent of total	Michigan	Wisconsin	Connecticut	New York
All functions	1,284	*100*	719(*56*)	363(*28*)	116(*9*)	86(*7*)
Education, libraries, and museums	323	25	212(*29*)	74(*20*)	25(*22*)	12(*14*)
Health and hospitals	262	20	175(*24*)	64(*18*)	11(*9*)	12(*14*)
Public works	247	19	91(*13*)	107(*29*)	34(*29*)	15(*17*)
Police	83	6	60(*8*)	0(*0*)	18(*16*)	5(*6*)
Fire	33	3	15(*2*)	11(*3*)	6(*5*)	1(*1*)
Public utilities	56	4	19(*3*)	29(*8*)	2(*2*)	6(*7*)
Parks and recreation	24	2	7(*1*)	9(*2*)	8(*7*)	...
Welfare and public assistance	29	2	13(*2*)	14(*4*)	2(*2*)	0(*0*)
Administrative services	197	15	96(*13*)	57(*16*)	18(*16*)	26(*30*)
Supervisory	31	2	20(*3*)	0(*0*)	2(*2*)	9(*10*)
All employees[b]	154	12	75(*10*)	40(*11*)	16(*14*)	23(*27*)
Other	45	4	16(*2*)	12(*3*)	4(*3*)	13(*15*)
Not available	9	1	5(*1*)	3(*1*)	0(*0*)	1(*1*)

Source: Data supplied by state agencies.

a. Total is less than sum of functions because some elections involved employees in more than one function.

b. Includes elections in all-city and all-county units of blue collar or white collar employees or both.

TABLE B-4. *Results of Representation Elections among Government Employees in Four States, by Organization and Size of Unit, 1962–69*

Organization and number of employees	Total elections	Elections won Number	Elections won Percent of total	Organization and number of employees	Total elections	Elections won Number	Elections won Percent of total
AFSCME				**FOP**			
1–25	299	249	83	1–25	3	2	67
26–50	153	110	72	26–50	2	2	100
51–100	113	86	76	51–100	1	1	100
101–200	64	47	73	101–200	...	...	...
201–1,000	38	25	66	201–1,000	...	...	...
Over 1,000	8	6	75	Over 1,000	...	...	...
SEIU				**ANA**			
1–25	35	27	77	1–25	37	33	89
26–50	25	23	92	26–50	10	9	90
51–100	17	10	59	51–100	9	8	89
101–200	15	11	73	101–200	4	4	100
201–1,000	15	6	40	201–1,000	3	1	33
Over 1,000	4	1	25	Over 1,000	...	...	...
Laborers				**Other unions**			
1–25	...	...	...	1–25	92	74	80
26–50	...	...	...	26–50	36	23	64
51–100	1	0	0	51–100	32	24	75
101–200	...	...	...	101–200	9	7	78
201–1,000	1	1	100	201–1,000	13	6	46
Over 1,000	...	...	...	Over 1,000	2	0	0
Teamsters				**Associations**			
1–25	70	56	80	1–25	94	74	79
26–50	43	32	74	26–50	50	37	74
51–100	31	25	81	51–100	41	25	61
101–200	13	6	46	101–200	19	10	53
201–1,000	10	5	50	201–1,000	22	12	55
Over 1,000	3	0	0	Over 1,000	7	6	86
Building trades				**No organization**			
1–25	20	19	95	1–25	624	78	13
26–50	1	1	100	26–50	280	36	13
51–100	...	...	...	51–100	201	20	10
101–200	3	2	67	101–200	99	11	11
201–1,000	1	1	100	201–1,000	66	9	14
Over 1,000	...	...	...	Over 1,000	14	1	7
IAFF							
1–25	13	12	92				
26–50	7	7	100				
51–100	2	2	100				
101–200	1	1	100				
201–1,000	...	...	...				
Over 1,000	...	...	...				

Source: Data supplied by state agencies.

TABLE B-5. *Results of Representation Elections among Government Employees in Four States, by Function and Winning Organization, 1962–69*

Function	All elections[a]		Number of elections and percent of total elections won by										
	Total	Percent of total	AFSCME	SEIU	Laborers	Teamsters	Building trades	IAFF	FOP	ANA	Other unions	Associations	No organization
All functions	1,284	100	523(41)	78(6)	1(*)	124(10)	23(2)	22(2)	5(*)	55(4)	134(10)	164(13)	155(12)
Education, libraries, and museums	323	25	144(28)	24(31)	0(0)	30(24)	2(9)	0(0)	0(0)	2(4)	54(40)	28(17)	39(25)
Health and hospitals	262	20	72(14)	30(38)	0(0)	6(5)	0(0)	0(0)	0(0)	55(100)	19(14)	34(21)	46(30)
Public works	247	19	115(22)	10(13)	1(100)	55(44)	3(13)	0(0)	0(0)	0(0)	26(19)	11(7)	26(17)
Police	83	6	39(7)	3(4)	0(0)	3(2)	0(0)	0(0)	5(100)	0(0)	5(4)	22(13)	6(4)
Fire	33	3	4(1)	0(0)	0(0)	0(0)	0(0)	22(100)	0(0)	0(0)	2(1)	4(2)	1(1)
Public utilities	56	4	17(3)	5(6)	0(0)	10(8)	8(35)	0(0)	0(0)	0(0)	8(6)	2(1)	6(4)
Parks and recreation	24	2	11(2)	2(3)	0(0)	6(5)	0(0)	0(0)	0(0)	0(0)	3(2)	0(0)	2(1)
Welfare and public assistance	29	2	17(3)	0(0)	0(0)	0(0)	0(0)	0(0)	0(0)	1(2)	0(0)	7(4)	4(3)
Administrative services	197	15	86(16)	9(12)	0(0)	8(6)	3(13)	0(0)	0(0)	0(0)	14(10)	51(31)	26(17)
Supervisory	31	2	8(2)	2(3)	0(0)	1(1)	3(13)	0(0)	0(0)	2(4)	0(0)	11(7)	4(3)
All employees[b]	154	12	74(14)	4(5)	0(0)	14(11)	2(9)	0(0)	0(0)	0(0)	16(12)	28(17)	16(10)
Other	45	4	18(3)	1(1)	0(0)	9(7)	7(30)	0(0)	0(0)	0(0)	5(4)	4(2)	1(1)
Not available	9	1	6(1)	1(1)	0(0)	0(0)	0(0)	0(0)	0(0)	0(0)	0(0)	0(0)	2(1)

Source: Data supplied by state agencies.

a. Total is less than sums of elections won because some elections involved employees in two or more functions.

b. Includes elections in all-city and all-county units of blue collar or white collar employees or both.

* Less than 0.5 percent.

TABLE B-6. *Results of Contested Representation Elections among Local Government Employees in Four States, by Winning and Losing Organization, 1962–69*

| Organization | Elections contested | | | | Organizations defeated and number of losses |
	Total	Won Number	Percent of total	Lost	
AFSCME	130	52	40	78	SEIU (3), Teamsters (17), FOP (1), ANA (2), other unions (7), associations (27), no organization (52)
SEIU	24	11	46	13	AFSCME (7), Teamsters (2), other unions (1), associations (3), no organization (11)
Laborers	2	1	50	1	AFSCME (1), no organization (1)
Teamsters	74	40	54	34	AFSCME (23), SEIU (1), other unions (4), associations (13), no organization (40)
Building trades	6	5	83	1	AFSCME (3), Teamsters (2), no organization (5)
IAFF	2	2	100	0	AFSCME (1), associations (1), no organization (2)
FOP	2	1	50	1	AFSCME (1), no organization (1)
ANA	13	8	62	5	AFSCME (3), associations (5), no organization (8)
Other unions	43	19	44	24	AFSCME (7), SEIU (1), Teamsters (3), other unions (1), associations (7), no organization (19)
Associations	116	51	44	65	AFSCME (26), SEIU (6), Laborers (1), Teamsters (9), building trades (1), ANA (3), other unions (6), associations (5), no organization (51)
No organization	199	9	5	190	AFSCME (6), SEIU (2), Teamsters (1), other unions (5), associations (4)

Source: Data supplied by state agencies.

Index

Advisory Commission on Intergovernmental Relations, 139, 142, 217

AFL–CIO. *See* American Federation of Labor–Congress of Industrial Organizations

Afro-American Patrolmen's Association, 61

AFSCME. *See* American Federation of State, County and Municipal Employees

AGE. *See* Assembly of Governmental Employees

Agency-shop clauses. *See* Union security

American Association of University Professors, 10

American Federation of Government Employees (AFGE), 91

American Federation of Labor, 56, 75, 91, 216

American Federation of Labor–Congress of Industrial Organizations (AFL–CIO): 2–6, 8, 19, 89, 101, 103; on collective bargaining by public employees, 98, 109, 116–17; COPE, 195, 198–200, 204, 207, 210; executive council, 30, 90, 97, 117, 196; factionalism, 195–96; and IAFF, 53–55, 64, 71, 110; Internal Disputes Plan, 19, 89, 93, 96–100, 112, 216; jurisdictional questions, 99–100, 216–17; and nurses, 104–05, 210; police organizations, 105–06, 112–13; political action, 195–201, 205–07, 210–11; on public employees, 108–13; and Jerry Wurf, 30, 196

—Councils, state and local: 31, 116–17; and AFSCME, 19, 109–10, 120, 135;

dues, 45, 71; IAFF affiliations, 54, 110; political action, 134, 196–99, 201; political influence of, 109–11; on public-employee collective bargaining, 110, 120; services of, 54; and Jerry Wurf, 111. *See also* Meany, George

American Federation of State, County and Municipal Employees (AFSCME): affiliates, 2n, 26, 101–02, 104; and AFL–CIO councils, 109–10, 120, 135; on AFL–CIO Internal Disputes Plan, 98; on arbitration, 189–90; area offices, 18–19; on bargaining units, 139–44, 157; charter, granting of, 91; on civil rights, 26, 195; on civil service, 115–16; and Coalition of Public Employee Organizations, 111, 113, 211, 216–17; on collective bargaining, 35–36, 96, 115–19, 128–30; contract negotiations, 131–35; delegate-voting issue, 17; dues, 45–47; factionalism, 16–17, 30–31; and IAFF, 74; and ICPA locals, 106; leadership, 30–31, 43; membership, 2–3, 17, 36; minority-group membership, 25–28, 30–31, 215; and NEA, 2n, 111, 211, 216–17; no-raiding agreements, 95; organization, 16–19, 43, 101; organizing costs, 38; prospects, 213; representation elections, 2n, 22, 27, 40, 152–55, 185; and SEIU, 38–39; staff, 25, 34–38, 40, 43; and state associations, 42

—Councils: 30, 130, 136, 141n, 142, 189, 196–98, 199; and associations, 43; decision-making role, 48; dues, 45–46; governance and activities, 18–19; Legis-

249

250 *Public Employee Unionism*

lative and Defense Fund, 197–98; staffs, 37

—Jurisdiction: 2–3, 14, 140, 147, 213; disputes over, 2n, 4, 19, 92–96, 98–102, 120, 216–17; positions on, 90, 98, 112, 216–17

—Locals: 28; affiliation with AFL–CIO bodies, 19; autonomy of, 19–20, 47, 49; dues, 45–47, 72; merger of, 18; minority-group membership, 26; political action, 196–99; roles of, 16–19; services to, 101; staffs, 37; structure and membership, 18–19

—Police locals: 6–7, 26, 105–06, 181–82; dues, 72–73; factionalism, 112; racial problems, 62–63, 215; services to, 70; and strikes, 174

—Political-action programs: 194–99, 211; by councils, 118, 198; on Hatch Act, 194; PEOPLE program, 194–95; by police, 206; for uniformed services, 109

—Strikes: 26, 136, 142, 179, 181–82; attitudes toward, 106, 117–19, 172–75, 181; functions affected by, 162–65; union-recognition issue, 167. *See also* Mixed unions; Wurf, Jerry

American Federation of Teachers, 12, 111

American-Indians, 27–29

American Nurses' Association (ANA): and AFL–CIO, 210; on arbitration, 190–92; on bargaining units, 146–48, 157; on civil rights, 78, 209; on collective bargaining, 11, 78, 80–81, 83–84, 88, 125–27; Commission on Economic and General Welfare, 77, 80, 84–85, 186; compared with other organizations, 10–11, 87–88, 223; dues, 87; Economic Security Program, 84–87, 125; Governmental Relations Department, 209–10; House of Delegates, 76–77, 125; jurisdiction, 10; on labor laws, 126; leadership, 79–82; membership, 10, 76; minority-group membership, 78–80; organization, 77; political action, 104–05, 157, 208–11; professional and clinical interests, 76–77, 80; professional domination, 79–82; prospects, 214; purpose, 10–11, 81; staff, 85–86; strikes and strike policy, 175, 185–88, 192; on union security, 130–31. *See also* State nurses' associations (SNAs)

ANA. *See* American Nurses' Association

Arbitration, binding, 179

Arbitration, compulsory: 58, 176; attitudes toward, 188–91, 219; and civil service commissions, 123; and collective bargaining, 188, 192; laws on, 121, 189–

90, 219; prospects, 220; and uniformed services, 58, 109, 121, 190, 219

Arbitration, voluntary, 188–89

Assembly of Governmental Employees (AGE): bargaining units, 142–43; on collective bargaining and civil service, 21, 124, 137; income, 46; jurisdiction, 9; organization and leadership, 20–22, 33; on partisan politics, 207; on strikes, 21; and unions, 20, 223. *See also* Associations

Associations, local: autonomy, 9; civil-service ties, 9; on collective bargaining, 44, 124; contract negotiations, pattern of, 14; dues, 44, 46; jurisdiction, 9; leadership, 34; membership, 9, 29, 157; minority-group membership, 28–30; prospects, 213; staff, 43–44; and state associations, 12, 22; and unions, 12, 22, 102–04, 109–10. *See also* Associations, state and local

Associations, state: and AGE, 8–9, 20–21, 33, 46; on collective bargaining, 42–43, 123–25; dues, 22, 46, 131; impediments, 22; leadership, 33–34; and local associations, 12, 22; local chapters of, 46, 49; membership, 2–3, 22; minority-group membership, 28–30; organization, 22–23; organizing, 43; political action, 43, 207–08; prospects, 213; staff, 42–44; supervisory personnel in, 33–34; union-like activities, 9; and unions, 9, 20, 22, 46. *See also* Associations, state and local; Civil service; Collective bargaining; Collective-bargaining laws

Associations, state and local: arbitration policies, 191; on bargaining units, 142–43; on centralizing power, 16; on collective bargaining, 8–11, 214, 222; collective-bargaining laws, effects on, 34; dues, 46–48; finances, 44–48; forms of, 8–9; grievance procedures, 8, 43; group insurance, 8, 33, 43; jurisdiction, 8–9; local autonomy, 9, 20; minority-group membership, 28–30, 49, 215; mobility of membership, 33–34; objectives in founding, 8; political action, 8, 43, 46, 207–08; public relations, 43, 46; representation elections, 153–55; as social clubs, 8, 29; staff activities, 46, 48; strike policies, 183–85; supervisory personnel in, 217; on union security, 127–31

—Unions: affiliations with, 49, 223; attitudes toward, 8, 100–04, 221–22; comparisons with, 8–9, 20–21, 46, 48, 213–23;